Place-Based Science Teaching and Learning

40 Activities for
K–8 Classrooms

Place-Based Science Teaching and Learning

Cory A. Buxton
The University of Georgia

Eugene F. Provenzo, Jr.
University of Miami

Los Angeles | London | New Delhi
Singapore | Washington DC

Los Angeles | London | New Delhi
Singapore | Washington DC

FOR INFORMATION:

SAGE Publications, Inc.
2455 Teller Road
Thousand Oaks, California 91320
E-mail: order@sagepub.com

SAGE Publications Ltd.
1 Oliver's Yard
55 City Road
London EC1Y 1SP
United Kingdom

SAGE Publications India Pvt. Ltd.
B 1/I 1 Mohan Cooperative Industrial Area
Mathura Road, New Delhi 110 044
India

SAGE Publications Asia-Pacific Pte. Ltd.
33 Pekin Street #02-01
Far East Square
Singapore 048763

Library of Congress Cataloging-in-Publication Data

Buxton, Cory A.
Place-based science teaching and learning : 40 activities for K–8 classrooms / Cory A. Buxton, Eugene F. Provenzo, Jr.

p. cm.
Includes bibliographical references.

ISBN 978-1-4129-7525-4 (pbk.: alk. paper)

1. Science—Study and teaching (Elementary)—Activity programs. I. Provenzo, Eugene F. II. Title.

LB1585.B87 2012
372.35′044—dc22
2011011026

Acquisitions Editor: Diane McDaniel
Editorial Assistant: Theresa Accomazzo
Production Editor: Eric Garner
Copy Editor: Kim Husband
Typesetter: C&M Digitals (P) Ltd.
Proofreader: Carole Quandt
Indexer: Sheila Bodell
Cover Designer: Janet Kiesel
Marketing Manager: Katharine Winter
Permissions Editor: Adele Hutchinson

11 12 13 14 15 10 9 8 7 6 5 4 3 2 1

Contents

Part II: Activities to Promote Place-Based Science Teaching in the School Building

Preface

According to David Hutchinson, "Place-Based education is a philosophical orientation to teaching and learning that emphasizes the study of geographic context, particularly the local community, as a focus of elementary, secondary and higher education" (Hutchinson, 2009, p. 587). This book focuses on place-based education in elementary and middle schools and its uses in science education. Our purpose is to provide elementary and middle school science teachers with both a rationale and a set of ideas and activities for teaching science in a local or place-based context.

We feel that a place-based emphasis is timely and important as a counterbalance to the current overemphasis on standards-based teaching driven by high-stakes testing and accountability. Unfortunately, in recent years, science teaching around the country has become more and more generic with little regard for what is unique about any given environment. Just as main streets everywhere have become increasingly similar, with the same big-box merchandise stores and fast-food restaurants, so too are schools running the risk of losing their unique local flavor and identity. In this book, we hope to help teachers present their students with a vision of science that is rooted in their own communities and school sites, and thus, a vision of science that can be a more meaningful and engaging part of their lives.

This book is divided into three main sections:

1. An introduction to and rationale for place-based education

2. Forty activities for teaching place-based science

3. An annotated resource list for supporting place-based science teaching

The comprehensive introduction to place-based education begins with a rationale for teaching science in local contexts and why such an approach is critically important for meeting the science learning needs of all students in the 21st century. It also provides an analysis of the learning needs of culturally and linguistically diverse students, as well as students with exceptionalities, and how place-based science teaching can support the learning of all students. The introduction discusses our ideas about what it means to "think like a scientist" and how place-based science can enhance students' development of these important thinking skills. Fourth, the introduction addresses ways in which techniques and strategies for assessing science learning can be enhanced by place-based pedagogy. Fifth, we provide general suggestions for how the activities presented in Part II of this book can be modified to best meet the learning needs of students across the grade ranges of early elementary, late elementary, and middle school. Finally, we discuss how place-based education can serve as a valuable context for interdisciplinary teaching across the content areas.

The main portion of the book is composed of 40 examples of activities that teachers can use to enact place-based science learning with their students. This main portion is divided into five parts, which we view as a series of concentric circles or nested contexts (see Figure P.1). The inner circle is the classroom and the outer circle is the broader community, town, or city. The three intermediate circles represent the school building, the schoolyard or grounds, and the neighborhood within walking distance of the school. We provide a series of model activities that can be done within each of these contexts. For each activity, we include relevant scientific and cultural background information on the topic, a lesson plan with directions for how to conduct the activity, and examples of how the topic can support thinking like a scientist and teaching across the content areas. Each activity also provides an example of modifications based on grade level range, suggestions for individuals in the community who can provide additional information on the activity topic, and a list of relevant national standards from science, mathematics, language arts, and social studies that can be addressed through the activity.

Figure P.1	The nested contexts of place-based learning

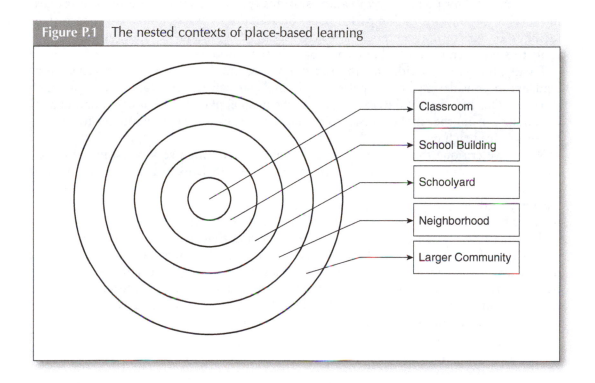

Part I focuses on *science in the classroom* and how elements of the local context can be brought into the classroom in unique ways. Examples of this type of activity could include interviewing scientists from local institutions about how their work contributes to science in the community (this could be done with live guest speakers or via video conferencing); analyzing data (meteorological, ecological, water quality, etc.) collected by local organizations (EPA, sewage and water board, etc.) and perhaps comparing those data to data collected by the class; and using various telecommunications to share ideas and data with students in other settings, both similar and different, nationally and internationally.

Part II focuses on *science in the school building* and how scientific inquiry can take place in many parts of the school such as the cafeteria, the gym, and even the water fountain. Examples of this type of study could include an ecological study of how the school building could be made more energy efficient, studying student nutrition, eating, and exercise habits, and comparing the taste and water quality of drinking fountain water to that of bottled water.

Part III focuses on *science on the school grounds* and helps teachers understand how taking the class outside of the school building and onto school playgrounds, ball fields, or even just the sidewalk can provide new opportunities for science learning. Examples of this type of activity could include planting and studying a school vegetable garden, bird watching in the schoolyard, and studying erosion and drainage patterns.

Part IV focuses on *science in the neighborhood* when the transportation needed for traditional field trips is not possible. Students can discover that there is still a lot of exploring to be done on foot in one's neighborhood. Examples of this type of activity could involve the study of water quality in a local creek, canal, or drainage, a wildlife census in a neighborhood park, or a study of the most common health problems in the community around the school.

Part V focuses on *science in the broader community,* when field trips requiring transportation are possible and students can get out of their daily surroundings to explore other parts of their community. Examples of this type of activity could involve studies in museum settings, in major parks, zoos, or aquariums, waste and water processing facilities, or agricultural centers. These activities may be infrequent, but they are memorable to students and can be built upon back in the school setting.

Finally, the book provides an annotated list of resources to assist both teachers and students in considering how a place-based emphasis can enrich science teaching and learning. This list of resources explores how the people, places, and things found in any community, from the smallest town to the largest city, can serve as resources for place-based science teaching.

While we critique the impact of science standards and high-stakes testing on classroom teaching practice in this text, we do not wish this text to be construed as a condemnation of standards or of assessment. Having clear and explicit standards for teaching and learning and rigorous assessments for measuring students' progress towards those standards is appropriate. What is inappropriate is when testing mandates and standards are used to generate scripted curricula that leave no room for teacher creativity or for exploration of local contexts or content. Teachers (and administrators) must learn how to use standards appropriately and to resist inappropriate uses. A place-based approach to teaching offers tools that both new and experienced teachers can use to help balance standards meant to create broad shared understandings with a focus on the local contexts that make every community unique.

Acknowledgments

We would like to thank the many people who have helped in writing this book. Asterie Baker Provenzo provided hospitality and her usual outstanding editorial skills. Jean-Marie Buxton provided encouragement, moral support, and most important, comedy during periods of stress. Jonah, Remy, and Lindy reminded us that the joy and the power of science come from asking "why" as often as possible. Diane McDaniel at SAGE helped us focus the project from its earliest conception and provided support and guidance throughout the process. Ashley Conlon, Theresa Accomazzo, Eric Garner, Kim Husband, and the production staff at SAGE helped keep us on track with our writing schedule and final production. Special thanks go to Katherine R. Baker, who helped her uncle, Eugene, develop the activities on urban gardening. Finally, we would like to thank the reviewers who gave us thoughtful feedback and suggestions at various points in the process.

Cory A. Buxton, The University of Georgia
Eugene F. Provenzo, Jr., University of Miami

The National Science Education Standards for Science Content

CONTENT STANDARD A: SCIENCE AS INQUIRY

All students should develop

A.1. Abilities necessary to do scientific inquiry
A.2. Understandings about scientific inquiry

CONTENT STANDARD B: PHYSICAL SCIENCE

All students should develop an understanding of

B.1. Properties and changes of properties in matter
B.2. Motions and forces
B.3. Transfer of energy

CONTENT STANDARD C: LIFE SCIENCE

All students should develop understanding of

C.1. Structure and function in living systems
C.2. Reproduction and heredity
C.3. Regulation and behavior
C.4. Populations and ecosystems
C.5. Diversity and adaptations of organisms

CONTENT STANDARD D: EARTH AND SPACE SCIENCE

All students should develop an understanding of

D.1. Structure of the Earth system
D.2. Earth's history
D.3. Earth in the solar system

CONTENT STANDARD E: SCIENCE AND TECHNOLOGY

All students should develop

    E.1. Abilities of technological design
    E.2. Understandings about science and technology

CONTENT STANDARD F: SCIENCE IN PERSONAL AND SOCIAL PERSPECTIVES

All students should develop understanding of

    F.1. Personal health
    F.2. Populations, resources, and environments
    F.3. Natural hazards
    F.4. Risks and benefits
    F.5. Science and technology in society

CONTENT STANDARD G: HISTORY AND NATURE OF SCIENCE

All students should develop understanding of

    G.1. Science as a human endeavor
    G.2. Nature of science
    G.3. History of science

National Council of Teachers of Mathematics: Principles and Standards for School Mathematics

STANDARD A: NUMBER AND OPERATIONS

A1. Understand numbers, ways of representing numbers, relationships among numbers, and number systems.
A2. Understand meanings of operations and how they relate to one another.
A3. Compute fluently and make reasonable estimates.

STANDARD B: ALGEBRA

B1. Understand patterns, relations and functions.
B2. Represent and analyze mathematical situations and structures using algebraic symbols.
B3. Use mathematical models to represent and understand quantitative relationships.
B4. Analyze change in various contexts.

STANDARD C: GEOMETRY

C1. Analyze characteristics and properties of geometric shapes and develop mathematical arguments about geometric relationships.
C2. Specify locations and describe spatial relationships using coordinate geometry and other representations systems.
C3. Apply transformations and use symmetry to analyze mathematical situations.
C4. Use visualization, spatial reasoning, and geometric modeling to solve problems.

STANDARD D: MEASUREMENT

D1. Understand measurable attributes of objects and the units, systems, and processes of measurement.

D2. Apply appropriate techniques, tools, and formulas to determine measurements.

STANDARD E: DATA ANALYSIS AND PROBABILITY

E1. Formulate questions that can be addressed with data and collect, organize, and display relevant data to answer them.

E2. Select and use appropriate statistical methods to analyze data.

E3. Develop and evaluate inferences and predictions that are based on data.

E4. Understand and apply basic concepts of probability.

IRA/NCTE Standards for the English Language Arts

The vision guiding these standards is that all students must have the opportunities and resources to develop the language skills they need to pursue life's goals and to participate fully as informed, productive members of society. These standards assume that literacy growth begins before children enter school as they experience and experiment with literacy activities—reading and writing and associating spoken words with their graphic representations. Recognizing this fact, these standards encourage the development of curriculum and instruction that make productive use of the emerging literacy abilities that children bring to school. Furthermore, the standards provide ample room for the innovation and creativity essential to teaching and learning.

They are not prescriptions for particular curriculum or instruction. Although we present these standards as a list, we want to emphasize that they are not distinct and separable; they are, in fact, interrelated and should be considered as a whole.

1. Students read a wide range of print and nonprint texts to build an understanding of texts, of themselves, and of the cultures of the United States and the world; to acquire new information; to respond to the needs and demands of society and the workplace; and for personal fulfillment. Among these texts are fiction and nonfiction, classic, and contemporary works.

2. Students read a wide range of literature from many periods in many genres to build an understanding of the many dimensions (e.g., philosophical, ethical, aesthetic) of human experience.

3. Students apply a wide range of strategies to comprehend, interpret, evaluate, and appreciate texts. They draw on their prior experience, their interactions with other readers and writers, their knowledge of word meaning and of other texts, their word identification strategies, and their understanding of textual features (e.g., sound–letter correspondence, sentence structure, context, graphics).

4. Students adjust their use of spoken, written, and visual language (e.g., conventions, style, vocabulary) to communicate effectively with a variety of audiences and for different purposes.

5. Students employ a wide range of strategies as they write and use different writing process elements appropriately to communicate with different audiences for a variety of purposes.

NCSS Curriculum Standards for Social Studies

I. CULTURE

Social studies programs should include experiences that provide for the study of culture and cultural diversity.

Human beings create, learn, and adapt culture. Culture helps us to understand ourselves as both individuals and members of various groups. Human cultures exhibit both similarities and differences. We all, for example, have systems of beliefs, knowledge, values, and traditions. Each system also is unique. In a democratic and multicultural society, students need to understand multiple perspectives that derive from different cultural vantage points. This understanding will allow them to relate to people in our nation and throughout the world.

Cultures are dynamic and ever-changing. The study of culture prepares students to ask and answer questions such as: What are the common characteristics of different cultures? How do belief systems, such as religion or political ideals of the culture, influence the other parts of the culture? How does the culture change to accommodate different ideas and beliefs? What does language tell us about the culture? In schools, this theme typically appears in units and courses dealing with geography, history, and anthropology, as well as multicultural topics across the curriculum.

During the early years of school, the exploration of the concepts of likenesses and differences in school subjects such as language arts, mathematics, science, music, and art makes the study of culture appropriate. Socially, the young learner is beginning to interact with other students, some of whom are like the student and some different; naturally, he or she wants to know more about others. In the middle grades, students begin to explore and ask questions about the nature of culture and specific aspects of culture, such as language and beliefs, and the influence of those aspects on human behavior. As students progress through high school, they can understand and use complex cultural concepts such as adaptation, assimilation, acculturation, diffusion, and dissonance drawn from anthropology, sociology, and other disciplines to explain how culture and cultural systems function.

II. TIME, CONTINUITY, & CHANGE

Social studies programs should include experiences that provide for the study of the ways human beings view themselves in and over time.

Human beings seek to understand their historical roots and to locate themselves in time. Such understanding involves knowing what things were like in the past and how things change and develop. Knowing how to read and reconstruct the past allows one to develop a historical perspective and to answer questions such as: Who am I? What happened in the past? How am I connected to those in the past? How has the world changed and how might it change in the future? Why does our personal sense of relatedness to the past change? How can the perspective we have about our own life experiences be viewed as part of the larger human story across time? How do our personal stories reflect varying points of view and inform contemporary ideas and actions?

This theme typically appears in courses that: 1) include perspectives from various aspects of history; 2) draw upon historical knowledge during the examination of social issues; and 3) develop the habits of mind that historians and scholars in the humanities and social sciences employ to study the past and its relationship to the present in the United States and other societies.

Learners in early grades gain experience with sequencing to establish a sense of order and time. They enjoy hearing stories of the recent past as well as of long ago. In addition, they begin to recognize that individuals may hold different views about the past and to understand the linkages between human decisions and consequences. Thus, the foundation is laid for the development of historical knowledge, skills, and values. In the middle grades, students, through a more formal study of history, continue to expand their understanding of the past and of historical concepts and inquiry. They begin to understand and appreciate differences in historical perspectives, recognizing that interpretations are influenced by individual experiences, societal values, and cultural traditions. High school students engage in more sophisticated analysis and reconstruction of the past, examining its relationship to the present and extrapolating into the future. They integrate individual stories about people, events, and situations to form a more holistic conception, in which continuity and change are linked in time and across cultures. Students also learn to draw on their knowledge of history to make informed choices and decisions in the present.

III. PEOPLE, PLACES, & ENVIRONMENTS

Social studies programs should include experiences that provide for the study of people, places, and environments.

Technological advances connect students at all levels to the world beyond their personal locations. The study of people, places, and human-environment interactions assists learners as they create their spatial views and geographic perspectives of the world. Today's social, cultural, economic, and civic demands on individuals mean that students will need the knowledge, skills, and understanding to ask and answer questions such as: Where are things located? Why are they located where they are? What patterns are reflected in the groupings of things? What do we mean by region? How do landforms change? What implications do these changes have for people? This area of study helps learners make informed and critical decisions about the relationship between human beings and their environment. In schools, this theme typically appears in units and courses dealing with area studies and geography.

In the early grades, young learners draw upon immediate personal experiences as a basis for exploring geographic concepts and skills. They also express interest in things distant and unfamiliar and have concern for the use and abuse of the physical environment. During the middle school years, students relate their personal experiences to happenings in other environmental contexts. Appropriate experiences will encourage increasingly abstract thought as students use data and apply skills in analyzing human behavior in relation to its physical and cultural environment. Students in high school are able to apply geographic understanding across a broad range of fields, including the fine arts, sciences, and humanities. Geographic concepts become central to learners' comprehension of global connections as they expand their knowledge of diverse cultures, both historical and contemporary. The importance of core geographic themes to public policy is recognized and should be explored as students address issues of domestic and international significance.

IV. INDIVIDUAL DEVELOPMENT & IDENTITY

Social studies programs should include experiences that provide for the study of individual development and identity.

Personal identity is shaped by one's culture, by groups, and by institutional influences. How do people learn? Why do people behave as they do? What influences how people learn, perceive, and grow? How do people meet their basic needs in a variety of contexts? Questions such as these are central to the study of how individuals develop from youth to adulthood. Examination of various forms of human behavior enhances understanding of the relationships among social norms and emerging personal identities, the social processes that influence identity formation, and the ethical principles underlying individual action. In schools, this theme typically appears in units and courses dealing with psychology and anthropology.

Given the nature of individual development and our own cultural context, students need to be aware of the processes of learning, growth, and development at every level of their school experience. In the early grades, for example, observing brothers, sisters, and older adults, looking at family photo albums, remembering past achievements and projecting oneself into the future, and comparing the patterns of behavior evident in people of different age groups are appropriate activities because young learners develop their personal identities in the context of families, peers, schools, and communities. Central to this development are the exploration, identification, and analysis of how individuals relate to others. In the middle grades, issues of personal identity are refocused as the individual begins to explain self in relation to others in the society and culture. At the high school level, students need to encounter multiple opportunities to examine contemporary patterns of human behavior, using methods from the behavioral sciences to apply core concepts drawn from psychology, social psychology, sociology, and anthropology as they apply to individuals, societies, and cultures.

V. INDIVIDUALS, GROUPS, & INSTITUTIONS

Social studies programs should include experiences that provide for the study of interactions among individuals, groups, and institutions.

Institutions such as schools, churches, families, government agencies, and the courts all play an integral role in our lives. These and other institutions exert enormous influence over us, yet institutions are no more than organizational embodiments to further the core social values of those who comprise them. Thus, it is important that students know how institutions are formed, what controls and influences them, how they control and influence individuals and culture, and how institutions can be maintained or changed. The study of individuals, groups, and institutions, drawing upon sociology, anthropology, and other disciplines, prepares students to ask and answer questions such as: What is the role of institutions in this and other societies? How am I influenced by institutions? How do institutions change? What is my role in institutional change? In schools, this theme typically appears in units and courses dealing with sociology, anthropology, psychology, political science, and history.

Young children should be given opportunities to examine various institutions that affect their lives and influence their thinking. They should be assisted in recognizing the tensions that occur when the goals, values, and principles of two or more institutions or groups conflict—for example, when the school board prohibits candy machines in schools vs. a class project to install a candy machine to help raise money for the local hospital. They should also have opportunities to explore ways in which institutions such as churches or health care networks are created to respond to changing individual and group needs. Middle school learners will benefit from varied experiences through which they examine the ways in which institutions change over time, promote social conformity, and influence culture. They should be encouraged to use this understanding to suggest ways to work through institutional change for the common good. High school students must understand the paradigms and traditions that undergird social and political institutions. They should be provided opportunities to examine, use, and add to the body of knowledge related to the behavioral sciences and social theory as it relates to the ways people and groups organize themselves around common needs, beliefs, and interests.

VI. POWER, AUTHORITY, & GOVERNANCE

Social studies programs should include experiences that provide for the study of how people create and change structures of power, authority, and governance.

Understanding the historical development of structures of power, authority, and governance and their evolving functions in contemporary U.S. society, as well as in other parts of the world, is essential for developing civic competence. In exploring this theme, students confront questions such as: What is power? What forms does it take? Who holds it? How is it gained, used, and justified? What is legitimate authority? How are governments created, structured, maintained, and changed? How can we keep government responsive to its citizens' needs and interests? How can individual rights be protected within the context of majority rule? By examining the purposes and characteristics of various governance systems, learners develop an understanding of how groups and nations attempt to resolve conflicts and seek to establish order and security. Through study of the dynamic relationships among individual rights and responsibilities, the needs of social groups, and concepts of a just society, learners become more effective problem-solvers and decision-makers when addressing the persistent issues and social problems encountered in public life. They do so by applying concepts and methods of political science and law. In schools, this theme typically appears in units and courses dealing with government, politics, political science, history, law, and other social sciences.

Learners in the early grades explore their natural and developing sense of fairness and order as they experience relationships with others. They develop an increasingly comprehensive awareness of rights and responsibilities in specific contexts. During the middle school years, these rights and responsibilities are applied in more complex contexts with emphasis on new applications. High school students develop their abilities in the use of abstract principles. They study the various systems that have been developed over the centuries to allocate and employ power and authority in the governing process. At every level, learners should have opportunities to apply their knowledge and skills to and participate in the workings of the various levels of power, authority, and governance.

VII. PRODUCTION, DISTRIBUTION, & CONSUMPTION

Social studies programs should include experiences that provide for the study of how people organize for the production, distribution, and consumption of goods and services.

People have wants that often exceed the limited resources available to them. As a result, a variety of ways have been invented to decide upon answers to four fundamental questions: What is to be produced? How is production to be organized? How are goods and services to be distributed? What is the most effective allocation of the factors of production (land, labor, capital, and management)? Unequal distribution of resources necessitates systems of exchange, including trade, to improve the well-being of the economy, while the role of government in economic policymaking varies over time and from place to place. Increasingly these decisions are global in scope and require systematic study of an interdependent world economy and the role of technology in economic decision-making. In schools, this theme typically appears in units and courses dealing with concepts, principles, and issues drawn from the discipline of economics.

Young learners begin by differentiating between wants and needs. They explore economic decisions as they compare their own economic experiences with those of others and consider the wider consequences of those decisions on groups, communities, the nation, and beyond. In the middle grades, learners expand their knowledge of economic concepts and principles, and use economic reasoning processes in addressing issues related to the four fundamental economic questions. High school students develop economic perspectives and deeper understanding of key economic concepts and processes through systematic study of a range of economic and sociopolitical systems, with particular emphasis on the examination of domestic and global economic policy options related to matters such as health care, resource use, unemployment, and trade.

VIII. SCIENCE, TECHNOLOGY, & SOCIETY

Social studies programs should include experiences that provide for the study of relationships among science, technology, and society.

Technology is as old as the first crude tool invented by prehistoric humans, but today's technology forms the basis for some of our most difficult social choices. Modern life as we know it would be impossible without technology and the science that supports it. But technology brings with it many questions: Is new technology always better than that which it will replace? What can we learn from the past about how new technologies result in broader social change, some of which is unanticipated? How can we cope with the ever-increasing pace of change, perhaps even with the feeling that technology has gotten out of control? How can we manage technology so that the greatest number of people benefit from it? How can we preserve our fundamental values and beliefs in a world that is rapidly becoming one technology-linked village? This theme appears in units or courses dealing with history, geography, economics, and civics and government. It draws upon several scholarly fields from the natural and physical sciences, social sciences, and the humanities for specific examples of issues and the knowledge base for considering responses to the societal issues related to science and technology.

Young children can learn how technologies form systems and how their daily lives are intertwined with a host of technologies. They can study how basic technologies such as ships, automobiles, and airplanes have evolved and how we have employed technology such as air conditioning, dams, and irrigation to modify our physical environment. From history (their own and others'), they can construct examples of how technologies such as the wheel, the stirrup, and the transistor radio altered the course of history. By the middle grades, students can begin to explore the complex relationships among technology, human values, and behavior. They will find that science and technology bring changes that surprise us and even challenge our beliefs, as in the case of discoveries and their applications related to our universe, the genetic basis of life, atomic physics, and others. As they move from the middle grades to high school, students will need to think more deeply about how we can manage technology so that we control it rather than the other way around. There should be opportunities to confront such issues as the consequences of using robots to produce goods, the protection of privacy in the age of computers and electronic surveillance, and the opportunities and challenges of genetic engineering, test-tube life, and medical technology with all their implications for longevity and quality of life and religious beliefs.

IX. GLOBAL CONNECTIONS

Social studies programs should include experiences that provide for the study of global connections and interdependence.

The realities of global interdependence require understanding the increasingly important and diverse global connections among world societies. Analysis of tensions between national interests and global priorities contributes to the development of possible solutions to persistent and emerging global issues in many fields: health care, economic development, environmental quality, universal human rights, and others. Analyzing patterns and relationships within and among world cultures, such as economic competition and interdependence, age-old ethnic enmities, political and military alliances, and others, helps learners carefully examine policy alternatives that have both national and global implications. This theme typically appears in units or courses dealing with geography, culture, and economics, but again can draw upon the natural and physical sciences and the humanities, including literature, the arts, and language.

Through exposure to various media and first-hand experiences, young learners become aware of and are affected by events on a global scale. Within this context, students in early grades examine and explore global connections and basic issues and concerns, suggesting and initiating responsive action plans. In the middle years, learners can initiate analysis of the interactions among states and nations and their cultural complexities as they respond to global events and changes. At the high school level, students are able to think systematically about personal, national, and global decisions, interactions, and consequences, including addressing critical issues such as peace, human rights, trade, and global ecology.

X. CIVIC IDEALS & PRACTICES

Social studies programs should include experiences that provide for the study of the ideals, principles, and practices of citizenship in a democratic republic.

An understanding of civic ideals and practices of citizenship is critical to full participation in society and is a central purpose of the social studies. All people have a stake in examining civic ideals and practices across time and in diverse societies as well as at home, and in determining how to close the gap between present practices and the ideals upon which our democratic republic is based. Learners confront such questions as: What is civic participation and how can I be involved? How has the meaning of citizenship evolved? What is the balance between rights and responsibilities? What is the role of the citizen in the community and the nation, and as a member of the world community? How can I make a positive difference? In schools, this theme typically appears in units or courses dealing with history, political science, cultural anthropology, and fields such as global studies and law-related education, while also drawing upon content from the humanities.

In the early grades, students are introduced to civic ideals and practices through activities such as helping to set classroom expectations, examining experiences in relation to ideals, and determining how to balance the needs of individuals and the group. During these years, children also experience views of citizenship in other times and places through stories and drama. By the middle grades, students expand their ability to analyze and evaluate the relationships between ideals and practice. They are able to see themselves taking civic roles in their communities. High school students increasingly recognize the rights and responsibilities of citizens in identifying societal needs, setting directions for public policies, and working to support both individual dignity and the common good. They learn by experience how to participate in community service and political activities and how to use democratic process to influence public policy.

Source: National Council for the Social Studies, *Expectations of excellence: Curriculum standards for social studies* (Washington, DC: NCSS, 1994). This book may be purchased by calling 800–683–0812. Electronic copies of it are not available.

Introduction to Place-Based Science Teaching and Learning

INTRODUCTION

Science education in elementary and middle schools was not widely taught in the United States until the beginning of the 20th century. At that time, science began to be integrated into instruction as part of the Progressive Education Movement. Individuals such as John Dewey included science instruction as a central feature of his curriculum. As explained in his 1922 book, *Democracy and Education*, "The chief opportunity for science is the discovery of the relations of a man to his work—including his relations to others who take part—which will enlist his intelligent interest in what he is doing." (Dewey, 1922, n.p.) In other words, science in the schools connects the child to the real world of work and others. As a result, science not only serves to teach students practical skills, but group and social skills as well.

Students at the University of Chicago Laboratory School creating a garden, 1904

Dewey included science activities, such as raising animals, gardening, cooking, and examining the workings of everyday machines, at the Laboratory School he started in 1892 at the University of Chicago. This represented perhaps the earliest inclusion of placed-based science in primary schooling in the United States, the integration of locally relevant scientific knowledge with the experience of the child. This differed significantly from the standard practice of the day, which, according to Dewey, isolated "science from significant experience." Dewey felt strongly that most students learned a type of science that was not connected in meaningful ways to their world. As a result, the child "acquires a technical body of information without ability to trace its connections with the objects and operations with which he is familiar—often he acquires simply a peculiar vocabulary" (Dewey, 1922, n.p.).

Dewey's criticisms resonate strongly with the condition of contemporary science education in the United States with its overemphasis on generic standards and teaching to a single high-stakes assessment. While the reforms of the last few decades in science education have emphasized the importance of laboratory experiences and hands-on inquiry science, they have not adequately connected scientific curricular content to the lived experience of students beyond the classroom. Indeed, many students still complete their education in science having primarily learned that science is little more than a "peculiar vocabulary." Once again, Dewey's ideas about science in *Democracy and Education* become extremely relevant. Arguing that while laboratory experimentation was "a great improvement" on exclusive textbook instruction, it was not sufficient to promote scientific learning that would become part of the student's larger experience and worldview. As he explained: "Physical materials may be manipulated with scientific apparatus, but the materials may be disassociated in themselves and in the ways in which they are handled, from the materials and processes used out of school" (Dewey, 1922, n.p.).

This is the key to the importance of place-based education in science. For elementary and middle school students, science will be more likely to take on significant meaning when it is related to the communities in which those students live and to other aspects of their day-to-day life. That students rarely see this meaning in their school science education is reflected in the current academic performance of American students in science.

TRENDS IN CURRENT SCIENCE ACHIEVEMENT IN THE UNITED STATES

Overall, U.S. students have not performed well in recent decades on international measures of science achievement. In the largest study of its kind, results from the 1995 Third International Mathematics and Science Study (TIMSS) indicated that U.S. students did not perform competitively with students in other developed nations (Schmidt, McKnight, & Raizen, 1997). While 4th-grade U.S. students scored within the cluster of top-performing nations, 8th-grade students scored only slightly above the international average, and 12th-grade students scored among the lowest-performing nations. In other words, the longer students studied science in U.S. schools, the farther they dropped in international comparisons.

The 1999 TIMSS-Repeat (TIMSS-R) was meant to provide a more detailed comparison of science performance, but it involved only 8th-grade students. As was the case with the 1995 administration of the TIMSS, 8th-grade U.S. students ranked slightly above the international average, placing 18th out of 34 nations (National Center for Education Statistics, 2000). Dishearteningly, American students showed no significant change in science performance between 1995 and 1999, despite the emphasis on implementing systemic science education reforms in U.S. schools during this time period. Additionally, when the TIMSS-R data were disaggregated to show the 14 U.S. school districts that participated in the study individually, striking differences were seen. Several of the more affluent suburban districts scored on par with the highest-achieving nations such as Singapore and Japan, whereas the lower-SES urban school districts performed significantly below the international average, on par with less-developed countries such as Bulgaria and Tunisia.

The most recent administration of the TIMSS was conducted in 2007 and again showed no significant changes for 4th- and 8th-grade U.S. students in international comparisons. Thus, despite major investments in science reform efforts over the past 15 years, science achievement, as measured by the TIMSS, has remained stagnant.

The other major international assessment of science learning is the Program for International Student Assessment (PISA), which tests 15-year-olds. PISA was administered to students in 43 countries in 2000, 2003, 2006, and 2009. PISA assesses students in reading and mathematical and scientific literacy and, unlike TIMSS, strives to assess problem solving and relevant life skills related to the disciplines in addition to basic content knowledge. When it comes to applying science in meaningful ways, such as using scientific evidence, identifying scientific issues, and explaining phenomena scientifically, U.S. 15-year-old students performed in the bottom half of the international PISA comparisons during each of its four administrations (2000, 2003, 2006, and 2009; National Center for Education Statistics, 2009).

At the national level, the National Assessment of Educational Progress (NAEP) provides assessment of U.S. students' academic performance over time for 9-year-olds, 13-year-olds, and 17-year-olds. NAEP science data from the assessments in 1996, 2000, and 2005 show similar trends to those seen in the TIMSS data for U.S. students. Fourth-grade students continued to make steady progress in science. Scores for 8th-grade students remained flat across the three tests, and scores for 12th-grade students in 2005 decreased slightly when compared to both the 1996 and 2000 achievement levels (National Center for Education Statistics, 2005). Again, the pattern emerges that, despite an increased focus on science education in recent years, the longer our children study science in U.S. schools, the less growth is seen in their test performance. One interpretation of these test results that is sometimes given by science educators is that the increased efforts to promote hands-on inquiry science may be improving student learning, but not in ways that are reflected in the assessment items used on large-scale comparative tests such as TIMSS and NAEP. The results of the PISA assessment, however, which goes to great lengths to assess problem solving and real-world application, would seem to refute this interpretation.

In fact, the evidence is that the strongest force currently influencing science teaching in U.S. classrooms is not the push for inquiry-based practices supported by the national professional organizations or the results of national or international comparisons such as TIMSS, PISA, or NAEP, but rather the state-level tests that have resulted from No Child Left Behind (NCLB) and Race To The Top (RTTT) legislation. With the release in 2010 of the Common Core State Standards for mathematics and language arts and their immediate adoption by more than half the states in the nation, the promise of even more curricular and assessment uniformity is on the horizon. While the type of accountability for meeting academic standards emphasized in NCLB and RTTT has a place in education, the reduction of this goal to the simple desire to achieve higher test scores, without sufficient attention to what those scores actually mean in terms of student learning, has become the primary focus in far too many schools and districts. In such a learning environment, the value of local knowledge becomes increasingly marginalized, as it is unlikely to be tested on a statewide assessment.

Standardized test

We are concerned that more and more, students are being trained to become expert test takers rather than engaged learners and creative problem solvers. The world that today's students will live in will require creative problem solving and persuasive communication if we are to overcome the many challenges we will face as a nation and as a planet. Some of those challenges are known, such as climate change and increasing population pressures on natural resources. Other challenges will emerge in the next generation that we cannot conceive of in the present day. In both cases, a large part of the solution to these challenges will reside at the local level. Even global challenges are often most effectively addressed by local action. Climate change, for example, which affects our entire planet, can be ameliorated by small lifestyle changes made by individuals in their communities—changes that can be understood through a focus on place-based science education. Thus, in a very real sense, the current focus on standardized test scores as the only relevant outcome measure of student learning is not only misguided educationally but is also counterproductive to our future well-being. This concern was a primary motivation for us to create a book that promotes placed-based science learning in elementary and middle grade classrooms.

A HISTORY OF PLACE-BASED EDUCATION

Place-Based education is not a new idea. Its roots can be traced back to antiquity and to the Greek philosopher Aristotle's (384–322 BC) notion of *topos*—i.e. (Greek "place"; *pl.* topoi). *Topos* is the root of the English word *topology*, "the study of a given place." Place-Based education was practiced widely during the 19th century. Childhood educators, such as the Swiss Johann Heinrich Pestalozzi (1746–1827) and the German Friedrich Froebel (1782–1852), included models of place-based learning in their early childhood programs. Froebel, the founder of the modern kindergarten, for example, included nature study, gardening, folk tales, and similar types of localized content in his curriculum. In the

United States, John Dewey (1859–1952) included place-based knowledge as an essential part of his Progressive curriculum. According to Dewey:

> From the standpoint of the child, the great waste in the school comes from his inability to utilize the experiences he gets outside the school in any complete and free way within the school itself; while on the other hand, he is unable to apply in daily life what he is learning in school. That is the isolation of the school–its isolation from life. When the child gets into the schoolroom he has to put out of his mind a large part of the ideas, interests and activities that predominate in his home and neighborhood. So the school being unable to utilize this everyday experience, sets painfully to work on another tack and by a variety of [artificial] means, to arouse in the child an interest in school studies. . . . [As a result there is a] gap existing between the everyday experiences of the child and the isolated material supplied in such large measure in the school. (1956, pp. 75–76)

At the Laboratory School of the University of Chicago, Dewey and talented teachers such as Katherine Kamp and Georgia F. Bacon developed models of place-based education for both science and social studies. The first day of the school's operation was chronicled by Dewey as follows:

> The building No. 389 57th Street is a new house; has large windows, sunny rooms and is surrounded by a playground. The work of the first morning began with a song followed by a survey of the premises to test the knowledge of the children regarding the use of garden, kitchen, etc. as well as their powers of observation. At the end of the morning each child had completed a paper box for pencils and other materials. A story was told by one of the children and physical exercise concluded the program. (Dewey, 1896, p. 707)

Children learned about regional geography in their social studies lessons, taking field trips to the mouth of Lake Michigan and studying maps in order to understand why Chicago was built where it was and why it became a major commercial and transportation hub. In the science classes, students tended gardens and raised animals such as rabbits.

Sixth-grade students at the University of Chicago Laboratory School building a tabletop town (1904). Students designed and constructed scale models of a topological map (right), a 3-D neighborhood map (left), and a fully constructed home with interiors (center). Courtesy of University of Chicago Laboratory School

In addition to being place based, Dewey's curriculum was also highly interdisciplinary—another model of instruction that has been deemphasized in contemporary schools. Like the child's life, Dewey felt that the curriculum should not be compartmentalized. As a result, activities in science flowed into social studies and literature and *vice versa*. The educational models that Dewey developed at the Laboratory School made their way into other educational settings—both public and private. One of the most interesting was the development of the Country Day Movement in private education.

In 1911, Dewey, who had moved to Teachers College, Columbia University in New York City, was contacted by a group of parents from Buffalo, New York, about establishing a private school based on his educational theories. In 1912, the Park School of Buffalo was founded under the leadership of Mary H. Lewis, one of Dewey's students at Teachers College, and a former teacher at the Horace Mann School, which was the Laboratory School for Columbia University.

A first-grade "farm" at the Park School of Buffalo, 1915

Lewis's educational experiment in Buffalo began in a single house in the city, similar to the Chicago lab school, but later moved to the 60-acre farm in suburban Snyder, a suburb of Buffalo. Lewis recounted her work developing the first Park School in her 1928 book *An Adventure with Children*, a book that is still relevant today for prospective teachers. Lewis's teaching model is grounded in place-based education, an idea she traced back to her work with Dewey at the Horace Mann School. For example, one day she requested from her principal a carpet for her classroom on which she could sit and work with her students. This "magic carpet" transformed her classroom by breaking down the artificial barriers between teacher and students created by traditional rows of desks and blackboards. While today this may seem a common thing for an elementary teacher to do, in 1928, such an approach was unheard of. As Lewis described:

> The attitudes of the children changed completely the moment they set foot on that rug. Language lessons became confidential chats about all sorts of experiences. One day the rug became early Manhattan Island; another day it was the boat of Hendrick Hudson. Unconsciously it began to dawn upon me that the thing I wanted to do was to break up as far as possible the formality and artificiality of my classroom. (Lewis, 1928, p. 4)

Lewis also believed in "open-air education," the idea that children should learn as much as possible outdoors. This was partially due to a concern about unhealthy closed classroom environments, which encouraged the spread of illnesses, but also out of a desire to teach children in more natural settings that would promote curiosity. On the farm in Snyder, Lewis implemented an outdoor-based curriculum in which the children took care of farm animals and raised vegetables and flowers, as well as conducting science experiments in the school's marsh and pond.

The Park School led to the founding of other private schools around the country, including the Park School of Cleveland, the Park School of Baltimore, the Harley School in Rochester, the Park School of Boston, and the Shady School in Cambridge. Lewis's innovative work as an educator is widely considered to be the origin of the Country Day School Movement in the United States (Provenzo, 1998). Her approach represented an early example of place-based education. While this model has remained a cornerstone of the teaching philosophy in many private schools, such as among members of the National Association of Independent Schools, the model has rarely found a foothold in American public schooling.

One exception to this was the Life Adjustment Movement, which gained some popularity in public schools following the Second World War. This movement emphasized the need for students to develop personal identity and life skills—many of which were linked to community activities. This place-based movement spread through parts of the country from the late 1940s through the mid-1950s. The launch of the Soviet satellite Sputnik in 1957, however, led to a push for more "rigorous" mathematics and science education and the rejection of the Life Adjustment Movement in Education.

Another attempt at place-based education was reintroduced into American schools a few decades later. In the early 1970s, Eliot Wigginton, a high school teacher at the Rabun Gap-Nacoochee School, a small private school in Northern Georgia, began a program called Foxfire. Named after a local plant, Foxfire engaged students in producing a series of magazines and books based on their interviews with local community members as a way of preserving local knowledge and folk traditions. The Foxfire model replicated many of Dewey's and Lewis's ideas. Specifically, Wigginton felt that the traditional curriculum failed to engage and motivate students to learn in meaningful ways. He advocated a model rooted in the local community and with a cross-disciplinary focus as a way to generate excitement in his students and provide an authentic purpose for learning.

Students film Joseph and Terry Dickerson in the process of making tar from pine knots at the headquarters of the Foxfire Fund, Inc., c. 1970, Mountain City, Georgia. Courtesy of the Georgia Archives

Even though the Foxfire model was developed specifically in the context of rural Northern Georgia and in a private school setting, the model has been applied in other settings as well—rural and urban, public and private. The Foxfire model promotes "core practices" that are fundamentally place based in nature. These practices include the ideas that learning must be active, that there must be an audience for student work and projects beyond the classroom, that what is learned in the classroom or school must be connected to the surrounding community and ultimately to the broader global environment, and that imagination and creativity must be a central part of students' learning process (Foxfire Fund, 2009).

During the 1990s, groups such as the National Science Foundation and the Annenberg Foundation funded initiatives to support the revitalization of rural education, including a number of projects that built upon place-based models of instruction. More recently, the need for place-based education, especially in science, has been supported by the pressing need for more ecological education in the face of global ecological crises. Individuals such as C. A. Bowers have argued that students need to access the wisdom and knowledge systems of elder generations (such as through the Foxfire model) as well as embracing new ideas and technologies in order to promote "ecojustice." Ecojustice is the idea that social justice is inseparable from questions regarding ecological well-being (Bowers, 2005). Bowers describes ecojustice as including five elements that are particularly relevant to educators:

1. Eliminating the causes of eco-racism;

2. Ending the ecological exploitation of developing nations by the developed nations;

3. Revitalizing public spaces (the "commons") to enhance community life;

4. Ensuring that resources and opportunities are available for future generations based on the ecological choices we make today; and

5. Promoting "Earth democracy"—that is, the right of natural systems to reproduce themselves rather than to have their existence contingent upon the demands of humans. (Bowers, 2005)

Place-Based education clearly resonates with many of Bowers's ideas. While place-based education has sometimes focused more explicitly on social studies education (oral history interviews and local geography) and at other times has focused more explicitly on science education (animal husbandry or gardening), a framework centered on eco-justice tends to be more integrative, emphasizing the connections between culture and nature and therefore between social studies and science. Global ecological challenges are likely to produce major sociopolitical crises in the coming years, and our educational system should be proactive rather than reactive in preparing today's students to be able to respond to these challenges.

Other theoretical support for place-based education comes from the research on psychological and anthropological perspectives on learning in context. Cognitive psychologist Ann Brown and cultural anthropologists Jean Lave and Etienne Wenger put forward the idea of "situated learning" in the late 1980s, claiming that learning is inseparable from its physical and cultural setting. They argued that learning can best be promoted through an apprenticeship model where the learner gradually moves from newcomer to expert status within a community of practice. A community of practice could be composed of the students in a classroom, but it could also be a family on a picnic, a Girl Scout troop on a camping trip, or a bunch of kids at a neighborhood swimming pool. In essence, situated learning emphasizes an awareness of authentic contexts, meaningful activities, and worthwhile assessments along with guidance and mentoring by a teacher who serves as a "master learner" and who models learning strategies rather than dispensing knowledge. This view of "situated learning" can be seen as synonymous with place-based education.

Thus, there is a strong historical and theoretical basis for promoting place-based teaching as an important component of modern education. First, such an approach is engaging and motivating for students and teachers. Second, it is relevant to the skills and ways of problem solving that today's students will need as tomorrow's citizens. Third, it provides a needed counterbalance to the testing-driven model of instruction that has become dominant in public schools today. Finally, it is more equitable because students in "exclusive" private schools continue to receive this type of engaging education, while students in public schools are increasingly getting an education that focuses on passing an annual series of tests.

While we want students (and teachers) to have fun using a place-based model of science teaching, we also wish to highlight the role that a place-based approach can play in addressing serious educational, social, economic, and scientific challenges. As Thomas "Tip" O'Neill, a longtime Speaker of the House of Representatives in the U.S. Congress, once stated, "All politics is local." We can help our current students and future leaders get prepared to address the big challenges they will face by helping them explore these challenges today at the local level. This approach has sometimes been referred to as "critical place-based pedagogy" (Buxton, 2010; Gruenewald, 2003) because it combines the traditional local focus of place-based teaching with the attention to social inequities and injustice common in critical pedagogy.

Teachers who take up this model of place-based teaching and learning should be prepared for a change in their classroom and their students. Once we begin to treat our students as the capable thinkers and problem solvers who will be asked to confront tomorrow's global challenges, it is difficult to go back to traditional fact-driven education. In a sense, if you adopt the approach we are advocating, you are opening up Pandora's Box and your students are unlikely to let you put the lid back on.

PLACE-BASED SCIENCE AND DIVERSE LEARNERS

The school-aged population in the United States continues to grow more racially, ethnically, socioeconomically, and linguistically diverse (U.S. Census Bureau, 2005). For example, the 2007 racial and ethnic makeup of students in U.S. schools was 55% White, 21% Hispanic, 17% Black, 5% Asian/Pacific Islander, and 1% American Indian/Alaska Native (National Center for Education Statistics, 2008). While these figures already represent the lowest percentage of White students and the highest percentage of Hispanic students in U.S. schools to date, this is a demographic shift that is almost certain to continue for the foreseeable future. In terms of socioeconomic status (SES), in 2007, 42% of the nation's K–12 students received free or reduced-price lunch, indicating students coming from homes where the family income was less than $38,200 for a family of four during the 2007–2008 school year (NCES, 2008). Free and reduced lunch data over the past decade indicate an increase in student poverty that is also likely to continue, given both demographic and economic trends.

Today's classroom

Along with the increased growth of minority representation in the U.S. student population is the steady increase in English language learners (ELLs), who can now be found in virtually every school in the nation. Currently, more than 20% of U.S. residents speak a language other than English at home. More than 5.5 million, or 11%, of public school students are categorized as ELL students (NCES, 2008).

There are nearly 9 million Hispanic students in U.S. schools, of which approximately 4.4 million are Spanish-speaking ELL students (U.S. Department of Education, 2007). While Spanish speakers make up approximately 80% of the U.S. ELL student population, there are more than 400 different languages spoken by U.S. students. Increasing concentrations of ELL students have spread into geographic regions of the country that lack a history of educating linguistically diverse populations. Most notably, the 12-state Southeastern region has seen the largest percentage increase of ELL students in the last decade (National Clearinghouse for English Language Acquisition, 2007).

This increasing student diversity is coupled with an increase in the importance of knowledge about science and technology in today's world. In addition to the growing number of professions that require a working familiarity with scientific concepts and technological tools, the future well-being of our society may well be determined by decisions made on the basis of general scientific literacy, as well as more specialized scientific knowledge. Systematic reduction of greenhouse gases, controlling the spread of pandemic viral infections, and combating the obesity and diabetes epidemics in the U.S. are just a few examples of critical social issues that can only be adequately addressed by a scientifically literate public. A model of science education that fosters academic achievement and scientific literacy for all students requires an awareness of cultural and linguistic diversity as it applies to teaching and learning.

For example, with ELL students, instruction in science, mathematics, and social studies can and should explicitly support English language and literacy development (Teachers of English to Speakers of Other Languages, 2006). In reality, however, ELL students frequently are required to engage in academic learning through a yet-unmastered language without the instructional support they need. As a result, ELL students often fall behind their English-speaking peers in content-area learning.

If we believe that all students are capable of high academic performance, then gaps in academic outcomes across racial, ethnic, cultural, linguistic, or SES groups must be understood in terms of inequitable learning opportunities, inequitable resources, and/or differences in engagement and motivation to learn. What, then, as educators, can we do to create more equitable and more engaging science learning environments?

At least part of the answer may lie in place-based education. A major challenge facing many teachers is the disconnection that students often feel between school practices and out-of-school practices. What students are asked to do and how they are asked to speak and behave in school may be very different from their actions, behaviors, and language outside of school. While this is at least somewhat true for all students, it is especially true for many students of color, ELL students, and students from low-SES backgrounds. Students are less likely to actively engage in schooling if they do not see their learning experiences as relevant and meaningful to their lives beyond school. All students bring funds of knowledge from their homes and communities that can serve as resources for academic learning (González, Moll, & Amanti, 2005), yet teachers often miss out on ways to build upon this knowledge. Using a place-based approach, academic learning can be connected to activities that occur in day-to-day living, both in and out of school. When these connections are made explicit and actively promoted, all students are likely to find new reasons to engage in science learning.

Bilingual street sign

For example, Rodriguez and Berryman (2002) have worked with academically at-risk students in U.S.–Mexican border communities, using a curriculum they developed collaboratively with students, to investigate local water quality. Students who participated in the project showed an increased enthusiasm for their science classes and an increased understanding of science content. Perhaps more significantly, they also found that a number of the participating students took additional action beyond school-situated projects, such as testing water in their homes and investigating ways to improve water standards in their communities. Students changed their own water use practices and informed their families of ways to conserve water at home. Having come to see science as relevant to their lives and communities, students then considered scientific investigations as worthwhile activities.

In another example, Rahm (2002) created and studied an inner-city youth gardening program. Participants were middle-school students who had been identified as being at risk of dropping out of school. The research took place as part of a summer 4-H community youth program in which the students earned money by gardening and then selling their produce at a community market. Rahm found that working together in the garden supported youth-initiated planning and decision making, as well as enabling connections among science learning, the community, and authentic work. A wide range of science content emerged naturally from participants' engagement in the gardening activities that the students considered valuable and meaningful. Some students volunteered to continue their gardening projects after the summer program was over.

These modern examples show the value of place-based science education for promoting both student engagement and academic science learning. The approaches share characteristics with Dewey's and Lewis's work from nearly a century ago, as well as

White House Garden

qualities of more recent efforts such as Foxfire and Bowers's model of ecojustice. Modern place-based education fosters community connections in ways that build on local funds of knowledge and develop students' intellectual curiosity and motivation in ways that lead to sustained interest in science. Sustained interest is demonstrated when students pursue self-motivated explorations outside of the classroom or use science in an ongoing way to improve, expand, or enhance an activity to which they are already deeply committed. It could be argued that this kind of ongoing and self-directed engagement is the best evidence of place-based science being a worthwhile instructional approach. As a classroom teacher, however, you must naturally be concerned about how to assess student learning that results from a place-based approach. In the following section, we present a wide range of assessment techniques that can be used with place-based instruction.

ASSESSING PLACE-BASED SCIENCE TEACHING AND LEARNING

Place-Based science teaching benefits greatly from a broad view of classroom assessment that includes teacher-directed assessments in addition to the mandated state and district testing. Here, we consider the multiple roles that assessment should play in your classroom and how assessment should be conceptualized in relation to teaching and learning.

Assessment should be viewed as an integrated part of science teaching and learning. The metaphor of a three-legged stool is sometimes used to describe this relationship among curriculum, instruction, and assessment—if the three legs are not in balance or are of unequal length, then the stool will at best be wobbly or worse, completely dysfunctional. When teaching, learning, and assessment are conceptualized and practiced as an integrated system, then the metaphorical stool is likely to be balanced. Too often today, the assessment leg seems to be out of balance with the other two, leading to unsound teaching and learning. While we have integrated assessment into the activities in Parts I through V, we wish to explore the idea that practicing place-based science teaching may require teachers to rethink their classroom assessment practices at the same time that they rethink their curriculum and instruction. Given the current assessment pressures, this may make some teachers nervous, but the research evidence seems clear that place-based science instruction will help students meet the science standards to which they are currently held accountable at the same time that it provides additional benefits.

When students are engaged in projects over time, and when they care about what they are learning, then they are likely to retain that knowledge for a prolonged period. When the tests that count are cumulative, end-of-year tests, then knowledge retention becomes a critical piece of student success. Even if the tests fail to assess higher-order thinking, problem solving, reasoning, or communication skills that are also taught through place-based learning, students are still more likely to retain factual information that they learned 6 months earlier during a stream-monitoring project than facts they learned 6 months earlier from reading a textbook chapter on water quality. The learning that takes place through place-based instruction can be further solidified through a teacher's thoughtful and strategic use of varied assessment strategies.

TEACHER-DIRECTED ASSESSMENTS

It is understandable that teachers today may sometimes perceive assessment of student learning as being out of their hands. On one level, this may well be true. State-level assessments have the most visibility and the most significant consequences, both positive and negative, for students and teachers. However, teachers still maintain a great deal of control over their daily classroom assessment and should consider ways in which they can use this teacher-driven assessment as an integral part of students' science learning. Using the stool metaphor we referred to earlier, effective teachers find ways to bring the assessment leg of their practice into balance with the teaching and learning legs. To do this, teachers must come to see assessment not just as something that is done to students but also as a form of knowledge sharing that is done with students.

Norm-referenced and criterion-referenced standardized tests are just two variations of one form of assessment (the on-demand, cumulative test). While these tests are an inevitability, teachers can do much more to conceptualize an assessment system along with their students—one that includes diagnostic assessment of prior knowledge, formative assessment of ongoing learning, and summative assessment of major learning goals and that takes into account skills, dispositions, beliefs, and other measures besides factual knowledge. Multiple uses of assessment have unique objectives that come together to both paint a picture of and contribute to student learning. A focus on place-based teaching can and should influence each element of this assessment system.

Diagnostic Assessment and Place-Based Science Learning

Diagnostic assessments are meant to provide teachers and students with a sense both of students' prior knowledge and of their misconceptions about a topic before beginning a learning activity. It is often the case that many students in a class are already familiar with at least some aspects of a topic and that these parts can be treated more as a review than as a new idea. On the other hand, a diagnostic assessment sometimes reveals that many students in a class do not have a working knowledge of a topic that a teacher assumed was clearly understood. In this case, a responsive teacher backs up and reviews that material before proceeding. For example, in order to engage students in a study of the effects of acid rain on a local pond ecosystem, the students need to have a working understanding of the pH scale. A diagnostic assessment may show that some students have a clear understanding of the pH scale, how it is tested, and how it is related to acid rain, while other students may need some instruction and an opportunity to practice testing and interpreting the pH of substances in the classroom before they are prepared to begin the pond study.

Diagnostic assessment can also provide a baseline for later consideration of how much learning has taken place once a unit or project has been completed. There has been a dramatic increase in the number of district or state diagnostic, or benchmark, tests that are aligned to state academic content standards. These assessments are meant to provide teachers (and school administrators) with tools for checking the progress of students toward meeting state standards and are often meant to serve as predictors of end-of-year testing results. Diagnostic assessments for this purpose are generally of the forced-response (multiple-choice) variety. This is because they are quick, easy, and cheap to score on a large scale. Teachers should not limit themselves to this form of diagnostic assessment in their classrooms. Diagnostic assessments can also support place-based teaching and learning and take a variety of forms, including:

Quizzes—quizzes are well known to all of us from our own days as students. The typical quiz has traditionally been used as a mini-summative assessment, for the purposes of grading, or to promote student motivation and keep the class on task. However, quizzes can also serve as a diagnostic assessment when they are given at the start of a unit of study to assess students' prior knowledge. Diagnostic quizzes can support place-based learning when they are used at the start of a project to gauge what directed instruction might be needed to support students' successful learning during the project.

Concept maps—Concept maps provide visual models of a student's thinking about a given topic. They are meant to show the relationships that an individual or small group perceives between key concepts. In a concept map, concepts are connected by arrows (often called links) that should be labeled to clarify the nature of the relationship perceived by the student. The purpose of a concept map is to make student thinking visible. They are flexible assessment tools that can be used as diagnostic, formative, or summative assessments. By focusing on the links between key concepts, concept maps help clarify how well students understand the hierarchy of ideas related to the topic of study. Concept maps not only serve to assess but also to teach. For example, concept maps can help develop student abilities to draw reasonable inferences from observations, to synthesize and integrate information and ideas, and to learn concepts and theories in the subject area. Concept maps as diagnostic assessments can support place-based learning by providing a map of student understanding of a topic before the start of a project. The map can be revisited, edited, and expanded at the end of the project to allow the students to see how their ideas have evolved.

Journal entries—Journaling provides a safe way for students to express what they may already know about a topic in a private way, without having to risk sounding foolish in front of classmates. Additionally, students have the time to craft a clear statement with supporting details that may be missing from an oral response to a question. Journal responses can provide a range of insights into the depth or lack of student understanding of a particular concept or set of skills. The journal entry can be done the day before the start of a new unit of instruction so the teacher can check the range of student prior knowledge and plan to introduce the topic accordingly. A journal response makes a good diagnostic assessment for a place-based project because it provides an open format for students to share their past experiences relevant to the topic of the project. For example, before beginning a project on where our food comes from, a student could share her experiences with gardening (a question the teacher might think to ask explicitly) but could also share that her father is a truck driver and is gone for a week at a time when he carries produce from Mexico or California (relevant but unexpected prior knowledge).

Interviews/small-group discussions—Interviews can be conducted with individual students or in small groups to explore their depth of knowledge on a topic that will be studied. The key to using interviews or small-group discussions effectively as diagnostic assessment is in asking good questions—questions that probe for both relevant experiences and depth of understanding. Asking students if they have ever planted a garden before is important to know before starting a gardening project but by itself tells the teacher very little about what students actually know about gardening. Individual interviews take a lot of time for a full class of students, so they are generally impractical as a diagnostic assessment. Small-group discussions can be done more easily as the rest of the class is engaged in independent work.

Whole-class discussion—While whole-class discussions are among the most common teacher-lead informal diagnostic assessments, they are generally not highly recommended. They are used because they are quick and give feedback right away; however, they rarely give a balanced picture. This is because the students with the most prior knowledge on the topic are likely to volunteer what they know and students with less prior knowledge are likely to remain quiet. This usually gives a false impression of the typical amount of prior knowledge in the class.

Formative Assessment and Place-Based Science Learning

While diagnostic assessment focuses on what students already know, formative assessment is primarily concerned with the question of how students learn. Formative assessments take place during a learning activity to provide the teacher with ideas about how well students are making sense of the learning goals and key ideas of a lesson, activity, or unit. Formative assessments can be seen as evidence that learning is taking place but should also be viewed as learning opportunities in their own right. Nearly all teachers intuitively use some types of formative assessment as they teach, most typically whole-group questioning, to try to be sure that the class is following the lesson. As was mentioned in the discussion of diagnostic assessment, however, whole-group questioning has serious limitations, primarily because not every student will be questioned, and a small number of students will typically push to answer every question. Additionally, many students do not effectively demonstrate what they know in this format of on-the-spot answers in front of all their peers. Other types of formative assessments are available that may provide a clearer picture of how student learning is progressing. For example:

Think Aloud—In a think aloud, students are asked to say out loud whatever they are thinking while they are working on a problem or task. Think alouds can be used with individual students, pairs, or small groups (generally no more than four students in a group). When using pairs or groups of students, it is generally best to ask one student to act as the problem solver and the other student(s) to act as listeners, asking clarifying questions as needed. The teacher can circulate and listen to students thinking aloud as they work on their problem. While the think aloud strategy is most often used in mathematical problem solving, it is very appropriate for place-based science activities as well. The strategy can be used out in the field or back in the classroom. The important thing is for students to narrate their thinking as they do their work. Note that this is different than a small-group interview in that the students are not responding to questions from the teacher but rather talking aloud to describe their thinking as they work on a problem or project.

Lesson Study—In lesson study, two or more teachers jointly plan, teach, and observe a lesson and collectively analyze student work. One member of the group teaches the lesson, while the other(s) observes students and collects evidence of their learning. After the lesson, the teachers discuss the student learning that was taking place and consider how to build upon that learning in subsequent lessons. Unlike the other formative assessments discussed here, in lesson study the students are not explicitly asked to perform an assessment task. Instead, the presence of additional teachers who are focused on studying student learning during the lesson can provide insights about that learning to the teacher who was running the lesson. Paraprofessionals and other adult volunteers in the classroom can also be taught to do lesson study in order to help the teacher get a better understanding of the learning that is taking place in her classroom. Lesson study is especially appropriate for place-based science projects that involve leaving the classroom since these trips will generally require additional adults for supervision in any case. Those adults can do more than just supervise; they can also help to provide formative assessment.

Exit slips—An exit slip (also known as a "ticket out the door") is a short form of formative assessment that can be used at the end of a lesson to help the teacher gauge student understanding of one or two big ideas that were presented in the lesson. This insight can then guide planning for the subsequent lesson. Students write a one-sentence summary on a slip of paper of what they feel was the most important thing that they learned during the day's lesson and hand it in on their way out the door. Alternatively, the teacher can ask one question for the students to respond to on their exit slip. Teachers will get a clear and immediate picture of whether or not they successfully conveyed the big idea they were trying to present in the lesson. A journal entry can be used in much the same way but to capture a bit more detail. Using an exit slip on a regular basis also gets students in the habit of summarizing what they are learning in their own minds as the lesson progresses, since they know that they will be asked to write this down at the end of class. Exit slips are appropriate for place-based teaching since they provide the flexibility for the students to choose for themselves what they feel the most important idea of the lesson was. Putting more responsibility on students for thinking about the value of what they are learning is well aligned with the goals of place-based education.

Performance assessments—In a performance assessment, students are asked to demonstrate their ability to use a particular tool or technique. Performance assessments are common in science classes that emphasize experimentation since the proper use of the tools and techniques is essential to successfully doing experiments. Typical examples of a performance assessment would be demonstrating the ability to focus a microscope and identify an amoeba or being able to do a hardness test to differentiate between the minerals quartz and calcite. While performance assessments are common in college lab science courses, they are less common in K–12 teaching. Additionally, the current push toward more fact-driven science standards has further decreased the perceived value of performance assessments in many cases. Performance assessments are appropriate as formative assessment during place-based learning, however, due to the emphasis on the use of tools and techniques that often go along with place-based projects. Tracking the weather, monitoring water quality, using bird identification charts, and many other activities presented in this book require students to master the use of tools.

Summative Assessment and Place-Based Science Learning

Summative assessments are meant to provide a measure of cumulative learning over time and are given at the end of a unit of study to assess mastery of key concepts or ideas. Summative assessment is what generally comes to mind first when assessment is discussed. The most traditional methods of summative assessment are written unit tests and term papers, but a range of other summative assessments are possible. There has been a push in recent years for teachers to model their summative assessments after the state high-stakes tests that students will take at the end of the year to give them more practice with this format. While students do need practice with these formats, the increase in district- and state-mandated benchmark tests means that students will already get plenty of practice with standard forms. As a teacher, you should guard the flexibility that you still have when it comes to assessment. Be sure to use that freedom to ensure that your students get access to a balanced variety of assessment styles, as this will improve their learning and your teaching. The following list is certainly not exhaustive, but it provides examples of varied summative assessments that can support the goals of place-based teaching and learning. Additionally, some of the assessment styles that were discussed under diagnostic and formative assessments above can be extended over time to serve multiple assessment purposes, including as a summative assessment. The example of concept maps used in this way is given below.

Multimedia presentations—Multimedia presentations using PowerPoint or other similar software have become a ubiquitous part of teaching, replacing the traditional notes presented on the chalkboard. More and more, students are being asked to do the same kinds of presentations to demonstrate their learning. Such presentations can foster creativity and problem solving and show the connections students are making between school learning and the real world, but they rarely do. Instead, student multimedia presentations frequently just summarize and restate factual content without reflection or synthesis of ideas. As a way to assess place-based learning, teachers can encourage students to create multimedia presentations that both document activities that were done beyond the classroom and reflect on what was learned from those activities. The rest of the class can participate in assessing how well the presentation moves beyond the restatement of facts to include the synthesis of ideas.

Video or photo projects—A video or photo project can be used to document student learning in a visual format. This format may allow some students to more easily share what they have learned. All students must learn to express their understanding in writing, but since most assessments will continue to be in written form, using assessments that draw on a wider range of media can provide a clearer picture of what students have learned and makes for a fairer assessment system. Some teachers are hesitant to use video or photo projects as assessments because students sometimes spend too much time working on the aesthetics of the project and fail to dedicate enough time to the substance they are presenting. Usually, this problem can be addressed by giving clear assessment guidelines and a clear rubric that is explained to students in advance. There are many assessment rubric templates available on the web for project-based multimedia that can be easily modified to meet your needs. The most important thing, however, is that the video or photo project should demonstrate how the students made sense of what was learned. Place-Based education is well suited to this type of assessment since the focus will generally be on a project that encourages students to take ownership of their learning and apply it in some way.

Series of concept maps—Concept maps were described earlier as a form of diagnostic assessment, but in fact, they are quite flexible assessment tools. They were designed to serve multiple instructional and assessment purposes. Concept maps can provide a visual image of what students already know about a topic (diagnostic assessment). They can then be revisited, edited, and expanded during instruction to serve both as a teaching tool and as a formative assessment. Finally, new concept maps can be drawn at the end of a project or unit of study and compared to earlier maps to document growth and development of understanding of a topic. Assessing learning through a series of concept maps can be aligned with the goals of place-based education in that concept maps highlight the relationships between ideas, and place-based teaching encourages students to make connections between their local environment and academic learning.

Exhibits or museum-style displays—In Part V we use the example of museum visits as a source of place-based learning in the community. When students visit a museum, they notice that there is a style to the learning that takes place there that is different from classroom learning. It is more flexible and free flowing. You are free to wander about and spend as much or as little time as you like thinking about and perhaps interacting with a certain topic. Students will also notice that some museum exhibits draw them in to learn more while other exhibits cause them to walk by. This understanding of how and why we learn in informal contexts can be put to use in student assessment. Having your students construct their own science museum exhibits and then sharing them with parents or other classes can be both a powerful learning experience and a powerful summative assessment tool. Students can design interactive exhibits to specifically address topics that they found confusing or challenging when they were learning them. This can help the students to develop a deeper understanding of a topic they struggled with as they consider how to teach this idea to others. A good science museum exhibit is informational and engaging and leaves you wondering something as you walk away. These serve as good evaluation criteria for a summative assessment and are well-aligned with the goals of place-based education.

Mock scientific conferences—Once students have engaged in a place-based science learning project, they should have something to share about what they learned. This could be information about plant growth in a garden, rock types in buildings downtown, the duck population in a local park, or any of a wide number of topics. Students should learn that when scientists have findings to share, the first thing they usually do is present those findings at a scientific conference. This allows them to present their results to an informed audience who will ask them questions and push their thinking. In the same way, a mock scientific conference in the classroom makes a meaningful summative assessment that can be informative and fun. A conference allows students to share opinions, support ideas with evidence, and demonstrate their understanding of key issues. It also provides an opportunity to teach the importance of skills such as listening carefully, respecting others' ideas, communicating clearly, evaluating ideas, and asking good questions. A mock scientific conference is well aligned with a place-based teaching model since students are asked to take ownership of the assessment rather than just being passive recipients of a test.

Peer teaching lesson to younger students—It is an old saying that the best way to be sure that you understand something is to try to teach it to someone else. Having students teach a lesson on what they have learned to other students a year or two younger than they are can serve as a powerful summative assessment. Students will learn that it takes a lot of preparation to teach a lesson even once they have figured out what they want to teach. It is generally best to have students try this in groups of three or four, and the class of younger students may also be split into smaller groups. Be sure to give your students ample time to prepare so that you are not setting them up to fail. Help them think about setting a reasonable learning goal, the materials needed, the timing of the lesson, and even how they might assess their "students'" learning in a creative way. Be sure that they have something active for the younger students to do. As a class, discuss how peer teaching demonstrates their own learning and how that could be assessed. Peer teaching as summative assessment can support the goals of place-based education because, like the other examples given here, it places some of the responsibility for considering how they will demonstrate their learning on the students themselves.

ASSESSMENTS AND NONMAINSTREAM STUDENTS

Given the high-stakes nature of science assessment in our schools today, it is crucially important to consider whether assessments are fair for all students. In particular, concerns have been raised about the fairness of assessments given the increasing cultural and linguistic diversity of students in U.S. schools. Are the assessments we are using to decide students' futures biased in ways that we are not considering? These questions are true for state-level standards-based tests, but they are also true in your own classroom-level assessments. Are the assessments you are using fair? Fairness in this context can be thought of as the probability that a given assessment will allow all students to adequately demonstrate what they have learned about the topic being assessed. Assessments that are aligned with place-based teaching may improve the fairness of assessments for nonmainstream students. This is because place-based teaching more easily builds on students' prior knowledge from family and community settings. If assessments, whether diagnostic, formative, or summative, also build on these community-based experiences, then they are likely to provide better and fairer measures of what and how well non-mainstream students are leaning.

Assessments should be particularly attentive to social, cultural, and linguistic influences that might affect some students' ability to understand and respond to assessment items more than others. Students of differing cultural backgrounds may express their ideas in ways that hide their knowledge and abilities in the eyes of teachers who are unfamiliar with the linguistic and cultural norms of students' homes and communities. While all students, including mainstream students, are subject to cultural influences, the linguistic and cultural knowledge that mainstream students use to express their understanding is more likely to be aligned, or congruent, with the language and culture of teachers, researchers, and test developers. Thus, the backgrounds of mainstream students are more likely to support their performance on assessments than to interfere with it, while the opposite may be true for many nonmainstream students.

Since teaching, learning, and assessment all mutually reinforce each other (remember the three-legged stool), instruction that is better aligned with students' experiences and communication patterns may also improve assessment outcomes for those students. Place-Based teaching, because it can be readily situated within the communities, experiences, and discourse patterns of a given teacher's students, can lead to the development of meaningful place-based assessment measures. Results of these assessments, can, in turn, guide subsequent place-based instruction. It is important to remember the critical role of assessment "for" learning as well as assessment "of" learning. That is, when assessment is thoughtfully done, it contributes to students' learning rather than simply measuring that learning.

Assessments that aim to be equitable should consider the knowledge and abilities that students bring from their home and community cultures while also measuring the science standards that are expected of all students. Traditional science assessments have generally made few, if any, connections to nonmainstream students' lived experiences. In most cases, this is not due to a desire to be unfair but rather to the fact that few teachers or test developers have an in-depth knowledge of nonmainstream students' cultural and linguistic beliefs and practices. Also, because science is usually thought of as being universal and culture free, the idea that cultural backgrounds might influence science instruction or assessment may seem alien to many teachers and test developers. However, a growing number of assessment experts have come to understand that the inclusion of authentic tasks drawn from students' real-life situations can motivate students, more accurately reflect their knowledge, and actually enhance their performance (García & Pearson, 1994; Solano-Flores & Li, 2008). Place-Based teaching can provide the context to support these kinds of more equitable assessments.

In addition to considering the content of assessments, it is important to consider the formats used for assessing student achievement. Traditional multiple-choice tests have been criticized for failing to adequately measure the types of knowledge and abilities that scientists and science educators feel it is most important for science students to learn (National Research Council, 2000). Instead, performance assessments and other alternative assessments, such as the kinds discussed above, have been proposed as better measures of meaningful science learning. Advocates of more varied science assessments claim that this variety provides students with flexible and multiple opportunities to demonstrate their knowledge, are more consistent with cultural preferences, may be less heavily dependent on academic language proficiency in English, and permit students to communicate their ideas in multiple ways. The overarching goal for using a place-based approach to science teaching is to promote more meaningful and engaging learning experiences for our students (remember Dewey, Lewis, and the other place-based educators discussed earlier). Using a range of diagnostic, formative, and summative assessment strategies can be an important part of this learning experience.

PLACE-BASED SCIENCE AND THINKING LIKE A SCIENTIST

One of the advantages of a place-based approach to science teaching is that it supports students in developing the skills of thinking like a scientist. What does it mean to think like a scientist? More than anything else, thinking like a scientist means learning to use scientific inquiry practices when studying the natural world. Science inquiry has many definitions, but following Kuhn (2005), the definition we prefer is this: *The ability to coordinate hypothesis and evidence through the study of controlled, cause-and-effect relationships.* This definition highlights three key inquiry practices that can be readily taught through a place-based approach to science teaching:

1. Coordinating hypothesis and evidence

2. Controlling variables

3. Studying cause-and-effect relationships

Focusing on these three inquiry practices will help students learn to think like a scientist. Below, we discuss each of these practices in turn. In each of the 40 place-based science activities in the second part of this book, we highlight one of these practices and how the activity can help students master this practice as they learn to think like a scientist. If students participate in a number of the place-based science activities in this book, one thing they will learn is how to think like a scientist.

COORDINATING HYPOTHESIS AND EVIDENCE

We all have personal hypotheses about many of the things we experience in life. What the best streets are to drive on during rush hour to avoid traffic, what temperature to set your air conditioning to minimize your electrical bill, and how long to microwave a bag of popcorn to get the most kernels to pop without burning them are just three everyday examples of personal hypotheses. Scientists also work with hypotheses on a daily basis. A scientist might hypothesize that igneous rocks are harder than sedimentary rocks, that tall people have faster heart rates that short people, or that bikes with skinny tires will roll faster than bikes with fat tires.

A hypothesis is basically an expectation of what should happen barring unforeseen circumstances. We develop hypotheses over time based on our personal experiences and things that other people tell us that we choose to believe. Hypotheses, however, cannot stand alone. They need to be supported by evidence. Children (and many adults too) have a hard time distinguishing between hypothesis and evidence. People also have a hard time connecting the two. Sometimes our hypotheses can't account for the evidence we gather. The highway with heavy rush hour traffic still gets us home faster than the surface road with less traffic. We find a piece of sandstone (a sedimentary rock) that is harder than a piece of pumice (an igneous rock). Students must learn that when our hypothesis fails to accommodate our evidence, the hypothesis needs to be refined, revised, or totally replaced. This can be quite difficult for people to do, especially if they have held onto their hypothesis for a while.

There is a good deal of research in psychology showing that most people are very resistant to giving up ideas they already believe to be true when confronted with evidence to the contrary. Scientists work hard to train themselves to become better at this—to test their hypotheses by gathering and critically examining evidence and then refining, revising, or totally replacing their hypotheses based on that evidence. This is difficult for students and takes lots of practice. In many of the activities in this book, students will be asked to gather evidence and then use it to generate or revise a hypothesis about how things work in the natural world. Because place-based activities tend to be engaging for students, they are a good way to support the development of challenging thinking such as coordinating hypothesis and evidence.

CONTROLLING VARIABLES

A variable is anything that can change. This can be in a science experiment or in life more generally. The weather, the speed of a bike going down a hill, and the height of students in your class are all variables. When we think about inquiry practices, the only way to be sure that we correctly understand what we observe is if we account for all the possible variables.

When we conduct science experiments, we usually manipulate one variable to determine the effect of this manipulation on another variable. Any other variables that could possibly affect the experiment need to be kept constant or controlled. The variable we manipulate is usually called the independent variable. The variable we want to observe is usually called the dependent variable (because what happens to this variable *depends* on the changes we make to the first variable). The other variables we wish to control are usually called controlled variables or constants.

If we consider a question such as what is the effect of nitrogen fertilizer on the growth of bean plants, the independent variable would be fertilizers with different amounts of nitrogen (what we would manipulate). The dependent variable would be a measure of bean plant growth (where we would look for change). We would try to control all other possible variables that could influence bean plant growth, such as soil type, amount of sunlight, size of container, amount of water, and other ingredients in the fertilizers. Another way to say this is that we would make sure that each variable such as soil type, amount of sunlight, and amount of water would be the same for every bean plant. The only thing we would want to be different for each plant is the amount of nitrogen in the fertilizer (the independent variable). When all these variables are controlled, we can logically conclude that the differences we see in bean plant growth are likely due to changes in the nitrogen level in the fertilizer.

Controlling variables can be difficult for students because not all of the variables that could cause a change are always obvious. It can also be hard to plan for keeping many possible variables controlled at the same time. When we do experiments in the natural world, sometimes it is impossible to control all the variables we would like to. Learning to control variables to the best of our ability takes practice and planning. The place-based activities in this book will give students ample opportunity for just this kind of practice.

STUDYING CAUSE-AND-EFFECT RELATIONSHIPS

The third inquiry practice we wish to emphasize is the study of cause-and-effect relationships. While cause-and-effect reasoning may seem to be a fairly simple skill, it is actually more abstract and more complex than it may appear. Particularly for children and young adolescents, this is generally a new way of thinking that takes time and practice to develop. It is worth the time to help students develop this skill because it is useful in everyday life and not just in the study of science. A simple definition is that *a cause-and-effect relationship exists when one event, the cause, brings about another event, the effect, through some mechanism.*

Sometimes people assume that when two events occur together, then one of the events must have caused the other. Sometimes this is the case—when we see lightning we almost always hear thunder and so we conclude that the lightning causes the thunder. Sometimes, though, two events may occur together but not be linked by a cause-and-effect relationship. When the weather gets cold in the winter, people are more likely to get the flu, so we may conclude that cold weather causes the flu, but this turns out not to be the case. The onset of winter and the increase in flu cases occur together because when the weather turns cold, people are more likely to stay inside and in close proximity to each other, allowing viruses and bacteria to more easily pass from person to person. So cold weather can be linked to flu season but not in a direct cause-and-effect relationship. Research has shown that humans naturally try to construct cause-and-effect relationships as a way to explain our observations of the world around us. These mental models help us to predict and control our environment. We do this even when not consciously thinking about it, probably as a survival mechanism.

The goal of studying cause-and-effect relationships through place-based science is to make these subconscious practices conscious and explicit. When we study cause-and-effect relationships, we learn to think critically and to focus on identifying the actions, events, or conditions (the causes) that lead to or create specific consequences (the effects). Multiple activities in this book will give students the chance to practice making these connections. Practicing cause-and-effect reasoning, like learning to control variables and learning to coordinate hypothesis and evidence, provides students with rich opportunities to think like a scientist, skills that are very useful for navigating the world as well as for succeeding in science class.

MODIFYING ACTIVITIES FOR GRADE RANGE AND OTHER LEARNER DIFFERENCES

Considering how to modify activities (often called "differentiated curriculum" or "differentiated instruction") based on the grade range of students is not as simple or as straightforward as it may first appear. Every experienced teacher can testify that within any class or grade level, there exists a wide range of student abilities and experiences. For example, the typical elementary or middle school science class today is likely to include students with physical or cognitive special needs, students who are English language learners, students from multiple cultural, ethnic, and racial backgrounds, students with a range of previous academic success, students with a range of attitudes toward science and toward school in general, students with a range of reading levels, and students with different learning style preferences, as well as other types of student diversity. Thus, to say that students at a particular grade level need a certain type of instruction is a gross oversimplification of the reality of teaching children. Every teacher at any grade level needs to think about how to differentiate her lessons to meet the unique learning needs of the students in her class. These modifications can take a number of different forms, including modifications to the content, the conceptual difficulty, the intended learning goals, the methods of instruction, and the methods of assessment, among others.

For example, English language learners may need the same content with the same conceptual difficulty as native English speakers but with modifications to methods of instruction and assessment, while a gifted student may require an increased cognitive difficulty and a modification to the learning goals. To further complicate the issue, a student might be both an English language learner and gifted. Thus, there is much more to modifying curriculum and instruction than just considering the grade level of the student. That said, it is also true that there are developmental differences that occur as students grow and develop through the elementary and middle school years. For this reason, in the activities in the second part of this book, we present suggestions for curricular modifications for lower elementary grades, upper elementary grades, and middle school grades as well as for other learner differences. For each of the 40 activities, we present a sample curricular modification based on one or more type of learner difference. Teachers should take these ideas as a starting point for discussions about the broader range of learner differences in their classrooms.

INTERDISCIPLINARY TEACHING THROUGH PLACE-BASED SCIENCE

As we have mentioned several times in this introduction, place-based education is quite conducive to interdisciplinary teaching or teaching across the content areas. Interdisciplinary teaching can play a critical role in addressing the wide range of content standards that teachers are responsible for covering and that students are responsible for learning. When these lists of standards are considered separately, they can be daunting to teachers and students alike, because there are so many topics that need to be covered in each of the core content areas. However, when the standards are considered in unison across the content areas, there are ways in which multiple standards from different content areas can be addressed simultaneously in the same lesson. For example, language arts standards for expository reading and writing, math standards for data representation and analysis, and social studies standards for civics could all be addressed along with relevant life science standards during a place-based science activity on the role of exercise in life-long heath and wellness.

Interdisciplinary teaching may look quite different at the elementary and the middle school levels, but it can be done at both levels (and beyond). In elementary schools, where one teacher is generally responsible for teaching multiple content areas, a decision to try more interdisciplinary teaching can be made and carried out by a single teacher (although it can often be easier to do this using a team planning approach). In middle schools, where most teachers teach only one content area, interdisciplinary teaching will require a team effort with multiple teachers planning activities together and then each carrying out his or her part to contribute to the larger goal. In either case, place-based science can serve as a centerpiece for this approach.

In each of the 40 place-based science activities in the second part of this book, we highlight one example of how the activity can lend itself to interdisciplinary connections. While many of the science activities could be connected to multiple content areas in meaningful ways, we provide one example of an interdisciplinary connection and encourage the reader to use this example as a starting point for considering additional interdisciplinary connections.

Throughout this book, we try to provide the reader with as many resources as we can for making placed-based science instruction possible. Interdisciplinary connections, modifications for grade range and other learner differences, and support for thinking like a scientist included with each activity are three of those resources. In the remainder of this book, we provide a series of 40 activities that can be used to enact place-based science teaching with elementary and middle school students in both formal and informal settings. The Appendix at the conclusion of this book includes a catalogue of resources (many Internet connected) that can be found in most communities to help provide settings for worthwhile placed-based science instruction.

REFERENCES

Bowers, C. A. (2005). *EcoJustice dictionary.* Accessed July 18, 2009, at http://www.cabowers.net/dicterm/CAdict010.php.

Bruner, J. (1962). *The process of education.* Cambridge: Harvard University Press.

Buxton, C. (2010). Social problem solving through science: An approach to critical, place-based, science teaching and learning. *Equity and Excellence in Education, 43*(1), 120–135.

Dewey, J. (1896, January). The Model School. *University of Chicago Weekly* (Vol. 16), 707.

Dewey, J. (1922). *Democracy and education: An introduction to the philosophy of education.* New York: Macmillan. Available online at http://www.gutenberg.org/etext/852.

Dewey, J. (1956). *The child and the curriculum and the school and society.* Chicago: University of Chicago Press.

Foxfire Fund Website. (2009). Core practices. Accessed July 18, 2009, at http://www.foxfire.org/index.html.

García, G. E., & Pearson, D. P. (1994). Assessment and diversity. In L. Darling-Hammond (Vol. Ed.), *Review of research in education: Vol. 20* (pp. 337–391). Washington, DC: American Educational Research Association.

González, N., Moll, L. C., & Amanti, C. (2005). *Funds of knowledge: Theorizing practices in households, communities, and classrooms.* Mahwah, NJ: Erlbaum.

Gruenewald, D. A. (2003). The best of both worlds: a critical pedagogy of place. *Educational Researcher, 32*(4), 3–12.

Hutchinson, D. (2009). Place-Based education. *The encyclopedia of the social and cultural foundations of education* (Vol. 2.). Thousand Oaks, CA: SAGE.

Kuhn, D. (2005). *Education for thinking.* Cambridge, MA: Harvard University Press.

Lewis, M. H. (1928). *An adventure with children.* New York: Macmillan. Reprinted in 1985, Eugene F. Provenzo, Jr. and Therese M. Provenzo, editors. Lanham, MD: University Press of America.

National Center for Education Statistics. (2000). *Highlights from the trends in international mathematics and science study (TIMSS) 1999.* Washington, DC: U.S. Department of Education.

National Center for Education Statistics. (2005). *The nation's report card: Science 2005.* Washington, DC: U.S. Department of Education.

National Center for Education Statistics. (2008). *The condition of education, 2008.* Washington, DC: U.S. Department of Education.

National Center for Education Statistics. (2009). *The condition of education, 2009.* Washington, DC: U.S. Department of Education.

National Clearinghouse for English Language Acquisition. (2007). *The growing numbers of limited English proficient students: 1996–2006.* Washington, DC: Author.

National Research Council. (2000). *Inquiry and the national science education standards: A guide for teaching and learning.* Washington, DC: National Academy Press.

Piaget, J. (1971). *To understand is to invent.* New York: Viking.

Provenzo, E. F. (1998). An adventure in learning: The Park School of Buffalo and American progressive education. In Susan F. Semmel & Alan R. Sadovnik, Eds., *Schools of tomorrow today* (pp. 103–119). New York: Peter Lang.

Rahm, J. (2002). Emergent learning opportunities in an inner-city youth gardening program. *Journal of Research in Science Teaching, 39*(2), 164–184.

Rodriguez, A. J., & Berryman, C. (2002). Using sociotransformative constructivism to teach for understanding in diverse classrooms: A beginning teacher's journey. *American Educational Research Journal, 39*(4), 1017–1045.

Schmidt, W. H., McKnight, C. C., & Raizen, S. A. (1997). *A splintered vision: An investigation of U.S. science and mathematics education.* Dordrecht, the Netherlands: Kluwer Academic Publishers.

Solano-Flores, G., & Li, M. (2008). Examining the dependability of academic achievement measures for English-language learners. *Assessment for Effective Intervention, 33*(3), 135–144.

Teachers of English to Speakers of Other Languages. (2006). *PreK–12 English language proficiency standards*. Alexandra, VA: Author.

U.S. Census Bureau. (2005). *2005 American community survey*. Washington, DC: U.S. Department of Education.

U.S. Department of Education. (2007). *Participation in education: Elementary and secondary education*. Washington, DC: U.S. Department of Education.

PART 1

Activities to Promote Place-Based Science Teaching in the Classroom

Look back at Figure P.1 on page xix where we presented to idea of place-based science as a series of concentric circles, with the classroom in the center and the circles extending out into the broader community. We begin in the science classroom, the site of traditionally distant and removed science learning, and consider instead a model of science learning that recognizes both the importance and the intrinsic interest that comes from studying place-based science. Themes and activities that will be studied beyond the classroom in the later parts of this book can be grounded in and supported by classroom activities.

For example, Activities 1 and 2 can easily be connected to the planting of a school garden that is described in Part III. Growing a garden provides a range of opportunities for studying different aspects of plant biology. In this way, a focus on place-based teaching and learning can also be connected with a number of other science standards to which students are held accountable. The focus can be on the value of place-based science learning and the other standards can be met along the way. Activities 3 and 4 relate to water both as a resource and as an environmental risk. They can lay the foundation for ideas that are raised in other place-based contexts such as in Part II during the water taste test, in Part IV during the stream monitoring project, and in Part V during the trip to the local water treatment plant.

Activity
1

Monocot Versus Dicot Plants

SCIENCE BACKGROUND

Flowering plants have evolved into two subdivisions known as monocots and dicots. The classification depends on the structure of the plant's leaves. Monocots have leaves with parallel veins that are usually organized in groups of three. Dicots have leaves with veins that branch in netlike structures and are usually organized in groups of four or five. Monocot veins are long and run parallel to one another. Dicot veins are netlike and connected. Each represents a very different type of plant structure. Dicot leaf growth is at the top or leading edge of a leaf, while monocot plants grow from their leaf base. Examples of a monocot plant include a blade of grass and a cornstalk. Examples of a dicot plant would be a maple, oak, or rosebush.

CULTURAL CONNECTIONS

Plant leaves provide a common theme in design. Acanthis leaves, for example, can be found in corbels (decorative supports under 19th-century roofs), on wallpaper, in furniture carving, and so on. Have students see where they can find plant shapes in design. Can they identify the types of plants being used? If possible, have them determine if they are monocot or dicot.

MONOCOT OR DICOT?

In the following activity you will learn to classify plants that surround your school as either monocots or dicots.

MATERIALS YOU WILL NEED FOR THIS ACTIVITY

- Samples of various kinds of leaves
- Magnifying glass

WHAT YOU WILL DO

Before the Activity

Go into the schoolyard and collect four or five examples of different dicot and monocot leaves. Have at least two examples of each.

If a school garden is already growing, then the leaves can be picked very carefully from plants in the garden. If the garden has not been planted yet, then leaves can be taken from other plants growing around the schoolyard. (Be careful not to take too many leaves from any one plant so as not to damage it.)

Take the leaves back to the classroom for classification.

Autumn leaves

During the Activity

Observe each leaf with your naked eye and then with a magnifying glass. Using what you have learned, decide whether each leaf comes from a monocot or dicot plant. Do some research on the web about where monocot and dicot plants are most common.

THINKING LIKE A SCIENTIST—HYPOTHESIS AND EVIDENCE

What is your hypothesis for why both monocot and dicot plants exist?

What are some of the advantages for the plant to being a monocot or a dicot? Why, for example, do grasses stand up straighter than the leaves on dicot plants? Where do grasses suffer the greatest damage from weather and animals?

What evidence could you collect to test your hypothesis about why some plants are monocots and others are dicots?

Which types of plants are more common in different parts of your schoolyard, monocots or dicots? Does this evidence support your hypothesis? Why our why not?

SAMPLE GRADE-LEVEL MODIFICATION—MIDDLE SCHOOL

The study of leaves tends to be considered an elementary activity. Ask middle schoolers to study a number of leaves and then create their on dichotomous key for indentifying the types of leaves commonly found on the school grounds.

SAMPLE INTERDISCIPLINARY CONNECTION—LANGUAGE ARTS

After students have studied thier schoolyard leaves, have them make a leaf collage and then write a poem inspired by their collage. Have students include at least five science words from their leaf study in their poems.

SCIENTISTS IN YOUR COMMUNITY

Individuals in your community who might be knowledgeable about leaves include botanists, horticulturalists, farmers, gardeners, and plant nursery employees.

Correlation With National Standards

NSES Science: A1; C1; C5

NCTM Math: C1

NCTE Language Arts: 12

Activity 2

Germinating Seeds

SCIENCE BACKGROUND

Much like the embryo of an animal, growing inside its mother or in an egg, a seed contains a plant embryo waiting to emerge, grow, and develop into an adult plant. Unlike most animals, however, a seed has no one to protect it or feed it, so it must protect and feed itself. Thus, seeds have a hard seed coat for protection and contain food for the plant embryo to survive until it can grow leaves and begin to produce its own food through photosynthesis. Seeds wait until the environmental conditions are right before they begin to germinate, or grow. Seeds germinate when they absorb water, causing the hard seed coat to swell and burst. Seeds also need heat and light to germinate. This combination of water and heat starts a series of chemical reactions and the beginning of growth and development of the plant embryo. Seeds contain stored energy in the form of starch that is changed to sugar during germination. Germination begins with the appearance of a root tip, followed by leaves and stem. The process of germination can be most easily studied using a large seed like an avocado.

CULTURAL CONNECTIONS

Spouts are common foods in many cultures. The Chinese have been growing mung bean sprouts (nga choi) for approximately 3,000 years. Have students sprout mung beans and try them out to eat. (Go online to find out about sprouting seeds to eat. Type "sprouting" into a search engine to find instructions.) If they want to be particularly adventuresome, students can locate and try out different mung bean recipes.

GROWING AN AVOCADO

MATERIALS YOU WILL NEED FOR THIS ACTIVITY

- Envelopes for collecting seeds
- Magnifying glass

- Microscope
- Glass jar
- Mature avocado seed
- Toothpicks
- Water

Growing an avocado

WHAT YOU WILL DO

Before the Activity

Collect as many different types of seeds as possible from the school grounds. The class can do this as a group or the teacher can do this in advance of the lesson.

During the Activity

Examine the seeds that were collected from the school grounds. Use your naked eye, a magnifying glass, and a microscope.

Discuss how they are similar and how they are different.

Discuss whether there is a relationship between the type of plant the seed comes from and what the seed looks like.

Wrap a sample of each of the different seeds in a moist paper towel and place in a resealable plastic bag. Carefully check the seeds every few days to see if some of them have sprouted. If the paper towel gets dry, moisten it again.

Have students germinate an avocado by following the instructions below:

1. Poke three toothpicks 120 degrees apart around the top quarter of an avocado seed.

2. Rest the seed in a jar of water so that the bottom of the seed is submerged but the top is not.

3. Observe the seed every day to see the roots begin to sprout and develop (you may want to take a picture every day so that you can create a stop-action movie).

4. Change the water in the jar at least once a week so that the plant can receive fresh oxygen.

5. When the plant develops a good root system (at least 2–3 inches long) and a stalk and foliage (usually in 6–8 weeks), students can transfer the plant to a pot with soil.

THINKING LIKE A SCIENTIST: CONTROLLING VARIABLES

What are some of the variables that are involved in seed germination? Make a list. If you wanted to study the effect of one variable, such as temperature, how would you design your experiment? What are all the other variables you would want to control?

Why did some of the schoolyard seeds sprout in the paper towel but others did not? How might seed size and shape be variables that influence seed germination? With the avocado, consider why the seed still sprouted even though it was not planted in soil. What would happen to the plant if you continued to leave it in the water jar and did not plant it in the soil? Consider how an avocado seed is similar to and different from the other types of seeds you investigated. What are some of the variables that make it different? What variables affect seeds' germination? How could you test the effects of each variable on germination?

SAMPLE GRADE-LEVEL MODIFICATION—UPPER ELEMENTARY

Studying seed germination is often considered a lower-elementary-grade activity. Upper elementary and middle school students can increase the scientific rigor of this activity by tracking multiple dimensions of seed germination and studying these ratios. When you change certain variables, how does this affect the rate and speed of seed germination? Covered or uncovered? Type of seed? Seed size? Amount of water? Temperature? Type of light?

SAMPLE INTERDISCIPLINARY CONNECTION—MATHEMATICS

As described in the grade-level modifications section above, there are many possible applications of mathematics to a study of seed germination. Multiple variables can be tracked and then compared to each other using tables, charts, and graphs. Students can study which of these variables seem to be related to each other.

SCIENTISTS IN YOUR COMMUNITY

Individuals in your community who might be knowledgeable about seed germination would include botanists, forestry workers, horticulturalists, farmers, gardeners, and plant nursery employees. Invite one or more of these indivuduals to your class to ask them questions about seeds and to share what you have learned.

Correlation With National Standards

NSES Science: A2; C2; C5

NCTM Math: D2; E4

NCTE Language Arts: 5

NCSS Social Studies: 7

Activity
3

How Will Global Warming Affect You?

SCIENCE BACKGROUND

The Earth's climate is a dynamic system—it does not stay the same over time. Scientific data from glaciers, coral reefs, fossils, and other sources tell us that the climate in any particular place on Earth has changed many times in the past and will continue to change in the future. In the past, there have been heat waves and ice ages that have lasted thousands of years. These climate changes are a natural part of the interactions between the different Earth systems and would happen regardless of humans or what we do. Thus, climate changes can be natural—but they can also be human made. Today, the scientific evidence is that the Earth's climate is warming very quickly and that this warming is at least partially a result of actions by people. This rapid climate change is known as global warming.

There has been a lot of political debate about whether the current global warming is a natural climate change like the Earth has experienced in the past or whether this climate change is something new that is caused by humans and our actions. Although this political debate continues, there is little scientific debate. The vast majority of climate scientists are in agreement that human action is producing much of the current global warming. There is clear evidence that carbon dioxide gas in the atmosphere traps the sun's heat and warms the Earth. Humans are producing much more carbon dioxide gas now than ever before. Coal-burning power plants and car exhaust are the two biggest producers of carbon dioxide gas. At the same time, the decrease in forests around the world—also a condition caused by humans—means that there are fewer trees to absorb the increasing levels of carbon dioxide. If this pattern of global warming continues, there are likely to be dramatic and rapid changes in weather and climate patterns. The most serious result of these changes may be a rise in sea level caused by the melting of glacial ice. In both the northern and southern hemispheres, icebergs are melting more quickly than in the past.

In the following activity, you will investigate how scientists track climate change and you will build a model to see the effects of sea level rise on an island. Then you will explore what effects different amounts of sea level rise would have where you live.

CULTURAL CONNECTIONS

Disaster movies based upon the theme of climate change have been a favorite subject for Hollywood directors in recent years. The 1995 film *Waterworld* starring Kevin Costner takes place in a world where the polar ice caps have melted, forcing earth's few surviving people to wander the oceans searching for dry land. In 2006, former vice president Al Gore released the documentary *An Inconvenient Truth,* which looked at the consequences of global warming. In *The Day After Tomorrow* (2004), a new ice age is caused by global warming. Have students watch and discuss film clips from these or other eco-disaster movies. Many clips are available on sources such as YouTube.

SEA LEVEL RISE

MATERIALS YOU WILL NEED FOR THIS ACTIVITY

- 1 plastic shoebox-sized container
- 1 box modeling clay or play dough
- Sand and gravel
- Plant clippings, sticks, or other natural decoration
- 1 measuring cup
- 1 ruler
- Water

WHAT YOU WILL DO

Before the Activity

Watch the video "Melting Ice, Rising Seas" on the website of the American Museum of Natural History:

http://www.amnh.org/sciencebulletins/?sid=e.f.melting_ice.20070514&src=e

As you are watching the video, respond to these questions:

1. What evidence do scientists have that the global temperatures are higher today than they were 50 years ago?

2. What evidence do scientists have that sea levels were higher at other times in the past than they are today?

Icebergs forming from pieces of Dawes Glacier

During the Activity

1. Use the modeling clay to form the shape of your island. Consider whether it is flat or mountainous. Maybe it has a volcano? Place your clay island in the plastic shoebox. You can decorate your island with small pieces of plants to represent trees, add some sand for the beaches, and so on. Be creative!

2. Create a data table like the one below for recording your data.

3. Before you begin to add water to the box, what is the depth of the water? What percentage of the island is covered by water? Record the amount of water, depth of water, and percentage of island covered. Record the data in row one for 0 cups of water.

4. Measure one cup of water in the measuring cup and gently pour it into the box. Use the ruler to measure how deep the water is in the box. Estimate the percentage of the island that is under water. Record the data in row 2 for 1 cup of water.

5. Repeat step 3 a total of 5 more times until there are 6 cups of water in the shoebox. For each cup of water added, fill in the next row of the data table.

When you have finished collecting your data, answer the following questions:

1. Did each cup of water added to the shoebox raise the water level the same amount? Why or why not?

2. Did each cup of water added to the shoebox cover the same percentage of the island with water? Why or why not?

Amount of Water Added	Depth of Water	% of Island Covered
0 cups		
1 cup		
2 cups		
3 cups		
4 cups		
5 cups		
6 cups		

After the Activity

1. Look at the following interactive map of sea level rise: https://www.cresis.ku.edu/research/data/sea_level_rise/index.html. It shows the actual effects of a sea level rise between 1 and 6 meters around the world. How are these maps similar to or different from your model island?

Thinking Like a Scientist—Cause and Effect

How are the effects of sea level rise related to climate change? What evidence is there to support the claim that current sea level rise is at least in part a result of human activity? Think about the sea level rise shown on the interactive map above. Assuming that you are not in an area directly affected by flooding due to sea level rise, what indirect effects would this flooding have on your community? Think about things like the economic impact and the question of refuges from flooded areas.

How would the type of relocation that happened in New Orleans after Hurricane Katrina be different if flooding happened simultaneously in several big east coast cities like New York, Boston, Washington, and Miami?

SAMPLE GRADE-LEVEL MODIFICATION—EARLY ELEMENTARY

Climate change is a topic that is not typically raised in schools until a middle school Earth science course. Given the importance of understanding climate change for our future well-being, this topic should be introduced in the earliest grades. If both the questions and the data table are reworked and simplified, students in the younger elementary grades could still conduct the sea level rise activity and discuss what happens during a flood to people, plants, animals, houses, and so forth.

SAMPLE INTERDISCIPLINARY CONNECTION—SOCIAL STUDIES

People, politicians, and governments in different countries have responded to the threats of climate change and global warming in different ways. Ask students to pick two different countries in differnt parts of the world. First consider what the possible effects of sea level rise on this country would be and then research what the country has committed to do to address the problem. Do you see a relationship between the country's risk and its proposed response?

SCIENTISTS IN YOUR COMMUNITY

Individuals in your community who might be knowledgeable about climate change and global warming would include climate scientists, meteorologists, TV weather broadcasters, geologists, and perhaps elected officials or other government workers who can make policy that relates to this topic. Invite one or more of these individuals to your class to ask them questions about climate change and global warming.

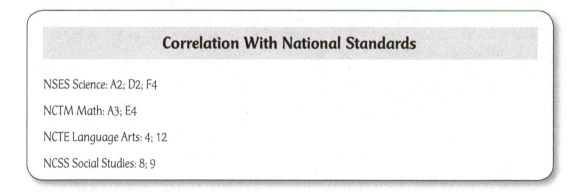

Correlation With National Standards

NSES Science: A2; D2; F4

NCTM Math: A3; E4

NCTE Language Arts: 4; 12

NCSS Social Studies: 8; 9

Activity

4

Your Water Footprint

SCIENCE BACKGROUND

A water footprint may sound like something that you leave behind after you've been walking through puddles, but it actually has a different meaning for people who think about environmental science. Your water footprint is the amount of water you use both directly and indirectly. This water footprint is much larger than just the amount of water that you actively use to drink, cook, shower, and flush the toilet. This is known as your direct water use. Beyond direct water use, there is also the water used to create things you use and eat. It may not be obvious how water is used in this way. Ecologists call this "virtual" or indirect water use to represent the amount of water it takes to grow or manufacture something. This is sometimes called "hidden water" to emphasize that we are often unaware of this water use. Understanding how much water it actually takes to grow a plant or manufacture an item is essential to understanding how much water we actually use and how we can protect our water resources.

The average person in the United States consumes about 500,000 gallons of water per year—that's about the same amount of water as there is in an Olympic-size swimming pool! Where does all that water go? Much of it is virtual or hidden water. For example, to make a cup of coffee actually takes about 37 gallons of water. How is this possible when you only see 12 ounces of water in your coffee cup? The rest of the water went into irrigating the coffee plants on the coffee farm and washing, processing, roasting, packing, and transporting the coffee beans. Similarly, the actual amount of water needed to manufacture a car is approximately 100,000 gallons, and to build a new house requires roughly 1.25 million gallons of water.

In the following activity you will do research to more accurately compare your personal direct and indirect water usage.

CULTURAL CONNECTIONS

Water is sacred in many religions throughout the world. Point out to students how water is used in baptism in the Christian faith and used with blessings (Holy Water) in the Catholic faith. Ritual bathing or cleansing is important in Judaism, Hinduism, Islam, and in Shintoism, the indigenous religion of Japan. Discuss with students why water is such an essential element of so many religions.

EXPLORING YOUR WATER FOOTPRINT

MATERIALS YOU WILL NEED FOR THIS ACTIVITY

- Home water usage data collection form

WHAT YOU WILL DO

Before the Activity

Have students complete the following survey of bathroom water usage.

How much water do you use in the bathroom? Seventy-five percent of all direct water use takes place in the bathroom. Answer the following questions to determine how much water you use every day.

Showerhead and water

1. How many times per day do you brush your teeth?

    _____ × See below = _____.

If you turn off water while brushing, write 1 quart. If you leave the water running while brushing, write 4 gallons.

2. How long do you spend in the shower (in minutes)?

    _____ × See below = _____.

If you have a low-flow showerhead, write 2 gallons; if you have a standard showerhead, write 5 gallons.

3. How many times per day do you flush the toilet?

    _____ × See below = _____ If you have a low-flush toilet, write 3 gallons. If you have a standard toilet, write 5 gallons.

Calculate your total daily bathroom water usage = _____
Calculate your annual bathroom water usage = _____

During the Activity

The numbers above may seem high to students. You can use the following simulation to check the accuracy of one piece of the calculation. If you have a sink in your classroom, have students leave the water running full blast and ask each of them to pretend to brush their teeth. Instead of running the water down the drain, collect it in gallon milk bottles and measure the amount of water that has been used. Now repeat the process having them pretend to wet their toothbrush, turn off the water while brushing, and then turn it on long enough to rinse their brush and get a drink.

Have students calculate how much more water they use by leaving the tap running vs. turning it off during brushing. Calculate the difference this causes in direct water usage in one week. In one year. In an 80-year lifetime.

To estimate your total water usage, including indirect usage, you can visit the website of the organization WaterFootprint.Org and use their water footprint calculator:

http://www.waterfootprint.org/?page=files/home

There are two versions of the calculator, a "quick calculator" and an "extended calculator." If you have time to use the extended calculator, it will give you a much better sense of the things you do that consume water, indirectly as well as directly. If you don't know your family's annual income, use the figure of $50,000 (an approximation of the U.S. median family income in 2010) for your "gross yearly income." The calculator estimates in cubic meters. Use a meter stick in the classroom to better visualize how much water fits in a cubic meter.

After the Activity

Using the calculator, determine the water footprint for someone in the United States, Egypt, Fiji, Turkey, and China.

THINKING LIKE A SCIENTIST: HYPOTHESIS AND EVIDENCE

What is your hypothesis about why there are such large differences in water usage between some countries and others? If you wanted to explore your hypothesis, what kinds of evidence would you need to collect? Could you collect this evidence without having to actually travel to the country you wanted to study? How could you do this?

If water is a limited and finite resource, what are the possible long-term consequences of allowing some countries to consume much more water than others?

If water is a limited and finite resource, are all uses of water equally justifiable, or are some uses of water better than others? Explain?

If we buy and use more locally produced items, how would this affect our water footprint?

SAMPLE GRADE-LEVEL MODIFICATION—EARLY ELEMENTARY

The concept of indirect water usage and especially its calculation may be too abstract for many early-elementary-grade students. However, the focus on direct water usage and ways this can be conserved is both concrete and powerful for young children. In fact, elementary-age children can often be the most persuasive advocates in a family for changing basic conservation practices such as not leaving the water running during teeth brushing and dishwashing. Simplify the activity by focusing on direct water usage, but we recomend at least introducing the concept of "hidden" water usage even with young children. There is something exciting and curious about this idea that can spark young imaginations.

SAMPLE INTERDISCIPLINARY CONNECTION—MATHEMATICS

It should be obvious that the potential mathematical connections in this activity are plentiful. There is a lot of basic arithmatic, but there is also the need to organize data for purposes of comparison as well as many opportunities to chart and graph data as well as to use some basic statistics to analyze it. Once students have studied their data, ask them to write their own applied math problems and then share them with another class to see if they can solve them.

SCIENTISTS IN YOUR COMMUNITY

Individuals in your community who might be knowledgeable about water usage would include water treatment plant workers, managers of factories that do manufacturing, employees of the local water management district, and local government officials. Invite one or more of these indivuduals to your class to ask them questions about water usage in your community and to share with them what you have learned about your own water usage.

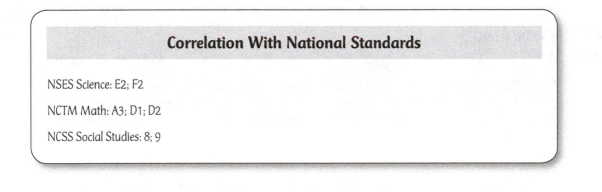

Correlation With National Standards

NSES Science: E2; F2

NCTM Math: A3; D1; D2

NCSS Social Studies: 8; 9

Activity

5

Where Did My Juice Come From?

SCIENCE BACKGROUND

The following activity is related to several other activities in this book that all explore questions about the foods we eat. In Part V we will study where the food that our community eats comes from and in Part II we will study the quality of the food that we eat in our school. This activity combines both of those topics by asking where the juice that is served in our school cafeteria comes from, how it gets to us, and what the implications are for our environment.

In addition to the idea of the water footprint that we discussed in Activity 4, scientists also think about the related idea of our carbon footprint. A carbon footprint considers the impact all of our actions have on the production of greenhouse gases. Your carbon footprint is the total amount of greenhouse gases produced to directly and indirectly support your activities.

For example, when you drive a car, the engine burns fuel that then creates carbon dioxide (CO_2), the primary greenhouse gas. The amount of CO_2 produced depends on the mileage of the car and the driving distance. Additionally, when you heat your house with oil, gas, or coal, you generate additional CO_2. Even if you heat your house with electricity, the generation of the electrical power is usually responsible for a certain amount of CO_2—unless your electricity is produced by solar, wind, or some other alternative energy source. The production, packaging, and transportation of the food and merchandise that you buy produce additional CO_2. Thus, your carbon footprint is the sum of all emissions of CO_2 that resulted from your activities in a given period of time.

CULTURAL CONNECTIONS

While foods like orange juice are frequently transported great distances before they are consumed, many foods are local in nature. For example, in Louisiana, unique shrimp dishes like shrimp etouffee or shrimp jambalaya reflect the history of the region and the use of local resources. Explore with students what foods are unique to their part of the country. Using resources on the Internet, help increase your school's awareness of local food festivals and local traditions of eating.

Where Did My Juice Come From?

Materials You Will Need for This Activity

- Variety of juice cartons and containers from the school cafeteria and juice containers that students bring from home

- Blank world map handouts

What You Will Do

Orange juice

Before the Activity

1. Have students collect juice containers from their school cafeteria and ask students who wish to bring other juice containers from home to do so.

2. You can limit the activity to a single type of juice such as apple juice or orange juice or let students bring containers from different kinds of juice. Limit students to 100% juice, not drinks that contain some juice but that are mostly sugar water.

3. Have students research what juice concentrate is and how it is made.

During the Activity

1. Have students read the side of the container and list the countries where the juice concentrate has come from. For example, a typical brand of apple juice may have juice concentrate from Argentina, Austria, Chile, Germany, Hungary, and the United States.

2. Have students use an atlas to locate the countries where the concentrate comes from and label them on a blank outline map of the world.

3. Determine how far the concentrate had to travel to get to your school.

4. Describe all the things that contribute to the carbon footprint of the juice that is sold in the school cafeteria. Calculating the actual carbon footprint of a product is quite difficult because CO_2 is produced at many steps in a product's life cycle. There are companies now, however, that specialize in doing these calculations to help other companies reduce the carbon footprints of their products—for one example, check out the following website:

   www.carbonfootprint.com/productlifecycle.html

For example, the typical consumer product, such as a carton of juice, produces CO_2 emissions at five different points during its life cycle: creating/gathering raw materials, manufacturing, distribution, consumer use, and disposal.

1. CO_2 emissions from creating raw materials come from processes such as mining, farming, fertilizers, transporting raw materials, and so forth.

2. CO_2 emissions from manufacturing come from processes such as processing machines, packaging, lighting, storage, temperature control, and the like.

3. CO_2 emissions from distribution come from processes such as air, ground, or ocean transport, as well as retail storage and display in a store.

4. CO_2 emissions from consumer use come from processes such as energy used during storage, preparation, or maintenance.

5. CO_2 emissions from disposal/recycling come from processes such as transport, storage, and processing of waste.

In the case of apple or orange juice concentrate, try to determine what the main sources of CO_2 emissions would be at each point of the life cycle.

After the Activity

Come up with possible ways to reduce the water and carbon footprints of the juices that are served in your school. As a class, pick one of these possible solutions and then decide how you could inform people about the issue and your possible solution. Write a letter to the school principal, your school board, and/or the school district's office of food and nutrition and propose your solution.

THINKING LIKE A SCIENTIST—CAUSE AND EFFECT

There are good reasons why juice concentrate is produced, transported, and sold in the way that it is. However, these reasons are generally business reasons and not environmental or scientific reasons. Some environmental groups have proposed a CO_2 tax that would be charged to companies based on the amount of CO_2 that they use in the production, distribution, and sale of their products. If a law were passed to do this, what do you think the effects would be on the foods in our local grocery store? Why? Could it change the juice options you have in your school cafeteria? How?

In addition to concerns about the distance traveled, concerns have also been raised that the laws governing pesticide use are very different in different countries and that fruits may be treated with pesticides that are not considered safe in this country. Do some research to see if you can find any information on pesticide use in the countries where your school juice concentrate comes from.

SAMPLE GRADE-LEVEL MODIFICATION—EARLY ELEMENTARY

Certain aspects of this activity may be too abstract for many early elementary students. Working together, the class can still find out which countries provide the juice concentrate for the juice in their cafeteria, identify those countries on a world map, and discuss the questions such as the pros and cons of transporting juice concentrate from those distant places.

SAMPLE INTERDISCIPLINARY CONNECTION—SOCIAL STUDIES

There are multiple possibile connections that can be made between the study of CO_2 footprint and social studies. The connections to geography are perhaps the most obvious. To understand the impact of CO_2 footprint, students need to have a better sense of where the materials we use on a daily basis actually come from and how they get to us. There are also clear connections to ecomomics—understanding the processes of production, transportation, distribution, and sale of goods is essential to understanding why we have the CO_2 footprint issues that we do.

SCIENTISTS IN YOUR COMMUNITY

Individuals in your community who might be knowledgeable about CO_2 footprint, how it has changed in recent years, and the related issues of global trade would include environmental scientists, geographers, economists, and managers of businesses that are involved in international trade. Invite one or more of these indivuduals to your class to ask them questions about the growth of our CO_2 footprint in recent years.

Correlation With National Standards

NSES Science: C4; E2; F2

NCTM Math: A3

NCTE Language Arts: 1; 5; 12

NCSS Social Studies: 3; 7; 8

Activity 6

Distance Learning: Reaching Beyond One's Classroom

SCIENCE BACKGROUND

Distance education provides students with a remarkable opportunity to extend their science learning beyond their local school and community and to reach out to others on a global level. One of the interesting things about scientific principles and the laws of nature is that they act the same everywhere in the world. Students can compare their observations of natural phenomena in different places and the "rules" for making sense of those observations will be the same. While studying place-based science in one's community is engaging for most students, studying science in very different places can also be engaging, especially when students can have direct contact with peers in those different places.

CULTURAL CONNECTIONS

While many people think that distance learning was only made possible by the Internet, it was actually first begun in elementary schools in France and Italy in the mid-1920s. At that time, the French educator Célestin Freinet and the Italian educators Mario Lodi and Bruno Ciardi began to exchange student-created materials through the mail. Through these exchanges, the students in Freinet's and Lodi and Ciardi's classes learned about each other despite the fact that they lived hundreds of miles from each other and spoke different languages.

However, distance learning does not necessarily involve place-based connections, especially in science. In Australia, for example, because of the huge distances between communities, colleges have a long history of using distance education. In the 1980s, Monash University created a video-based physics course that involved sending students a kit of physics equipment along with their books and videos. The lab materials were used by the students and then mailed back to the university. The program was successful, but the physics course itself was very traditional.

Distance learning exchanges have become much more widespread as a result of the Internet and World Wide Web. Having Internet pen pals, (now often called "key pals" because students are likely to use a keyboard rather than a pen for their communication) has been particularly exciting for students, because they can easily exchange correspondence with children elsewhere in the world at little or no cost and on an almost instantaneous basis. The following activity provides one example of how to have your students communicate online with students in another country to share information about a place-based science project that you are engaged in.

DISTANCE LEARNING: REACHING BEYOND ONE'S CLASSROOM

MATERIALS YOU WILL NEED FOR THIS ACTIVITY

- A computer with access to the Internet

WHAT YOU WILL DO

Connect online to a student in another country to exchange information from a science project or report.

Binary code

Before Contacting a Foreign Pen Pal

Have students choose a project they have already done involving place-based science education.

Create a multimedia report based on this project that can be sent as an e-mail attachment to someone in another country.

Think about the kinds of images and descriptions that would help to explain your local environment to someone living in a different part of the world, including someone who may not speak English.

Make contact with another school to set up a science "key pal" exchange. Some websites that can help facilitate this process are (there are many others as well):

International Pen Pals Europa

http://www.europa-pages.com/school_form.html

International Pen Friends

http://www.ipf.net.au/

School-to-school International

http://www.sts-international.org/pen_pals.html

ePals

http://www.epals.com/

Writing a Letter to a Key Pal and Exchanging Scientific Reports

Once you have contact information for students overseas, write them a letter offering to exchange information on how they learn about science.

Ask them about what they have been learning in their science classes and share what you have been learning about place-based science. Ask if they ever use their local environment for science studies, and if so, in what ways.

Send your key pals the report about the project you have done and ask if they can send a report on one of their own projects.

Continue this dialog for as long as both classes remain interested and engaged. See if you can spread the word about place-based science learning. See what you can learn about how place-based science is done elsewhere in the world.

Thinking Like a Scientist: Hypothesis and Evidence

Do people in different parts of the world think about scientific problems in the same way or differently? What is your hypothesis about this and why it might be that way? How can you gather evidence through your and your classmates' conversations with your key pals to support or disprove your hypothesis about how people in different places think about scientific problems?

How is what you have been doing with your key pals similar to what scientists do when they share their work with international colleagues?

Discuss with your classmates the importance of accurately reporting what you find during a scientific investigation. Discuss the same topic with your key pals and compare the answers from the two groups.

Sample Grade-level Modification—Middle School

Pen pals have typically been used as an activity with elementary-age students as a way to motivate them to practice writing for an authentic purpose, but that purpose has generally been to learn about children their age living in another place. By focusing the commuication between key pals on more substantive content such as scientific investigations, the idea of writing to key pals can be made more grade appropriate for middle school students. It still serves to give an authentic purpose for written communication and can be motivating for students who don't enjoy writing.

Sample Interdisciplinary Connection—Language Arts

Content area reading and content area writing are important language arts skills in the middle school grades. Language arts teachers sometimes struggle to find ways to support the development of these skills in the content areas of science and mathematics. Distance education, such as using key pals to compare the results of place-based science projects, provides a meaningful way to connect science and language arts learning goals.

Scientists in Your Community

Individuals in your community who might be knowledgeable about distance learning and creating meaningful communication with students in other places might include information technology specialists, international businesspeople, a foreign language teacher in your school, or any scientist who works with international colleagues. Invite one or more of these individuals to your class to ask them questions about communicating information, and especially scientific information, to people in distant places.

Correlation With National Standards

NSES Science: E2; G1

NCTE Language Arts: 5; 10; 12

NCSS Social Studies: 1; 3; 9

Activity
7
Interviewing a Scientist

SCIENCE BACKGROUND

Scientists play many important roles in local communities. A scientist is responsible for regulating your local water treatment plant, making sure that your drinking water is safe and clean to use. If you live in a city, there are meteorologists who work at the news station and at the airport. There are numerous scientists, in addition to the doctors and nurses, who work in your local hospital, collecting and interpreting data from complex scanning machines. Many types of scientists work at any college or university. Scientists can be found in many other places throughout your community as well.

CULTURAL CONNECTIONS

We tend to think of scientists as being people who wear white laboratory coats and conduct experiments in laboratories. While many scientists would indeed fit this description, there are many other scientists who wear jeans and a T-shirt or a wetsuit and who conduct their research in a desert or a wetland or in the ocean. Scientists don't just work in laboratories; they also work in health and sanitation departments, in hospitals, and as members of federal, state, and local governments. Have students see if they can identify different types of scientists who might not fit the scientist stereotype.

INTERVIEWING A SCIENTIST

MATERIALS YOU WILL NEED FOR THIS ACTIVITY

- Paper and pencil
- A computer with access to the Internet

WHAT YOU WILL DO

Before the Interview

Create a list of scientists. Go online and do a search for "types of scientists." Numerous websites will come up with lists of names such as:

- Astronomer
- Botanist
- Cytologist
- Epidemiologist
- Geneticist
- Geologist
- Geographer
- Marine biologist
- Meteorologist
- Microbiologist
- Paleontologist
- Physicist

Scientist at work

There are many, many others. Have students compile their own list and look up what some of the more unusual-sounding types of scientists do.

Next, combine students' individual lists into a master for the class.

Discuss whether the students think each type of scientist on the list could be found working in their community.

Have students research where these scientists might be found in their community and pick several types of scientists that the students agree they would be interested in interviewing.

Contact one or more community scientists and invite them to the classroom for an interview. Make sure they understand that they are not coming to give a presentation, but rather to be interviewed by the students.

Think about how you will document the interview. Will you video- or audio-record the interview or take notes? Prepare accordingly.

The interview questions below can get you started with your interview. Come up with your own additional questions as well.

It is a good idea to have students practice asking their interview questions with one another first. Decide who will ask what question when the scientist comes for the interview.

During the Interview

Welcome the scientist and tell her or him what you have been learning about in terms of place-based science.

Proceed to conduct your interview, using these and/or other questions that you have decided on in advance.

- What type of scientist are you?
- How did you become interested in being a scientist?
- Why is what you do important?
- How does what you do potentially affect other people?
- What do you like most about your work as a scientist? Least?
- How does what you do affect our local community?
- What do you wish that people in our community understood better about science? Why?

After Completing the Interview

Have students construct a poster, a PowerPoint presentation, or other way to document what they learned from the scientist interview.

Share this information with students from another class in your school.

Consider inviting another scientist with a different job in the local community to compare and contrast their ideas and experiences with those of the first scientist.

Thinking Like a Scientist—Hypothesis and Evidence

Have students consider what it is that makes a person a scientist. Is it the job that they do? The education they received? Some other quality or qualification? The way they think?

In this book, we present the idea that thinking like a scientist involves three key practices: coordinating hypothesis and evidence, controlling variables, and using cause-and-effect reasoning. As you reflect on your scientist interviews, do you see evidence in the scientists' responses that they use any of these three ways of thinking? Alternately, you can ask about these practices explicitly as part of your scientist interview. If you interview multiple scientists, compare and contrast their ideas about these practices. How similar or different are the responses? Why do you think that is?

Sample Grade-level Modification—Upper Elementary

Upper-elemenary-grade students are begining to go through the transition from learning to read and write to reading and writing to learn. In other words, the goal is now to use text and other types of language to learn new content, such as science knowledge. Thus, while upper-elementary-grade students will often require a lot of coaching to become good interviewers of adults such as scientists, they should be capable of learning to conduct interviews with professional people from the community, such as local scientists.

Sample Interdisciplinary Connection—Language Arts

Learning to conduct a good interview reinforces a number of important language arts skills. A good interviewer needs to be organized, must be a clear writer and speaker, a good listener, a good note taker, and more. Learning to do interviews about science topics requires all of these language arts skills and also enough science background to understand and ask questions about that science content.

SCIENTISTS IN YOUR COMMUNITY

This activity is all about finding and talking to scientists of any kind who live and/or work in your community. Students are likely to be surprised about how many scientists there are in even a medium-sized town.

Correlation With National Standards

NSES Science: G1

NCTE Language Arts: 4; 5; 12

NCSS Social Studies: 8; 10

Activity 8

Creating an Environmental Advocacy Press Kit

SCIENCE BACKGROUND

Teaching students to be aware of environmental issues is a basic part of most place-based education programs. A natural extension of creating environmental awareness is promoting environmental advocacy. While some may feel that teaching students to take a position and act on their beliefs is beyond the scope of basic education, we believe that it is an essential part of educating people to be engaged members of a democratic society.

Students need to reflect and think carefully about issues that might affect their lives. Is there a polluted stream that needs cleaning up in their community? Is there a water shortage that needs to be overcome where they live? Do they believe that animals need to be protected from abusive activities such as dog fighting? Are they concerned that the food that they eat in their school lunch program does not have enough fresh fruits and vegetables? Are they concerned that the vending machines in the school sell only soda, candy, and chips instead of water or fruit or vegetable juices?

CULTURAL CONNECTIONS

Students should begin with any of the various environmentally engaged, place-based activities in this book and then conduct additional research on the issue using local library resources and the Internet. The class should then develop a plan of action and a press kit, following the instructions below, that can bring about meaningful change in their community. In doing so, they will not only learn more about social issues involving science, but they will also gain basic research, writing, and communication skills. Additionally, students are likely to become more politically and socially active citizens, outcomes that are very rare in our current educational system.

There are many websites that focus on science and activism. Students will find a great deal of useful information and ideas at the Center for Science in the Public Interest (http://www.cspinet.org/). Also of interest as a model for health advocacy in the schools is the Healthy Schools Campaign (http://www.healthyschoolscampaign.org/), an independent not-for-profit organization, which is the country's leading advocacy group for creating more healthy school environments.

What You Will Do

Identifying a Cause

Students should have a class discussion of the various issues they have studied from a place-based science perspective. If they have not studied place-based science yet, use the table of contents of this book to consider some of the possible topics that could become a focus for this project. Students should have a values-based discussion about topics they think are important for the well-being of their community and that involve the environment. Continue the discussion until the class can agree on a topic. Remind the group that additional projects of this kind on other topics can be done in the future.

The future is in our hands

Researching a Cause

After identifying an issue, students can search for information concerning the cause or issue they are interested in. Doing a hands-on activity of the kind presented in this book is an important part of learning more about the issue. Students should clarify the scope of the problem or issue they are concerned with and why it is important.

Creating a Press Release

The following is a basic outline for a press release. Limit each release to a single page and have it begin at the top of the page with the statement "FOR IMMEDIATE RELEASE" or "PRESS RELEASE." Then do the following:

- Include contact information (name, phone number, online address)
- Include release time

Create a Headline

A headline should be in a type size at least twice as large as the main body of text. It should catch the reader's attention. For example: "Poor Nutrition Makes for Poor Learning!"

Create a Lead Paragraph

The lead paragraph should outline the basic issues of a problem or cause. An old reporter's trick is to use the five Ws—Who? What? When? Where? and Why?—to lead off the piece. This paragraph should grab the reader's attention. Also be sure to include the dateline, along with the city or town of origin.

Create a Main Body

Use two or three paragraphs to describe the subject of the news release in more detail.

Recap and Summarize

Recap the overall issue and its importance in a single brief paragraph.

Spread the Word

Send your press release to your city or town newspaper, local radio stations, and other news outlets that you can find in your community. You can send it to your school newspaper or newsletter as well, but think BIG. The point is to get this information out into the broader community, not to keep it in the school as a school project.

After you send out the press release, follow up in a few days with an e-mail or phone call to confirm that the news organization received the press release and to ask if they have any questions. Let them know that you would welcome a visit from a reporter to talk more about the issue you are concerned about. If a reporter is going to come, prepare for the interview and be ready to share your concerns.

THINKING LIKE A SCIENTIST—CAUSE AND EFFECT

How does science cause social change? Sometimes scientific information can lead people to change their behaviors. The use of seat belts and the dangers of smoking cigarettes are two examples, but in both cases it took more than just science to cause these changes. It also took advocacy by concerned citizens. Read about these two examples for more information—the stories are fascinating—and then consider the causes and effects involved in these episodes. Have students discuss the issue of what is scientific research and what is advocacy. Discuss with them how ethical advocacy needs to be responsible and based on scientific and accurate knowledge. Talk about the idea of propaganda and how it is different from advocacy. Examine the ethical issues involved in acting as an advocate for a cause.

SAMPLE GRADE-LEVEL MODIFICATION—EARLY ELEMENTARY

Are early-elementary-grade students too young to be advocates for something they beleive in? We say no. Young children have strong opinions, and with some practice and adult guidance, those opinions can be informed by scientific evidence. We know of cases where first graders have been involved in advocacy for issues such as butterfly gardens on the median strips of streets in town, school vegetable gardens, and local wetlands restoration projects. With help from teachers and other adults, young children can create a simple version of the press release described in this activity.

SAMPLE INTERDISCIPLINARY CONNECTION—LANGUAGE ARTS

Students must learn to write in both narrative and expository styles. Additionally, learning persuasive writing techniques is a common standard in nearly all language arts curricula. Creating a press kit and writing a press release is an engaging and meaningful way to practice persuasive writing. Writing in science tends to empasize detatched, third-person styles of writing where the voice of the author is largely missing. Writing science advocacy material allows for a diffent style of science writing where the authors' voices are clearly present.

SCIENTISTS IN YOUR COMMUNITY

Individuals in your community who might be knowledgeable about creating a press kit might include news reporters, political activists, representatives from local government, or small business owners. Invite one or more of these individuals to your class to ask them questions about communicating information for the purposes of advocacy. Ask them what they see as the difference between advocacy and science.

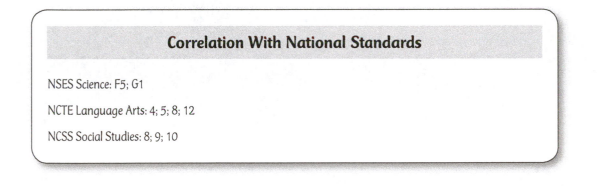

Correlation With National Standards

NSES Science: F5; G1

NCTE Language Arts: 4; 5; 8; 12

NCSS Social Studies: 8; 9; 10

Activities to Promote Place-Based Science Teaching in the School Building

As we move through the chapters in the second section of this book, we gradually trace larger concentric circles of activity as our sense of place moves outward from the classroom and into the community. While students will continue to spend most of their time in the classroom, one of the goals of place-based science teaching and learning is to look for ways to get students to both move and think beyond the classroom walls. The school building outside the classroom door presents the next context in which place-based science teaching and learning can be practiced. The school building includes places, such as the cafeteria, the gym, the library, and the auditorium, among others, where students engage in a range of academic, social, athletic, and community activities. Indeed, the school building provides multiple opportunities for helping students learn to form communities and to make choices about how to live their lives. In this chapter we focus on the many ways to enhance place-based learning within these school settings that are outside the classroom but inside the school.

Activity
9

Student Nutrition and Eating Habits at School

SCIENCE BACKGROUND

All students learn about the digestive system as part of their study of human biology. The following is a sample of what might typically be taught in a standards-based classroom:

We learn that we get the energy we need to function from the food we eat. The digestive system is made of the organs that break down food into smaller parts called nutrients. The digestive organs work together to turn food into energy, so our bodies can work and grow. We learn that the digestive system contains many structures and organs. Each has a special job. Parts of the digestive system include:

- Teeth and tongue—break down food into smaller pieces that you can swallow

- Esophagus or food pipe—the tube that carries your food into your stomach using a wave-like motion caused by smooth muscles

- Stomach—a J-shaped bag that works like a mixer, using smooth muscles to grind and crush the food into smaller and smaller pieces as they are bathed in acid

- Small intestine—a very long, narrow tube that breaks down the food mixture even more; food is digested here and then all the nutrients are absorbed into the blood

- Other important digestive organs such as the liver—send different liquids to the first part of the small intestine; these organs help to digest food and absorb nutrients

- Large intestine—a fatter, shorter tube than the small intestine; it absorbs water back into the blood; all that is left are the waste materials that leave the body

How does this type of learning connect with students in a meaningful way? Do students see any value in this knowledge? For many, if not most students, the answer to this question would be no. They are likely to learn this information for a test and then promptly forget it. Taking a place-based perspective can refocus a topic such as the digestive system in ways that can make science learning meaningful to many more students. Students typically learn all this information (and often much more) about the biology of eating in science class with only a minimal study of the importance of nutrition for life-long health. While problems with youth nutrition and childhood obesity have received attention in the popular press, little is actually being done in most schools to improve either students' nutrition education or their nutritional options. Nearly a quarter of elementary grade students in the United States are now considered to be overweight or obese, compared to about 15% of students two decades ago and less than

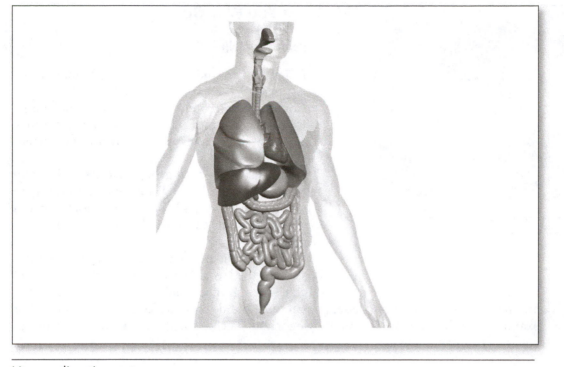

Human digestive system

10% of students four decades ago. What has caused this dramatic change? Nutritionists agree that the combination of a decrease in youth physical activity and changes in our diet are the two most significant factors.

CULTURAL CONNECTIONS

In 2004, Congress passed the Child Nutrition and WIC Reauthorization Act, which included a law requiring local education agencies to develop policies that address the growing problem of childhood obesity. These policies need to include nutrition education goals, physical activity goals, and nutrition standards for all foods available at school. Six years after this law was passed, however, most schools continue to offer a wide range of high-fat food choices as well as school day access to a range of low-nutrition snack foods and sugary beverages.

Considering the choices available and the choices that students make when it comes to eating at school can provide a fascinating and socially valuable opportunity for practicing place-based science learning that can serve to make the study of science topics such as the digestive system more personally meaningful for students.

ASSESSING NUTRITION AT SCHOOL

MATERIALS YOU WILL NEED FOR THIS ACTIVITY

- Paper and pencil
- Student-designed surveys

School lunch

WHAT YOU WILL DO

Before the Trip

Learn background material on the human digestive system. What happens to the food we eat?

Conduct background research on school nutrition programs in the United States. When did they start? How did they evolve? What are the current guidelines?

Break class into small groups and let each group select one of the following nutrition-related topics: school lunches, lunches brought from home, snacks available, vending machines, breakfast (at home or at school).

Each group should construct a survey or interview that can be used to gather data about its topic around the school. Questions can be designed to be asked of other students and/or of adults that are involved in the food purchase, preparation, and decision making for the school. For example, questions that the group studying school lunches could ask the cafeteria manager could include the following:

- What meals are served here at school?

- How much variety is there in the school meals?

- Have efforts been made to reduce the fat content of the foods prepared? How?

- Are there a la carte choices that are appealing and low in fat? What?

- What efforts have been made to encourage students to make healthy food and beverage choices?

- Is corn syrup found in many of the foods served?

- Is low-fat and skim milk available with every meal?

- Is soda available to students during lunchtime?

- Do students have enough time to eat their meals without rushing?

- Do you or other members of the food service staff ever collaborate with teachers to educate students about nutrition? How?

- Do you have opportunities for your own professional development to help you improve the food services you provide?

Student groups should come up with their own interview or survey questions depending on their topic and who they are interviewing or surveying (i.e., students or adults).

If the group is conducting a survey, it should decide how many people it would like to survey and make enough copies of the survey.

If the group is conducting an interview, it should decide how many people it will interview and how it will record the participants' answers (i.e., take notes, use an audio recorder or a video recorder). It should also determine how it can summarize the results.

On the Trip

The interviews or surveys can be conducted at lunch, before school, or after school, or groups can be allowed to make plans to conduct the interviews during class time.

When conducting the interviews, make sure that the participants understand the questions and that you understand their answers. Repeat or clarify as needed.

When you are done, ask participants if they have any questions for you. Use this as a opportunity to share some of what you have been learning about nutrition in schools.

Back in the Classroom

Groups should examine their data. They should consider the following questions:

- Are there patterns in the participants' responses?

- What kinds of nutritional choices are available in your school and what choices are students making? Why?

Create a way to share your data with other people beyond your class so that they can better understand the state of nutrition in your school. Consider making colorful posters or other visuals that show graphs of the data about the nutrition choices that are available and the nutrition choices that are being made.

Make a class commitment both to make healthier nutrition choices and to encourage the school to provide more healthy and appealing meal and snack options.

THINKING LIKE A SCIENTIST—CAUSE AND EFFECT

Some scientists worry that the eating habits that people form as children have a strong influence on what those people eat as adults. The eating habits of people in the United States have changed a great deal over the last few decades. What have been the effects of these changes? Do you think these changes are taking place in other countries as well? Explore this website, http://www.schoolfoodpolicy.com/ (then search for Country Watch), or others that you find, to consider the following questions:

- How are the school lunch options typical in other countries similar to or different from the options in the United States?

- How are the school day snack options typical in other countries similar to or different from the options in the United States?

- Which country's foods would you rather eat in school? Why?

- What are the causes of these changing food options, both in the United States and in other countries?

- If the United States does not change its school nutrition policies, what do you think the long-term effects will be?

SAMPLE GRADE-LEVEL MODIFICATION—EARLY ELEMENTARY

Younger students can still conduct school nutrition interviews or surveys with modifications. Instead of a survey with written answers, they can construct a survey that uses check boxes of what is available in the cafeteria. For an interview, invite subjects into the classroom and videotape the interviews, then watch the tape with the students, pausing it to ask relevant questions about the subject's responses.

Sample Interdisciplinary Connection—Social Studies

Studying traditional foods of other countries is a typical part of international social studies, but when this is done, connections are rarely made to the science of nutrition. Learn to think about traditional foods in other countries not just as an interesting part of their culture but also as a part of their health and well-being. What do we know about the diets of people in countries with the highest life expectancies? Compare things like the amount of fats and processed sugars in these diets.

Scientists in Your Community

Individuals in your community who might be knowledgeable about diet and nutrition would include doctors or nurses, nutritionists, cafeteria workers, or other food industry workers. Invite one or more of these individuals to your class to ask them questions about nutrition and to share what you have learned.

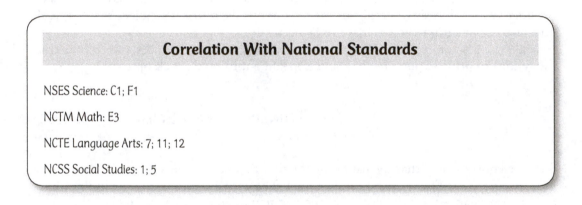

Correlation With National Standards

NSES Science: C1; F1

NCTM Math: E3

NCTE Language Arts: 7; 11; 12

NCSS Social Studies: 1; 5

Study of Student Exercise Habits

In the previous activity on school nutrition, we mentioned the relationship between nutrition and exercise. Just as students often learn about the digestive system in science class without making connections to the importance of nutrition, students likewise learn about the respiratory and circulatory systems without making connections to the importance of regular exercise for our long-term health and well-being. While there has been more of an emphasis on the importance of exercise in our schools than on the importance of good nutrition, there is still not enough done in most schools to promote physical fitness. For example, the trend to remove recess from elementary schools in order to increase academic instruction has occurred in many states in response to increased high-stakes testing and accountability. This combination of increased stress and decreased physical activity may well result in negative health consequences for students both in the short term and in the long term.

As with student nutrition, a place-based emphasis on teaching and learning about exercise and physical fitness can serve to connect academic learning with meaningful social action. In this activity, you will begin by surveying students and adults in your school about the exercise they get—how much, how often, and what kinds. Then you will develop a model exercise program to help meet the needs of people in your school (again, both students and adults) who are not finding ways to get sufficient exercise. Third, you will create a school advertising campaign to encourage people to participate in your program. Then, in the following activity, you will create the opportunity for people to participate in your program for a month and help them to monitor their fitness levels.

Exercise is not always about doing jumping jacks and push-ups. Many cultures have developed other types of exercise involving meditation and martial arts.

One of these exercise styles that has gained increased popularity in the West is the Chinese tradition of Tai Chi. Tai Chi literally translates as "boundless fist." It involves three primary elements: health, meditation, and martial arts. Have students explore how Tai Chi works as a total system as well as a type of exercise. Have them compare it with related types of meditation and exercise such as yoga.

DEVELOPING A SCHOOL EXERCISE PROGRAM

MATERIALS YOU WILL NEED FOR THIS ACTIVITY

- Paper and pencil

- Student designed surveys

Students exercising

WHAT YOU WILL DO

Before the Trip

As a class, design a short survey about people's exercise habits that students and adults in your school can take. The following sample questions can get you started. Some questions may have a numerical response, such as:

I typically exercise for at least 30 minutes how many times in an average week?

Some questions could be short fill-in-the-blank, such as:

The top 3 most common ways I get exercise are: 1._____ 2. _____ 3. _____.

Most questions should use a Likert scale for responses, such as Almost Always, Frequently, Sometimes, Occasionally, and Almost Never, or Strongly Agree, Agree, Unsure, Disagree, Strongly Disagree, such as:

I approach exercise as something fun and relaxing:	1. Almost always 2. Frequently 3. Sometimes 4. Occasionally 5. Almost never

I vary the types of exercise I get to include activities that build endurance, strength, and flexibility:	1. Almost always 2. Frequently 3. Sometimes 4. Occasionally 5. Almost never
It makes me feel good to exercise:	1. Almost always 2. Frequently 3. Sometimes 4. Occasionally 5. Almost never
When I exercise, I tend to overdo it, and then I feel pain afterward:	1. Almost always 2. Frequently 3. Sometimes 4. Occasionally 5. Almost never
I am satisfied with the amount and types of exercise that I do:	1. Strongly agree 2. Agree 3. Unsure 4. Disagree 5. Strongly disagree
I wish that I exercised more than I do:	1. Strongly agree 2. Agree 3. Unsure 4. Disagree 5. Strongly disagree
I prefer to exercise alone:	1. Almost always 2. Frequently 3. Sometimes 4. Occasionally 5. Almost never
I prefer to exercise with other people but in noncompetitive ways:	1. Almost always 2. Frequently 3. Sometimes 4. Occasionally 5. Almost never
I prefer to exercise through sports or in other competitive ways:	1. Almost always 2. Frequently 3. Sometimes 4. Occasionally 5. Almost never
When I exercise, it makes me also want to eat a healthier diet:	1. Strongly agree 2. Agree 3. Unsure 4. Disagree 5. Strongly disagree

(Continued)

(Continued)

I have trouble finding the time to exercise:	1. Almost always 2. Frequently 3. Sometimes 4. Occasionally 5. Almost never
I have trouble getting motivated to exercise:	1. Almost always 2. Frequently 3. Sometimes 4. Occasionally 5. Almost never
I would exercise more if I had a fun and convenient opportunity:	1. Strongly agree 2. Agree 3. Unsure 4. Disagree 5. Strongly disagree

Come up with other survey questions of your own, but keep the total number of questions under 20 so it does not take people too much time to fill out the survey.

Once you have designed your survey, decide who you would like to give it to. All the students and teachers in your grade? Younger or older students? All the adults in your school? Make copies and plan a time to administer the survey. Physical education class might be a good time to give the survey to students. Before or after school might be the best time to give it to teachers and other adults.

On the Trip

Take your survey directly to people and ask them if they will fill it out while you are there. If you leave if for them to fill out later, you will get a much lower response rate.

Tell them that you will be using the results of the survey to design a school fitness program that people can participate in voluntarily.

Encourage people to be honest in their responses since the survey will help to guide the design of the program.

Back in the Classroom

Look at your survey responses and compile the data. What patterns do you see in the responses? How do the people you surveyed feel about exercise? What are they currently doing? Would they like to exercise more? What kinds of exercise do they prefer?

Design an exercise and fitness program that builds on what you learned from your exercise survey. Here are some guidelines to consider when developing your program:

A balanced exercise program should include opportunities for exercise focusing on endurance (cardio training), strength (weight or resistance training), and flexibility (stretching). Knowing how to balance these different types of exercise can be confusing. Does the order matter? Should you do more than one type of exercise on the same day? Should you do cardio and strength training on the same day? Which one should you do first? This depends on your goals and how much time you have to exercise. The most important thing is to start slowly and allow for some recovery days in between exercise days.

Starting a program that meets for about 45 minutes 3 days a week is probably ideal. A typical program would begin with 5 to 10 minutes stretching followed by 30 minutes of some sort of cardiovascular training and ending with another 5 to 10 minutes of stretching or light resistance training. The details of exactly what to do are up to you to decide.

Once you have developed your exercise program, the next step is to get people to participate. It's time to do some advertising. Create posters with information about the program. Go on the morning announcements and make an announcement about the program. Send information home in the school newsletter and put it on the school website or listserv. Talk about it with your friends. See how many people, including students and adults, you can get to commit to participating in the program for one month.

Thinking Like a Scientist—Hypothesis and Evidence

Many people are likely to say that they know they do not get as much exercise as they should. What is your hypothesis about why people don't get more exercise? Use your survey questions to gather evidence about what people in your school say about the amount of exercise they get. Were the reasons you hypothesized common in the survey responses? Did people give reasons you did not think of? Were there differences between students' answers and adults' answers? Explain.

How can you use the survey responses to design an exercise program that meets the exercise needs of the people you surveyed? How are the activities that you planned in your program similar to and different from what you are doing in physical education class in school? Which do you think is more appealing? Why?

Sample Grade-level Modification—Middle School

Some middle school students have already decided that exercise is "not for them." Sometimes this is for social reasons such as that they do not want to be associated with the "jocks" in school. Spend some time talking with middle schoolers about the psychological and sociological side of exercise and how it relates to perceptions of identity. Brainstorm ways that adolescents can still get exercise without having to change the way they are perceived by their peers.

Sample Interdisciplinary Connection—Mathematics

Compiling and analyzing the data from a survey provides many opportunities for applying math skills. How should you total your data? What kinds of averages could you use and what would they tell you? Compare the mean, median, and mode of survey responses and interpret the differences between these three types of averages. What is the clearest way to express your findings? What sorts of charts or graphs could you construct? Would different types of graphs highlight different things in the data? Explain.

Scientists in Your Community

Individuals in your community who might be knowledgeable about exercise programs and their benefits would include doctors or nurses, personal trainers, fitness center workers, and your gym teacher, among others. Invite one or more of these individuals to your class to ask them questions about exercise and to share what you learned from your survey.

Correlation With National Standards

NSES Science: A1; C3; F1

NCTM Math: B1; E1; E2

NCTE Language Arts: 7; 11

NCSS Social Studies: 4

Activity
11

Study of Fitness Levels

On average, the U.S. population is getting older, more obese, and more sedentary. It has long been known that it becomes harder and harder for people to stay fit as they grow older. Endurance, strength, and flexibility all decrease as we age. Additionally, low fitness levels increase our risk of many diseases and eventually interfere with our ability to function and live independently. All of these changes are natural and, to some degree, unavoidable. There are many things we can do, however, to both slow and reduce the effects of this gradual physical decline. For example, maintaining a healthy body mass index (BMI), not smoking, and being physically active can all lead to higher life-long fitness levels.

It's very important, however, not to wait until you are an adult to begin addressing these fitness issues. While it is possible for a person who has not been physically fit to change his or her fitness practices later in life, it is both easier and more effective to develop healthy fitness practices when you are younger and maintain them throughout life. Additionally, there are benefits that come from physical fitness as a youth. For example, a recent study of the nearly 2 million students in Texas schools found that students who scored high on the state cardiovascular fitness test were more likely to do better academically, to have better school attendance, and to have fewer disciplinary referrals than students who scored low on the fitness test. In other words, there are both short-term and long-term benefits to starting a fitness program as a young person and then sticking with it.

In the previous activity, you developed a model fitness program based on information you gained from a survey of students and teachers in your school. Then you created an advertising campaign to encourage participation. In this activity you will help to run a fitness program in your school for a month and help students and teachers track their participation and their fitness levels.

CULTURAL CONNECTIONS

Exercise can provide not only physical benefits but mental benefits as well. The German philosopher Friedrich Nietsche, for example, said that "All truly great thoughts are conceived by walking." Explore with students the different aspects of exercise and its importance for physical and psychological well-being by discussing quotes on fitness and exercise found on the Internet (use the search terms "exercise quotes" and "fitness quotes"). For example, A. A. Milne wrote, in reference to his creation Winnie the Pooh, that "A bear, however hard he tries, grows tubby without exercise."

EXERCISE AND FITNESS LEVELS

MATERIALS YOU WILL NEED FOR THIS ACTIVITY

Materials depend on the type of fitness program designed—they could include exercise mats, jump ropes, resistance bands, hand weights, yoga balls, and other inexpensive exercise equipment. The following items are particularly useful:

- Stopwatch

- Meter stick

- Blood pressure monitor (optional)

- Fitness charts

- Attendance sheet

Exercising for improved fitness

WHAT YOU WILL DO

Before the Trip

Prepare the materials you will need for each fitness session. This will include any exercise equipment as well as any tools needed to monitor and record fitness level and an attendance sheet (be sure to have everyone sign in during each session using the attendance sheet).

On the Trip

During the first session of the fitness program, participants should do the following three tests to get an initial fitness measure in each of the three basic forms of exercise: *flexibility* (stretching), *endurance* (cardiovascular), and *strength* (lifting). Be sure to have everyone record their results so that they can compare these to their results at the end of the fitness program.

Flexibility Test

- Place a meter stick on the floor. Secure it by placing a piece of tape across the meter stick at the midpoint (the 50-centimeter mark).

- While sitting, place the soles of your feet even with the 50-centimeter mark on the meter stick.

- Ask a helper to place his or her hands on top of your knees to anchor them.

- Reach forward as far as you can, holding the position for 2 seconds.

- Note the distance you reached compared to the 50-centimeter mark. This could be a negative number if you cannot reach as far as the 50-centimeter mark or a positive number if you reach beyond the 50-centimeter mark.

- Repeat the test two more times.

- Record the best of the three reaches.

Endurance Test

To assess your aerobic fitness, take a brisk 1-mile walk. You can do the walk anywhere—on a track, around the school grounds, or even in the school building. Before and after the walk, check and record your pulse in your notebook or journal.

To check your pulse over your carotid artery, place your index and third fingers on your neck to the side of your windpipe. To check your pulse at your wrist, place two fingers between the bone and the tendon over your radial artery—which is located on the thumb side of your wrist. When you feel your pulse, look at your watch and count the number of beats in 10 seconds. Multiply this number by 6 to get your estimated heart rate per minute.

After you've recorded your pulse, note the time on your watch and walk 1 mile. After you complete the walk, check your watch and record the time it took you to finish. Then check and record your pulse once more.

Strength Test

Push-ups can help you measure muscular strength. If you're just starting a fitness program, do modified push-ups on your knees. If you're already fit, do classic push-ups. For both types:

- Lie facedown on the floor with your elbows bent and your palms next to your shoulders.

- Keeping your back straight, push up with your arms until your arms are extended.

- Lower your body until your chest touches the floor.

- Push your body upward, returning to the starting position.

Count each time you return to the starting position as one push-up. Do as many push-ups as you can until you need to stop for rest. Record the number of push-ups you complete in your notebook or journal.

After the initial fitness testing session, all subsequent sessions should begin with stretching for at least 5 to 10 minutes. The following site is one good resource for basic flexibility training. There are many others available online as well.

http://www.sport-fitness-advisor.com/flexibility-exercises.html

After stretching, the majority of your session's remaining time should be dedicated to cardiovascular training. This can take many forms and can be as simple as taking a brisk walk or jog, doing laps around the school for at least 20 minutes. Other possible types of cardio training that you could use in your fitness program could include cycling— either stationary ("spinning") or riding around the neighborhood—swimming, or sports that are cardio intensive, such as basketball or soccer. What you do should depend on participant interest, materials available, and the fitness level of the participants.

To avoid injuries, don't try to do too much too fast—work up to higher levels of fitness.

Depending on participants' fitness levels, follow the cardio training with some strength training or alternate between cardio training during one session and strength training during the following session. For strength training, you can use hand weights, resistance bands, or even just simple strength exercises such as push-ups and sit-ups.

The following site is one good resource for basic strength training. There are many others as well.

http://exercise.about.com/cs/exbeginners/l/blbegstrength.htm

Try to hold your fitness sessions three times a week for a month. During the last session, repeat the same three fitness tests that you did during the first session. Have participants record and compare their results to their results from the first session. Did everyone's fitness improve?

Back in the Classroom

Use the data from the beginning and ending fitness tests to draw conclusions about the effectiveness of the fitness program you developed. Look for patterns. Did participants show more growth in one of the three fitness areas than in the others? Did participants who attended more regularly show more growth than people who missed some sessions? Did kids or adults show more growth? Any differences between males and females? What other patterns can you find?

Prepare more posters to share the results of your fitness program and post them around the school. Share your success with the school in other ways such as on the morning announcements, web page, newsletter, and so forth.

Ask the participants if they wish to continue the fitness program for another month (maybe even all year). Keep at it and watch as everyone's fitness level improves!

THINKING LIKE A SCIENTIST—CAUSE AND EFFECT

In many areas of science, pre- and posttests are used to measure the effect of some action or event. If there is a difference between the pre- and posttest results, the events that took place between the two tests can probably be assumed to have caused the difference. In the case of the fitness tests that you gave at the beginning and the end of your exercise program, what can you conclude about the effects of your program on the participants?

What factors do you think influenced people's decisions about whether or not to stick with the program?

Based on what you learned, what are some things we could do in this country to support people in improving their fitness levels?

How is your fitness program an example of place-based learning?

SAMPLE GRADE-LEVEL MODIFICATION—EARLY ELEMENTARY

Students are never too young to learn about healthy exercise practices. Younger students will need more guidance to both develop and test out their fitness program. Additionally, young children must be especially careful with strength training exercises—it is better to focus on stretching and aerobic fitness. With the proper supervision and guidance, this activity, like nearly all of the place-based activities in this book, can be done in meaningful and rewarding ways with young children.

SAMPLE INTERDISCIPLINARY CONNECTION—LANGUAGE ARTS

The results of this activity lend themselves very well to a mock science convention poster session. Have small groups of students create a poster describing their project and showing their results. Hold an interactive poster session where students from other classes, parents, and family members or other members of the community come to learn about the fitness project. After the interactive session, the posters can be put on display somewhere in the school. Be sure that students use their best language arts skills as they create their posters.

SCIENTISTS IN YOUR COMMUNITY

Individuals in your community who might be knowledgeable about exercise programs and their benefits would include doctors or nurses, personal trainers, fitness center workers, and your gym teacher, among others. Invite one or more of these individuals to your class to ask them questions about exercise and to share what you learned as a result of implementing your exercise program.

Correlation With National Standards

NSES Science: A1; F1

NCTM Math: B4; E2

NCTE Language Arts: 6; 7

NCSS Social Studies: 4

Activity

12 Water Fountain Water Versus Bottled Water

SCIENCE BACKGROUND

Drinking bottled water has become increasingly popular in recent years in many countries. Why do you think this is? Most people who drink bottled water say that the number one reason is that it's convenient. Many people also believe that bottled water is cleaner or purer and that it tastes better than tap water from the sink or water fountain. Much of this perception is a result of advertising that emphasizes the idea that bottled water comes from crystal-clear mountain springs or the run-off of pure glacial water. Commercials and magazine ads for bottled water emphasize the "exotic" origins of this water and also imply that drinking this bottled water is a sign of high class and good taste. Some brands of bottled water now come in designer bottles that are often prominently displayed in fancy restaurants and gourmet food stores.

Research by groups such as the Natural Resources Defense Council (http://www.nrdc .org/), however, suggests that the bottled water sold in the United States is not necessarily purer or safer than most tap water. In a 4-year study, the NRDC tested more than 1,000 bottles of 103 different bottled water brands. They concluded that there was no significant difference between the content of municipal tap water and bottled drinking water.

In the following activity, students will research the question of whether bottled water actually tastes better than the water from the water fountains in their school. The class will set up a water taste challenge and have other students and adults in your school sample different bottled waters and water from water fountains in the school to determine which tastes the best.

CULTURAL CONNECTIONS

Water has many uses besides just for drinking and washing. It can also be used to create music. Have students line up eight glasses of the same size and then fill them up with different amounts of water. The first glass should be 1/8 of the way full and then each successive glass should be filled with an additional 1/8 of the height of the glass (1/8,

2/8, 3/8, 4/8, 5/8, 6/8, 7/8, 8/8). Each glass when struck with a spoon will sound like one of the notes on the music scale (do, re, mi, fa, sol, la, ti, do). With a little bit of tuning by the addition or subtraction of water from each glass, students should be able to play simple tunes by striking the top of each glass with a spoon.

DOES BOTTLED WATER TASTE BETTER?

MATERIALS YOU WILL NEED FOR THIS ACTIVITY

- Bottles of water collected from the school water fountains
- Several bottles of three different brands of bottled water (amount will depend on how many participants you plan on having)
- Small paper cups (four for each person participating in the test)
- Copies of water sample rating sheet

WHAT YOU WILL DO

Before the Trip

Have students find maps of the water resources in their community. Have them find out where the water comes from that they use in their home or in their school. This information can probably be obtained from the local water management district's website.

Next, consider these questions about bottled water: How does the bottling of water use valuable resources? Does the use of bottled water potentially contribute to the polluting of our environment? In what ways?

Do the following to prepare for the water taste test:

Bottled water

1. Announce to your school that you will be conducting a water taste test and determine when and where you will conduct the test and who you are asking to participate. You may choose to tell people that they will be comparing bottled water to water fountain water or you can choose to keep that a secret so as not to bias the participants.

2. You can make posters to advertise the event, time, and place.

3. Get your water samples together. Be sure to only get the water from the water fountain(s) just before the taste test because water that has been sitting around for a few hours or more will start to get a stale taste and will make for an unfair comparison. Also try to ensure that all the water samples are at about the same temperature because different temperatures can also bias the taste results. Most people can distinguish taste differences best if the water is cool but not cold.

4. Remove or totally cover the labels on each bottle and, using a permanent marker, number the bottles from 1–4.

5. Prepare a water sample rating sheet that participants can use to record the order of their taste preferences and any descriptions of the taste or smell of the samples (i.e., metallic, chlorine, and so on). Make copies of the rating sheet.

On the Trip

1. Travel around the school to get a range of participants.

2. Give each participant four numbered paper cups with a small sample (1–2 ounces) from each bottle.

3. Ask participants to taste each sample and then use the water sample rating sheet to rank order their preferences from 1–4 and make any notes they wish about the taste or smell of any of the samples. Try to get 100 participants if you can.

Back in the Classroom

Tally the results and then construct a bar graph based on participants' preferences.

How do the commercially bottled water samples compare with the tap water samples? Were there strong preferences? If so, can you form a hypothesis about why?

Have students create a presentation to explain their findings. This could take the form of a poster, a slide show presentation, a video, or any other format that you decide upon. Share your presentation with other people in the school.

THINKING LIKE A SCIENTIST—CONTROLLING VARIABLES

When performing a taste test of any kind, one of the most important things to think about is how to make the test as fair as possible. Creating a fair test is largely a question of controlling variables. If you want the tasters to only taste a difference based on the differences in the minerals or other chemicals in the water, then what other potential variables do you need to be sure to control? We have already mentioned temperature—can you think of others?

Have students research the production of one or more of the following commercially bottled waters and determine how far each bottle has to travel to be sold in a store in your neighborhood.

- Aqua Fiji, bottled in the remote highlands of the Pacific Fiji Islands

- Arrowhead Mountain Spring Water, bottled on the slopes of the San Bernardino Mountains in California

- Hawaiian Spring Water, bottled on the slopes of Mauna Loa Volcano in Hawaii

- Virga Pure Tasmanian Water, bottled water from the island of Tasmania, Australia

Have students describe the resources consumed in delivering the water, starting with plastic for the bottle, the gasoline to fuel the transportation for shipping the water, the "carbon footprint" of the product, and so forth.

SAMPLE GRADE-LEVEL MODIFICATION—UPPER ELEMENTARY

Upper-elementary-grade students should be able to plan and organize a water taste test with only limited organizational help from the teacher. While teachers want to be helpful, by fourth or fifth grade, the students should be able to carry out this project mostly under their own leadership. The more opportunities we give our students to take on project leadership, the better they will get at it and the more easily they will learn to accept that responsibility.

SAMPLE INTERDISCIPLINARY CONNECTION—SOCIAL STUDIES

As mentioned above, the more expensive bottled waters get their appeal from the exotic locations they come from. Use maps to locate the origins of these bottled waters, calculate the distance from the place of origin to where you live, and explore how the bottles of water are transported to distant markets. Discuss the economic benefits and the costs of this practice. Who wins economically and who loses? Do you think these practices are sustainable over the next few decades? Why or why not?

SCIENTISTS IN YOUR COMMUNITY

Individuals in your community who might be knowledgeable about water purification and bottled water would include water treatment plant employees, bottled beverage industry employees, health professionals, environmentalists, and chemical engineers. Invite one or more of these individuals to your class to ask them questions about water and to share what you have learned.

Correlation With National Standards

NSES Science: F1; F2; F4

NCTM Math: E1; E2

NCTE Language Arts: 7; 8; 12

NCSS Social Studies: 1; 3; 6

Activity 13

How Physical Space Is Used in Schools

SCIENCE BACKGROUND

The great British politician Winston Churchill (1874–1965) once wrote, "We shape our buildings and afterwards, our buildings shape us." Very few of us spend much time thinking about school buildings and how they shape us, but their impact on us is undeniable. School buildings often span several generations. It many parts of the country, it is common to go to a school that is 50 years old and often possible to attend one that is more than 100 years old.

Think about how most schools are designed. They incorporate many of the same features—many that have to do with control and regulation of both students and teachers. For example, think about the window that is included in most classrooms either in the main door or along the side of the door. The window is not of much use to see out from the classroom but is instead intended for seeing in. If you are sitting still in the classroom, the window in or at the door only allows you to see out to one fixed point. If you are walking in the hallway, however, you can scan the entire classroom from one end to the other—something a principal might find very useful. As another example, desks do not encourage sharing or collaboration. In many schools until the last generation, desks were actually bolted to the floor. This meant that only one type of instruction could go on, one that focused on the teacher at the front of the classroom.

CULTURAL CONNECTIONS

Think for a moment about the cafeteria. What types of exchanges does it encourage students to participate in? Are there cliques that meet together and control the space? What would happen if people were randomly assigned to eat at a specific table each week? What if food were served family style from the kitchen to the tables, as it's done in some private schools, rather than by having students move through a line? What if food were brought to the classrooms on carts and then served to each other by the students as it's done in Japan? Would the social dynamics of lunch change significantly?

Think about other spaces in the school. How is the library used? Hallways and commons areas? Have students discuss how changing the design of their school could improve the ways in which people interact and engage with each other.

DESIGN A SCHOOL

MATERIALS YOU WILL NEED FOR THIS ACTIVITY

- Paper
- Pencils and pens
- A computer with a printer connected to the Internet

WHAT YOU WILL DO

Before the Trip

Students will be divided into groups of three. They will be given the task of designing an ideal school. You might begin with a walking tour of the school and a discussion of why things might have been designed the way they were.

Students should then use the physical location of their own school but imagine that they are starting the design process from scratch. What types of things would they include to make the school function in the best ways possible for learning? Emphasize that they should not be silly—no shopping malls in the middle of the school—but that they should be trying to create what would be real school improvements for their community.

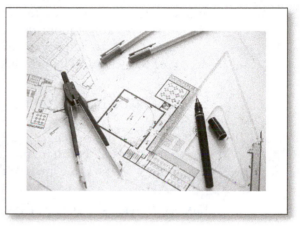

Architecture

Groups should draw a blueprint or map of their proposed school and write descriptions of the various parts and their uses.

During the Trip

Once students have outlines of their proposed schools, take another walk around the actual school and compare what exists to what the different student groups have designed. Discuss the pros and cons of different models.

Back in the Classroom

Give students a chance to modify their designs based on their experience on the walking trip and then organize a charette. A charette is a type of a collaborative review process that architects use when they build a building. Designs are presented and discussed with the actual potential users of the building that is being designed. Other students, teachers, and/or school administrators should be invited to participate.

Have each of the groups briefly present its design ideas for a new school. Conduct a discussion that guides them to combine the best ideas that they have developed. Have students redesign their schools based on the discussion that took place during the charette. Students can post their proposed designs as part of a bulletin board display in the classroom or in the hall or take this activity even further and present one or more of the designs at a PTO meeting or school board meeting to see if any aspects of the design can get support for actual implementation.

Thinking Like a Scientist—Cause and Effect

Does the learning environment actually have an effect on how well people learn? Have students design a series of experiments to consider this question. Experiment with different types of distractions (loud music, lots of talking, etc.) as well as with different ways to help students feel comfortable (add a sofa or some comfy chairs to the classroom, add some lamps instead of the fluorescent lights, etc.). What can students conclude from these experiments? How does this relate to other types of school redesign?

Have students think about how the school could be made safer, more energy efficient, and a more pleasant place to live and learn in. Have them see if there are ways that traffic patterns for student drop-off and pick-up, as well as pedestrian traffic in the hallways, could be improved. Could easier recycling opportunities be built into the design of the school? The possibilities are almost endless.

Sample Grade-level Modification—Early Elementary

For students in the younger grades, it will probably be best for the class to agree upon just one or two areas of the school they would like to design improvements for and then have all the groups work on those areas so that they can more easily share and compare their ideas.

Sample Interdisciplinary Connection—Mathematics

Design work such as architecture requires a lot more mathematics than most people think. For starters, it requires a lot of work with scale to be sure that things will fit correctly. As students work on their designs and models, make sure that they always think about and record their units of measure and the scale that they are using (i.e., 1 centimeter = 1 meter, etc.). Have groups check each other to be sure that the scales being used are realistic.

Scientists in Your Community

Individuals in your community who might be knowledgeable about topics related to school redesign would include architects, physical plant engineers, electricians, and custodians. Invite one or more of these individuals to your class to ask them questions about building design and to share what you have learned.

Correlation With National Standards

NSES Science: E1; E2; F5

NCTE Language Arts: 4; 7

NCSS Social Studies: 1; 5

Conducting a School Energy Audit

Activity 14

Doing a school energy audit provides students with an important means of learning to take responsibility for the energy that they consume while they are at school. In doing so, students not only learn basic ideas about energy but also develop energy conservation habits that will be useful throughout their lives.

Schools with effective energy conversation programs have been shown to save as much as 25% of their utility budgets per year. The most effective conservation programs are those that involve everyone in the school, including the students, staff, teachers, and administrators.

Many of the improvements that are possible by doing an energy audit are extremely simple to translate into action. For example, replacing incandescent light bulbs with energy-efficient compact fluorescent (CFL) light bulbs can save 80% of the energy used to produce an equally bright light. In other words, one cent of energy consumption with a CFL produces the same amount of light as five cents of energy consumption with an incandescent bulb.

Numerous websites are available to help students conduct an energy audit of their school. The National Energy Development Program (http://www.need.org/), for example, has a wide range of resources available at its site, including lists of student projects, as well as guidelines for developing a school energy audit. Another good site with similar types of information is the Alliance to Save Energy (http://ase.org/topics/education). Using these or other resources, have your class conduct a school energy audit.

CULTURAL CONNECTIONS

Have students consider what life would be like without electricity. When would their day begin and end? What would they do that would be different? Have them conduct an experiment where they use no electricity for a defined period of time (an hour, a half day, etc.). Discuss with them what would be lost and what might be gained.

CONDUCTING A SCHOOL ENERGY AUDIT

MATERIALS YOU WILL NEED FOR THIS ACTIVITY

- A computer connected to the Internet with a printer
- Paper and pencil
- A thermometer

Electric meter

WHAT YOU WILL DO

Before the Trip

Discuss with students what an audit is and some of the different kinds of audits that are possible. Discuss what an energy audit of the school would look like and what its goals would be.

Divide the class into groups that will focus on different types of energy-consuming devices such as computers, lights, and electrical appliances.

Using the questions below as a guide, have each group create a data collection form that it can use to collect data on school energy usage for its category of energy usage.

Lighting

- Are lights turned off when people are out of the room?
- Are more lights on in a room than are necessary for the task being done?
- Are there incandescent lights on that can be replaced with more energy-efficient CFLs?

Heating and Cooling

- Can air conditioners be turned down or heat lowered in most rooms? Most people are comfortable in rooms that are only heated to 68 degrees or cooled by air conditioning to 78 degrees. Have students take measures of the temperature of the classrooms throughout their building.
- Determine whether there are leaks in heating or ventilating systems, as well as doors and windows that leak or don't close properly.
- Are programmable thermostats in use—particularly for rooms like the cafeteria, which may not be used all day?
- Determine whether hallways are being kept cooler than classrooms in the heating season or warmer during air-conditioning weather. Doing so will keep energy costs down by not losing energy to the outside.
- See if air conditioner and furnace filters are being cleaned regularly.
- Find places where the addition or replacement of weather stripping, caulking, or insulation will help keep energy use down.

Computers

- Determine whether power management features on computers are being used.

- Determine whether computer equipment is being shut off at the end of the day.

- Determine what equipment is high-efficiency Energy Star equipment (computers, monitors, printers, fax machines, copiers, etc.) and what is not.

During the Trip

Using the data collection form that each group has constructed, go out in teams and conduct an energy audit of the school. It's a good idea for groups to do their audit over the course of several different days to look for patterns in behavior and usage. What you see on one particular day might not be typical.

Back in the Classroom

Teams should find different ways to represent the data they have collected. This could include various forms of tables or graphs.

Teams should then analyze the data and design a plan that improves energy conservation for their energy usage category in their school. Challenge them to identify 10 specific actions that they can take and/or encourage others to take to reduce energy usage.

Students can create posters and signs to remind students and teachers in their school to be more energy efficient.

Once these new practices have been attempted for a few weeks, repeat the energy audit to determine whether significant energy savings are being achieved compared to the initial audit.

THINKING LIKE A SCIENTIST—CAUSE AND EFFECT

Can simple energy conservation practices cause actual financial savings for the school? How much? Is it actually worth making those changes or are the savings so small that it isn't really worth the effort? This energy audit, combined with cost information that your class should be able to get from your school district, will help you to answer these questions. When you conduct your initial energy audit, ask the school district for the electrical bill information for your school. After your campaign to save energy in your school has been going on for several months, repeat the audit and get the new billing information. Remember that if the season has changed, uses like heating or air conditioning may have changed as well. How can you take this into account?

Discuss with students why it is difficult to change human behavior. Why, for example, is it a problem getting people to switch from using incandescent lights to using CFLs when it is clear that they can save money? Have students consider whether rational behavior always drives people in their actions. Discuss ways that people can be encouraged to change their behavior.

SAMPLE GRADE-LEVEL MODIFICATION—UPPER ELEMENTARY

Elementary school students rarely have the opportunity to present their ideas to adults in authentic settings where they will be taken seriously. With some coaching and practice, however, upper-elementary-age students can be prepared to do this. Once your class has compiled the findings from your school energy audit, see if you can get on the agenda for a school faculty meeting and have students share their findings and recommendations for increased energy efficiency with the adults in the school.

Sample Interdisciplinary Connection—Social Studies

While there are obviously many possible mathematics connections in this activity as well, the social studies connections are quite interesting. Some countries have been much quicker to embrace energy-reduction programs than others. Within countries, some regions and some populations have likewise been quicker than others. For example, in the United States, we currently have about 5% of the world's population, but we account for about 22% of the total world energy usage. How can this be explained? What, if anything, might cause us to begin to change these practices?

Scientists in Your Community

Individuals in your community who might be knowledgeable about energy efficiency include electricians, architects, builders, engineers, and environmental conservation consultants. Invite one or more of these individuals to your class to ask them questions about energy efficiency and to share what you have learned.

Correlation With National Standards

NSES Science: B3; E2; F5

NCTM Math: D2; E1; E2

NCTE Language Arts: 4; 8

NCSS Social Studies: 8; 9; 10

Water Drops and Water Loss

SCIENCE BACKGROUND

A drop is a small volume of liquid that falls into free or open space. Drops are very interesting in terms of studying patterns. Drops tend to be round like soap bubbles—this is because they are a minimal surface—essentially taking the most energy-efficient form possible. Liquid drips are periodic, meaning that they tend to drip at regular intervals. Dripping water has been used to create highly accurate clocks and timers—much the same way that sand can be used to record the passage of time in an hourglass.

Dripping water can be interesting to study, but it is usually not a good thing. Running toilets and dripping faucets waste large of amounts of water in homes and schools. A worthwhile place-based activity for students is to determine how much water is actually lost from a dripping faucet or a leaking toilet over the course of a year.

CULTURAL CONNECTIONS

The average person in the United States uses about 180 gallons of water a day for cooking, washing, bathing, and drinking. Have students consider what it would be like if they had to go to a well or a river (as do the majority of people in the world) and carry all of the water that they use in a day back to their home. Take gallon containers full of water out to the ball field and ask students to take turns carrying the containers back and forth across the field until they have simulated the equivalent of carrying 180 gallons. After the simulation, ask students how they think their water use would change if water were not so readily available.

WATER DROPS AND WATER LOSS

MATERIALS YOU WILL NEED FOR THIS ACTIVITY

- Paper and pencil
- A faucet in an easily accessible public space (a classroom, kitchen, or bathroom)

- A watch with a second hand

- A graduated cylinder or beaker

Drop of water

WHAT YOU WILL DO

Before the Trip

Discuss a drop of water. Ask students to describe a water drop. What does it look like? What does it sound like? How much water is in a drop? Is it always the same amount? Why or why not? You might have students look for other images of water drops in magazines or on the web.

On the Trip

Find a sink in the school and open the tap slightly so that the water drips out very slowly.

Place a graduated cylinder or beaker underneath the drip and time how long it takes to accumulate 100 ml.

Using the time it took to accumulate 100 ml of water from the dripping faucet, calculate how much water would be wasted by a dripping faucet in a day. In a month. In a year.

Walk around the school and have students count how many faucets there are in the school. How many of them are dripping? If they are left this way, how much total water will be wasted in the school in a year?

Now, look at the toilets in the school. Check to see if the toilets say how many gallons or liters of water are used per flush. The typical traditional toilet uses 3.5 gallons (or 13 liters) per flush. Newer, more efficient toilets use either 1.6 gallons (6 liters) or 1.4 gallons (4 liters) per flush.

Walk around the school again and count the number of toilets. If the typical toilet in the school is flushed a dozen times per day (this could be low or high depending on the number of students and bathrooms in the school), how much water is used each day for a traditional toilet? For a high-efficiency toilet?

How much water would be saved each day by switching from traditional to more efficient toilets? In a 180-day school year?

Back in the Classroom

Have students create a Saving Water Campaign for the school. Think about the number of faucets and toilets you counted in the school. How could you make a dramatic point about how much water is being wasted?

Create posters that can go in each bathroom in the school that say how much water can be saved if everyone pays a little more attention to conservation efforts.

THINKING LIKE A SCIENTIST—HYPOTHESIS AND EVIDENCE

What is your hypothesis about why so many people waste water without thinking too much about it? Is it because water is cheap? Because it is perceived in this country as being a nearly unlimited resource? What kinds of evidence do you predict would be most effective at getting people to change their practices? Economic evidence? Social evidence? Using your posters, try to determine what kind of evidence is most compelling? Does it matter who your audience is (kids or adults, etc.)?

How could you take what you learned from studying how water is wasted in your school and spread this message around the larger community?

How could you convince businesses, offices, and others in your community to replace their traditional toilets with low-flow models and to repair leaking sinks?

How could you convince people to make these changes in their homes?

SAMPLE GRADE-LEVEL MODIFICATION—MIDDLE SCHOOL

Extend the activity by connecting it with Activity 6—Distance Learning—and compare your findings about water usage in your school with findings from other schools in different parts of the country or the world. Look for patterns that might influence how people relate to water usage. Does geography matter? Economics? History? What can you conclude?

SAMPLE INTERDISCIPLINARY CONNECTION—LANGUAGE ARTS

Creating a poster campaign for saving water in your school provides students with an authentic reason to practice their persuasive writing. Come up with slogans and other short but persuasive statements that could be put on your posters to make readers think about how much water they waste and why it may be important to conserve water now to prevent serious water shortages in the future.

SCIENTISTS IN YOUR COMMUNITY

Individuals in your community who might be knowledgeable about water conservation could include plumbers, engineers, city employees who work at the waterworks or other water-related facilities, geologists, and other environmental scientists. Invite one or more of these individuals to your class to ask them questions about water conservation and to share what you have learned.

Correlation With National Standards

NSES Science: C4; F2

NCTM Math: A3; B1; D2

NCTE Language Arts: 4; 5; 12

NCSS Social Studies: 7; 10

Activity
16 Science Performances

SCIENCE BACKGROUND

There was a time in our history before the Internet, DVDs, TV, or even radio—and it was only a few generations ago. While it may be hard for today's media-saturated students to comprehend, people had to find other ways to get information until relatively recently in human history. When it comes to learning about science, one of these ways was to go see science lectures and demonstrations in the theater. These science presentations were partly educational and partly entertainment.

For example, the famous British chemist Michael Faraday gave a series of children's Christmas lectures at the Royal Institution of London beginning in 1860 in which he performed demonstrations with burning candles and other simple household materials to teach basic chemical principles. These 19th-century science performances later became the foundation for 20th-century science TV programs such as *Mr. Wizard* (Don Herbert) and more recently *Bill Nye the Science Guy*.

Even more recently, there have been efforts to recreate the genre of live science performances in a theater setting, but with the addition of 21st-century special effects. For example, in 2002, Professor Richard Wiseman of the University of Hertfordshire and Dr. Simon Singh created and performed the Theatre of Science at the Soho Theatre in London. The show was a mix of science demonstration, probability theory, and comedy. This performance was so popular that they created a second show in 2006 with a larger budget and more impressive special effects, including the generation of 6-foot-long bolts of lightning between two specially constructed transformer coils.

We don't recommend that you create giant lightning bolts in your school, but you can create and perform science theater. In the following activity, you will design an assembly for other students in your school in which you will present information based on one of the other place-based projects or activities that your class has done. The presentation should take the form of a dramatic performance. You should consider concluding the performance by making a proposal to the audience for a school-based project to address some aspect of a community challenge related to the information you presented.

CULTURAL CONNECTIONS

There are many great poems in literature that have science as their subject. An example is the following brief poem by Emily Dickinson (1830–1886):

> "Faith" is a fine invention
> When gentlemen can see—
> But microscopes are prudent
> In an Emergency.

Have students go online and search for interesting science poems by typing into their search engine "science and poetry" or "science poems." Have them write their own poems on a science topic of interest to them.

PERFORMING PLACE-BASED SCIENCE IN THE AUDITORIUM

MATERIALS YOU WILL NEED FOR THIS ACTIVITY

- Materials will depend on the project you are addressing in your performance, but you should think about materials that will help you make your presentation engaging and visually interesting for your audience

WHAT YOU WILL DO

Before the Performance

Review the various place-based activities that you have done as a class. Discuss which activities you found the most engaging, which ones had the most interesting results, and which topics you would like to see gain more attention in your school. As a class, agree on one topic to be the focus of your science performance.

Prepare a performance about your topic that aims to be both educational and entertaining. You may wish to talk to the theater, band, and or chorus teacher to get some tips about how to put on a good performance. Build any props, create costumes, and gather materials. Watch the excerpt below from Wiseman and Singh's Theatre of Science performance for a bit of inspiration:

http://www.psy.herts.ac.uk/wiseman/images/ToS.mov

Schedule your performance. Talk with the school administration to pick a time when you can perform in the school auditorium.

Student performance

Advertise your performance. Make an interesting poster and put it up around the school. Talk to other teachers and classes and invite them to the performance.

Do a dress rehearsal. If possible, practice your performance on the stage in the auditorium so that you get a sense of the spacing of things on the stage, where setting and props should go, and so forth.

During the Performance

Present your performance to other members of the school community. You may also consider doing an evening performance for family and community members.

Conclude the presentation with a proposal for a school-wide initiative for addressing some community challenge related to the information you presented. Try to get a commitment from your audience to help with this project.

Back in the Classroom

Discuss the performance and the response that you got from your audience.

What went as expected and what did not?

If you did a second performance, what would you do differently?

Make a plan for going around to groups who made up your audience for a follow-up conversation about the school or community project.

THINKING LIKE A SCIENTIST

You've been practicing three ways of thinking like a scientist—coordinating theory and evidence, controlling variables, and using cause-and-effect reasoning. As you developed your place-based science performance, did you find yourself building any of these three methods into your presentation? Are there ways that you could make these ways of thinking like a scientist more explicit for your audience? How? Was thinking scientifically part of the message you were trying to convey to your audience?

How was a live performance different from a TV show or a webcast?

Was it easier to engage the audience? To get them to agree to participate in the follow-up project? Why or why not?

Do you think live science performances could make a comeback as a way to teach about important science issues? Think about Al Gore's presentation of *An Inconvenient Truth* as one example. What are the strengths and limitations of performances of this kind?

SAMPLE GRADE-LEVEL MODIFICATION—EARLY ELEMENTARY

Younger children (and some older children too) may be intimidated about performing on the stage. They may also have trouble projecting their voices to be heard in a large space. It can be best to start by taking your presentation to other classrooms and starting on a smaller scale. As the students gain confidence and skill, they may decide that they would like to try a performance in a larger space and with a larger audience.

SAMPLE INTERDISCIPLINARY CONNECTION—LANGUAGE ARTS

Learning public speaking skills is an important part of language arts. While not everyone enjoys participating in theatrical performances, learning to speak clearly, to project one's voice loudly, and to learn the lines and actions that go with giving a live performance are important skills that are useful in many settings. Learning these skills from a young age can reduce anxiety about public speaking later in life.

SCIENTISTS IN YOUR COMMUNITY

Individuals in your community who might be knowledgeable about creating a science performance could include local theater performers, drama teachers, science teachers, and local TV personalities, among others. Invite one or more of these individuals to your class to share your presentation with them and to ask them about their own experiences with theater performance.

Correlation With National StAndards

NSES Science: F5

NCTE Language Arts: 4; 12

NCSS Social Studies: 8; 10

PART III

Activities to Promote Place-Based Science Teaching on the School Grounds

In the last chapter we focused on place-based science studies that can take place inside the school building but outside of the classroom to provide students with a wider range of contexts for considering the meaning of place-based education. A good deal of place-based education, historically, however, has taken place out of doors. In Part IV we will consider some of the places that we can take students to engage in place-based science learning that are typically within walking distance of the school. While such walking field trips can potentially be conducted on a regular basis, there can be circumstances, such as parent permission or hazardous walking conditions, that limit the availability or frequency of such neighborhood trips. Thus, as an intermediate step, in this chapter we explore the sorts of place-based science activities that can occur outside the school building while remaining on the school grounds. Such activities generally only require the permission of a school administrator and not parental permission. Thus, this chapter focuses on *science on the school grounds* and how taking the class outside of the school building and into school playgrounds, ball fields, or even just the sidewalk can provide new opportunities for place-based science learning.

Activity
17

Tracking Weather

SCIENCE BACKGROUND

Everyone experiences the weather on a daily basis, but today, we rarely pay close attention to our local weather patterns. We may check the forecast to see if we need to take our coat or our umbrella out with us or to know whether a ball game may be canceled, but we may not feel as if the weather plays a significant role in our daily lives. This has not always been the case.

Weather represents short-term changes in the atmosphere. Today, we know that scientists measure and collect weather data to look for patterns and changes and to make better weather predictions, but weather prediction is actually a very old science. For thousands of years, weather prediction has helped to guide farming practices like planting and harvesting, migrations, and even the timing of festivals. It was not until the 16th century, however, that tools like the thermometer, barometer, and anemometer were used to collect weather data scientifically. Today most people get their weather information from the news, such as TV weather reports, the radio, or the Internet. Few people actually collect their own weather data, look for patterns, and make their own predictions in the way that our ancestors did.

The first thermometer (*thermos* is Greek for heat and *meter* is Greek for measure) was invented in 1593 by the Italian scientist Galileo Galilei (1564–1642) to more accurately measure temperature. Thermometers work because changing temperatures cause the liquid in the thin, closed tube to expand or contract and thus rise or fall.

In 1644, another Italian scientist, Evangelista Torricelli (1608–1647), invented the first barometer (*baros* is Greek for pressure) to measure air pressure. He filled a dish with mercury and put a tube upside down in the dish. When the atmospheric pressure changed from day to day, the mercury in the tube moved up or down.

A third weather tool, the anemometer (*anemos* is Greek for wind), measures wind speed and was invented by the Italian architect Leon Battista Alberti. The anemometer uses small cups that spin around a central rod. The cups change speed depending on how fast the wind is blowing.

A fourth tool, the rain gauge, is a simple devise for measuring how much precipitation has fallen in a given period of time.

In this activity you will build an anemometer and a rain gauge and use them, along with a thermometer and barometer, to track your local weather over a 2-week period.

CULTURAL CONNECTIONS

Consciously or unconsciously, we track the weather almost every day of our lives. Many poets have done the same in their writings. F. W. Clarke in 1891, for example, published "An Ode to Pluviculture, or The Rhyme of the Rain Machine." Have students look up weather poems online. Have them choose a favorite to share and recite. Have them write their own weather-based poems.

TRACKING THE WEATHER

MATERIALS YOU WILL NEED FOR THIS ACTIVITY

- 1 thermometer
- 1 barometer

For rain gauge:

- Scissors
- 1-quart empty clear plastic water bottle
- An old ruler
- Masking tape
- Strip of duct tape or other strong tape

For anemometer:

- 2 plastic drinking straws
- Tape
- 4 small paper cups (the kind used in bathroom dispensers)
- 1 straight pin
- 1 pencil with a new eraser
- 1 marker
- Copy of the Beaufort wind scale

Weather icons

What You Will Do

Before the Trip

- Discuss weather and weather prediction and why it is important to different people.

- Discuss the weather and typical climate in your area and how this has affected the culture and history of the area over time.

Follow these directions for making a rain gauge:

1. Cut the plastic bottle at about 3/4 of its height from its base.

2. Tape the ruler to the side of the bottle. Its bottom should line up with the base of the bottle.

3. Place the rain collector in a safe open area on a flat surface that has no overhangs from buildings or trees nearby; those could interfere with the collection of rainwater. Secure the bottle to the pavement with the duct tape.

Follow these directions for making an anemometer:

1. Form a cross with two drinking straws. Tape the straws together where they cross.

2. Punch a hole in each paper cup about 2 cm below the rim.

3. Stick one cup to the end of each straw and secure it with tape. Make sure all the cups have their opening pointed the same way (right or left).

4. Push the straight pin through the center of the straws where they cross. Then push the pin into the eraser on the end of the pencil.

5. Use the marker to mark a large "X" on the side of one of the cups. This "X" will be a reference you can use to count the number of revolutions as the cups spin around in the wind.

6. Test your anemometer by blowing gently on it to be sure that it spins freely. Make adjustments as needed until it spins evenly.

7. To measure the wind speed using your anemometer, count the number of times it spins around in 10 seconds and then divide the number of revolutions by 3. This will give an estimated wind speed in miles per hour (for example, 15 revolutions in 10 seconds equals a wind speed of about 5 miles per hour).

8. Compare the results you measure using your anemometer with the observable effects using the Beaufort wind scale (below) to check the calibration of your anemometer.

	Wind Speed	Scale	Description (miles per hour) Observable Effects
0	Calm	Less than 1	Smoke will rise vertically.
1	Light air	1–3	Rising smoke drifts; weathervane is inactive.
2	Light breeze	4–7	Leaves rustle, can feel wind on your face, weathervane is inactive.
3	Gentle breeze	8–12	Leaves and twigs move around. Lightweight flags extend.
4	Moderate breeze	13–18	Moves thin branches, raises dust and paper.
5	Fresh breeze	19–24	Trees sway.
6	Strong breeze	25–31	Large tree branches move; umbrellas are difficult to keep under control.
7	Moderate gale	32–38	Large trees begin to sway; noticeably difficult to walk.
8	Fresh gale	39–46	Twigs and small branches are broken from trees; walking into the wind is very difficult.
9	Strong gale	47–54	Slight damage occurs to buildings; shingles are blown off of roofs.
10	Whole gale	55–63	Large trees are uprooted; building damage is considerable.
11	Storm	64–75	Extensive widespread damage.
12	Hurricane	Above 75	Extreme destruction.

On the Trip

Keep a daily record of the weather as recorded outside the school building.
Record your data in the nearby table.
This activity can be done for several weeks or extended over a longer portion of the school year.

Back in the Classroom

Students should work in groups to compile the data they have collected into tables and graphs.
Discuss the various options for how the data can be expressed.
Go to the website for Project Atmosphere Australia for one example of a group of schools that is sharing and comparing weather data from around the world. There are

other such projects as well. Consider becoming a partner school with another school somewhere else in the world and doing a comparative study of how weather influences how you live your life.

http://www.schools.ash.org.au/paa2/

THINKING LIKE A SCIENTIST—HYPOTHESIS AND EVIDENCE

The weather where you live is probably very different at different times of year. What hypothesis can you think of to explain this? How can collecting and charting your local weather over time provide evidence to either support or disprove your hypothesis? Consider that patterns you see when you look at the data over a 2-week period or longer. Which weather measures seem to be related to each other? Might this be evidence that helps you think about seasonal variations? What predictions can you make about the data you could collect 6 months from now?

SAMPLE GRADE-LEVEL MODIFICATION—EARLY ELEMENTARY

Weather study is a very appropriate activity for young children. Most kindergarten and early grades' classes check the weather every day as part of their morning meeting. Moving from reporting on the weather through simple observation to taking and recording weather measurements is an important step toward more rigorous science learning. Instead of taking four weather measurements (temperature, barometric pressure, wind speed, and rainfall), start with one or two measurements and then gradually work toward more complete weather study.

SAMPLE INTERDISCIPLINARY CONNECTION—SOCIAL STUDIES

Weather and climate affect everyone in the world. Our habits of dress, diet, architecture, and even our language are affected by the weather and climate where we live. How are weather and culture related? Have students pick cultures from different parts of the world and consider ways that weather and climate have shaped different aspects of that culture and how people in that region live. Do you think that modern technology is changing the relationship that exists between weather and culture? Discuss this with your class.

SCIENTISTS IN YOUR COMMUNITY

Individuals in your community who might be knowledgeable about local weather and climate would include local TV weather reporters, geographers or climatologists from a local college, older residents who have lived in the community for a long time, and amateur meteorologists. Invite one or more of these individuals to your class to ask them questions about weather and climate and to share what you have learned.

Class Weather Monitoring Data

Date/Time	Wind Speed	Temperature	Barometric Pressure	Rainfall

Correlation With National Standards

NSES Science: A1; D1

NCTM Math: D1; D2

NCSS Social Studies: 3

Activity
18

Soil Erosion and Runoff

SCIENCE BACKGROUND

Soil erosion is the process of soil particles being carried off by water or wind and deposited somewhere else such as into a stream or river. A common cause of erosion is runoff, or water that does not soak into the ground when it rains. Runoff flows over the ground and runs into another area, such as a stream or a storm drain. Runoff can wash fertilizer, trash, and other pollutants into streams and rivers along with soil. Erosion also removes nutrients from the soil, making it more difficult for plants to grow. Reducing erosion and runoff can make a significant difference in controlling local water pollution and protecting our soil and water supply.

While some degree of runoff and erosion will almost always occur, current development practices in many communities are increasing the problem of erosion. There are things that we can do in our communities, however, to reduce erosion and to better protect our soil and water. In this activity you will study soil erosion and runoff on your school grounds and create a plan for reducing erosion.

Erosion begins when rain or other flowing water (such as from a hose or sprinkler) loosens soil particles. When there is too much water to soak into the soil, the water begins to flow and carry away the loosened soil. Developed areas, with lots of roofs and pavement—such as a school—can increase erosion by channeling large amounts of water in a short time across small areas of soil that cannot absorb it quickly enough. The flowing water then carries the soil away.

You can begin your study of erosion in your schoolyard by walking around the grounds and looking for signs that erosion is taking place. These signs of erosion might include: gullies or channels in the soil, the roots of plants being exposed, sediment or soil collected on pavement or in low areas, and areas of bare soil. You can also observe the school grounds when it is raining or just after the rain has stopped to look for evidence of runoff and to identify spots where runoff is heavier. You are likely to observe that runoff and evidence of erosion usually occur together, since runoff is the primary cause of soil erosion. Pay special attention to what happens to water that runs off large paved areas like parking lots or ball courts.

One of the most common ways to reduce runoff and erosion is by planting additional plants in areas where runoff and erosion are occurring. The root structures of plants help the soil to absorb more water and help to hold soil in place, thereby reducing both runoff and erosion. Some types of plants are especially good for erosion control. *Ground cover* is the general name for any plant that covers the ground surface completely so that soil cannot be seen from above. Ground cover plants are the best form of erosion control because raindrops cannot hit the soil directly and loosen the soil particles. Many groundcover plants also require very little in terms of care and maintenance. Ground cover plants should be planted on slopes or bare areas to help control erosion and run-off. Ground cover plants also conserve soil moisture, reduce heat, and generally make the area look nicer. Below are some good ground cover choices for the southeastern United States region. You should talk with someone knowledgeable about local plants in your region (try calling a local plant nursery) to determine what some of the best ground cover choices are for your area.

Ajuga (*Ajuga reptans*)—Ajuga is a broadleaf, evergreen groundcover that forms a low, dense carpet of foliage. Ajuga is tolerant of a range of weather and soil conditions and has pretty purple flowers in the spring.

Dwarf Japanese Garden Juniper (*Juniperus procumbens*)—Dwarf garden juniper is an evergreen groundcover plant that starts in mounds and then spreads into a carpet. It has attractive blue-green foliage and generally needs a moist climate.

Lilyturf (*Liriope muscari*)—Lilyturf is an evergreen ground cover that grows in clumps with long grass-like leaves, but it is actually a type of lily and not a grass. Lilyturf can grow in a wide range of conditions.

In the next activity, you will explore erosion in your schoolyard and consider some of the factors that can increase or decrease soil erosion. These factors include soil type, slope, and plant cover. You will study the effect of planting local plants on erosion.

CULTURAL CONNECTIONS

Art is often created by processes that involve artificial rather than natural erosion. For example, carving a piece of marble to make a statue is very much the same as natural erosion, just at a must faster rate. Have students invent ways of creating art using erosion. This could involve running water, ink, or paint down a piece of paper to create patterns or combinations of shading and color, or blowing through a drinking straw on paint or ink on a piece of paper. See how many different techniques the students can propose.

STUDYING AND CONTROLLING RUNOFF AND EROSION

MATERIALS YOU WILL NEED FOR THIS ACTIVITY

- Camera
- Notebook
- Ground cover plants
- Garden tools

Erosion

WHAT YOU WILL DO

Before the Trip

Discuss the problems caused by excess runoff and erosion and how these problems may be affecting your community.

Discuss ways that runoff and erosion can be controlled and do some research on the Internet about ground cover plants that are suitable for your environment.

Research the best times and methods for planting ground cover plants.

On the Trip

Survey your school grounds and document sites where there is evidence of runoff and erosion. Take photos and make sketches.

Design a plan for reducing runoff and erosion in at least one part of the school grounds, such as through planting additional ground cover.

Back in the Classroom

Prepare a presentation for your school principal or other administrator outlining the problem and your proposed solution. Ask for your administrator's permission and support for enacting your plan.

You may consider a fundraiser to raise money to buy ground cover plants for your project. You may also consider contacting local plant nurseries, explaining your project, and asking them for some plant donations or for a discount on your plant purchases.

Back in the Schoolyard

Gather or purchase needed materials and work together to plant your ground cover plants. If the area where you are working to control erosion is on a slope, you should also consider making terraces on the slope for additional runoff and erosion control.

Take photos and make sketches after your project has been completed and compare these to the photos and sketches that were taken at the start of the project.

Periodically monitor your project area—especially during and after rainfalls—and document the degree of runoff and erosion that still takes place.

Back in the Classroom

If your erosion-control project was successful, consider how you could expand the project in your community. Consider going to other local schools and making a presentation on erosion control. Try to convince students in other schools to create their own project.

Make a presentation to a representative of your local government. Talk about the value of erosion control and of thinking about erosion when planning new development.

THINKING LIKE A SCIENTIST—CONTROLLING VARIABLES

Why are runoff and erosion a bigger problem in some places than in others? What are some of the variables that influence the rates of runoff and erosion? As you designed your plan to reduce runoff and erosion on the school grounds, what were some of the variables that you needed to consider? How successful were you in controlling extra variables?

In many parts of the country, groundwater is the source of people's drinking water. Groundwater needs to be recharged by water soaking through the soil and into the rock layers below rather than running off. How do development and construction impact the recharge of groundwater?

SAMPLE GRADE-LEVEL MODIFICATION—MIDDLE SCHOOL

The amount of science content can be increased in this activity to connect with more middle school science standards. One way is to do some additional research on the impact of chemicals that are often carried into the water supply by runoff—for example, nitrogen and phosphorus are common in lawn fertilizers and have been associated with many environmental problems, such as algae growth in ponds and lakes that can lead to depletion of the oxygen supply and the suffocation of fish and other aquatic creatures. Add this research to your presentation on why it is important to reduce runoff and erosion.

SAMPLE INTERDISCIPLINARY CONNECTION—LANGUAGE ARTS

Controlling runoff and erosion is as much a social issue as it is a science issue. If people do not see runoff and erosion as problems in their communities, then they are unlikely to do anything to reduce or prevent it. It is important for people who do see runoff and erosion as environmental problems to communicate clearly and convincingly about this issue to their friends and neighbors. In order to convince your school principal to let your class create an erosion-reduction plan for the school grounds, you need to make the case for why this is important. To do this, you need to organize your facts and build a sound argument. In doing so, you will be practicing a number of important language arts skills.

SCIENTISTS IN YOUR COMMUNITY

Individuals in your community who might be knowledgeable about runoff and erosion could include farmers, gardeners, soil conservation workers, foresters, geographers, and geologists. Invite one or more of these individuals to your class to ask them questions about runoff and erosion and to share what you have learned.

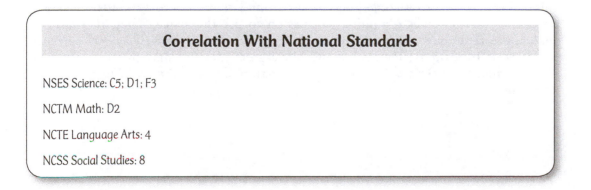

Correlation With National Standards

NSES Science: C5; D1; F3

NCTM Math: D2

NCTE Language Arts: 4

NCSS Social Studies: 8

Activity
19

Urban Gardens

SCIENCE BACKGROUND

Gardening has been an important part of school curriculums going back to the 19th century. The term *kindergarten* literally means "child's garden" in German. The founder of the kindergarten movement, the German educator Friedrich Froebel (1782–1852), included gardening as one of the main activities young children participated in as part of his educational program. The progressive educator John Dewey (1859–1952) included gardens as a major part of his experimental school curriculum at the University of Chicago. Dewey felt that gardening was a natural way to teach science and other subjects through a process of learning by doing. Gardening cannot be done successfully without an awareness of place. What can grow where, when, and how are fundamentally place-based concepts that are essential for successful gardening.

What can elementary and middle school students learn from gardening? Gardening is a valuable way to teach students social skills such as patience, responsibility, and concern for the environment and important science concepts, such as plant life cycles, human nutrition, and ecological effects of pollution.

Gardening can also be done in nearly any school setting. Around rural schools, farming and gardening may be ubiquitous. Suburban schools routinely have adequate green space for situating a garden on the school grounds. In urban schools, where green space may be scarce, container gardening is almost always an option. In recent years, urban gardening movements have developed in cities such as Chicago, Detroit, and Denver, and today most cities are actually full of opportunities to learn about gardening if you know where to look.

The first step student gardeners need to do is to map out the spaces where they might be able to grow something on or around their school grounds. First and foremost, this involves obtaining permission to use the space. They also need to make sure that they can get water to their garden easily, as well as other needed supplies. A rooftop garden may sound like a great idea but may prove impractical if the gardener doesn't have access to the materials necessary to keep the garden growing.

106

Things students need to consider when creating a garden:

- Is the garden site in a protected area where plants will not be damaged or trampled?

- Is there enough sunlight for the types of plants being considered?

- Is there good drainage?

- Is the soil of high enough quality that plants will grow in it? If so, what types of plants?

- Is the garden site easily accessible? Can fertilizer and topsoil be brought in easily?

- Is there water available at the garden site?

Once students have addressed these questions, they can then research what plants will grow at the garden site they have chosen.

A great website to become familiar with youth gardening is sponsored by the American Horticultural Society (AHS). It includes a national database of children's gardens as well as a Youth Garden Resource List.

American Horticultural Society (Youth Gardening):

http://www.ahs.org/youth_gardening/index.htm

Students can leave gardening questions that they want to have answered at the site as well as find lists of books and even share the experience of creating gardens with other children from around the world as part of the "The Growing Connection" program sponsored by the Society. Additionally, the AHS Partnership for Plant-Based Education provides various resources for educators who are interested in learning more about how local plants can be used to support students' science learning.

American Horticultural Society Partnership for Plant-Based Education

http://ahs.org/youth_gardening/plant_based_education.htm

There are many science activities appropriate for elementary and middle school students that can be done in conjunction with planting and tending a garden. Creating a school compost pile is a simple project that can support a school garden while also reducing the amount of trash that the school cafeteria throws away.

CULTURAL CONNECTIONS

The photographer Edward Steichen (1879–1973) did a famous series of photographs in which he took pictures from exactly the same spot for many years. They show a remarkable change of moods and seasons. Students can do the same by choosing a location (a garden, a landscape, a backyard) and setting their camera at exactly the same place with exactly the same settings to take a photograph. Depending on the effect one wants to achieve, this can be done every day, once a week, or once a month. Pictures can be placed in sequence for an exhibit or on a website where they can rotate through as a slide show.

CREATING A COMPOST PILE

Composting is an easy, economical, and environmentally friendly way to improve the quality of a school garden. *Composting* is defined as the decomposition of organic (i.e. plant) material as a result of aerobic organisms interacting with plant material. Compost is made from green (leaf) and brown (dried leaves, stalks, etc.) materials. Examples of green materials are grass clippings, vegetable peelings, and green leaves. Examples of brown materials include dried garden waste and dried leaves. A compost pile can literally be just a pile of plant material that is allowed to decay. Composting will be more efficient, however, in a contained structure or bin made out of wire or plastic. Instructions on making a wide range of compost frames or bins can be readily found by typing the phrase "How to make a compost bin" into an Internet search engine. In the following activity, you will learn to create a compost pile for your school garden.

MATERIALS YOU WILL NEED FOR THIS ACTIVITY

- Wooden stakes
- Chicken wire or strong plastic sheeting
- Hammer and nails or heavy staple gun
- Green materials (grass, vegetable peels, green leaves)
- Brown organic materials (small twigs, dry garden waste, and dry leaves)

Making compost at home

WHAT YOU WILL DO

Before the Trip

1. Research the uses of compost.

2. Pick a spot to create the compost pile. This can be in almost any area in a garden.

On the Trip

1. The composting project will be most effective if a composting frame is constructed first. Use the wooden stakes to outline the boundaries of your compost bin (at least 3 × 3 feet is recommended).

2. Use a hammer and nails or a staple gun to attach the chicken wire or heavy plastic sheeting to wooden stakes to complete your composting frame.

3. With or without a compositing frame, have students layer dead plant and organic material. A large pile of plant material is necessary—a minimum amount of 9 cubic feet (3 × 3 × 3 feet).

4. Water the pile of plant material for at least 3 minutes.

5. Every 2 weeks, use shovels and rakes to turn the pile.

6. When you turn the pile, take samples from the compost pile back to the classroom for observation. Note any changes taking place. Place these samples in airtight bags (squeeze out as much air as possible and save for later observation and comparison with the other samples from different points in time).

7. In about 3 months, the plant material will decompose into rich soil called mulch that can then be added back to the garden.

Back in the Classroom

Talk with the school cafeteria staff about setting up a special trash bin in the kitchen for collecting vegetable waste to add to the compost pile.

If they agree, create a poster that shows what sorts of items can and cannot be composted and discusses how compost helps a garden.

Put this poster with the bin in the cafeteria kitchen.

Make a plan with cafeteria staff for how often you should empty the bin and add its contents to the compost pile in the garden.

THINKING LIKE A SCIENTIST—CAUSE AND EFFECT

What is actually going on in the compost pile and why is this happening? What are the causes of the changes that you are observing in the compost over time and what are the effects? Do some additional research to answer questions such as the following: Why should a compost pile include both green and brown material? Why should you not put meat or other nonvegetable material in your compost pile? What did you observe about how compost changes over time?

SAMPLE GRADE-LEVEL MODIFICATION—UPPER ELEMENTARY

Upper-elementary-grade students start to be given more responsibility for taking care of certain things in the school. This includes acting as crossing guards and doing parts of the morning announcements. In U.S. schools however, students generally don't have responsibilities in the cafeteria. In some other countries students do a lot of the cafeteria work. See if you can get permission to put upper elementary students in charge of monitoring the compost bags, collecting them when they are full, and then taking the compost to the school compost bin.

SAMPLE INTERDISCIPLINARY CONNECTION—MATHEMATICS

Creating a compost pile has at least two concrete benefits. First, the compost that you create is an excellent fertilizer that can improve the quality of a school garden or other plants growing on the school grounds. Second, the compost pile reduces trash in the cafeteria when materials that would be disposed of as trash are placed in the compost bin instead. See if you can calculate how much less trash your school is throwing away because of the collection of compost. See if you can calculate the volume as well as the weight by which the trash is being reduced.

SCIENTISTS IN YOUR COMMUNITY

Individuals in your community who might be knowledgeable about composting could include farmers, gardeners, employees in agricultural supply stores, and environmental and conservation advocates. Invite one or more of these individuals to your class to ask them questions about composting and to share what you have learned.

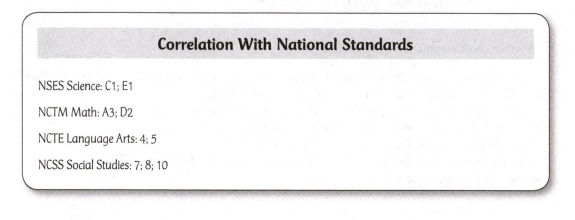

Correlation With National Standards

NSES Science: C1; E1

NCTM Math: A3; D2

NCTE Language Arts: 4; 5

NCSS Social Studies: 7; 8; 10

Bird Watching in the Schoolyard

SCIENCE BACKGROUND

There are many ways that we can involve our students in data collection during science, and our attempts to make these science activities place based may make them more relevant for our students. Students may find these activities to be enjoyable and they may learn a lot, yet they may still feel that they are just doing schoolwork for a grade rather than for some more authentic purpose. There are, however, some projects that have the goal of using data collected by students, clubs, or other community groups, in place-based contexts, to inform the work of practicing scientists. These scientists can then use the data in their ongoing research. Such projects have sometimes been referred to as citizen science projects. Perhaps the best known of these are the citizen science projects run by the Cornell University Lab of Ornithology (http://www.birds.cornell.edu).

Ornithology, or the study of birds, is a natural topic for citizen science projects, because birds exist in every environment where people can live (and even in some environments where people can't) and birds are both easy and enjoyable to observe. Students can track certain bird behaviors such as feeding patterns, migration patterns, and reproductive success and then submit their data to research scientists who are working on projects in these areas.

The following activity is based on a citizen science project that has students construct a bird feeder and then monitor it to track the bird species that visit the feeder. Feeder projects are especially important during the winter when nonmigratory species of birds have a much harder time gathering sufficient food. In the spring and summer, most songbirds eat a diet of mostly insects. In the fall, as the insects die off, this diet changes to mostly berries and seeds. In the winter, even berries and seeds become scarce and many birds struggle to find enough to eat. Thus fall and especially winter are the perfect seasons to stock and monitor a bird feeder.

CULTURAL CONNECTIONS

Have students systematically photograph birds that are attracted to a feeder that they have easy access to. Emphasize the idea of creating artistic compositions, as well as learning about science while studying the natural world. Exhibits and slide shows can be created from the photographs. An interesting exploration would be to have students compare their photographs with those the famous 19th-century naturalist John James Audubon (1785–1851), whose *Birds of America* (easily found on the Internet) provides a comprehensive catalogue of North American birds.

BIRD FEEDER OBSERVATION

MATERIALS YOU WILL NEED FOR THIS ACTIVITY

- Bird feeder (see below for discussion of types)
- Bird food (see below for discussion of types)
- Binoculars
- Bird tracking form
- Bird identification guide

Bird feeder

WHAT YOU WILL DO

Before the Trip

Research the bird species common to your region.

Research which of these species migrate away during the winter and which species are year-round residents.

Determine your "count site." A count site is an area with one or more bird feeders where you will observe birds on a regular basis. A good count site is convenient to observe, can be seen completely from one place, and has obvious boundaries, such as the borders of a ball field or a courtyard. An appropriate count site is about the size of a few tennis courts. Chose one count site, and stick with it for the whole season.

Buy or build one or more bird feeders for your count site. There are many different types of bird feeders, but the simplest is made by smearing pinecones with peanut butter covered by birdseed and then hanging them from tree branches.

Create a tally sheet on which you will record data such as the date and time for each trip to your count site, the weather each time, the types of birds seen, and the number of each bird type seen.

Plan a schedule for days and times that you will go to your count site and count birds.

On the Trip

Use a bird guidebook to identify the bird species you observe at your feeder. Typically, only a few different species of birds will visit your feeder during any given season, so you should be able to become familiar with the birds you see.

There are multiple possible ways to count birds. The Cornell lab projects generally use a method known as "index of abundance." When running your own bird count, you can use whatever method you decide upon as a class. The only important thing is that once a method is chosen, everyone must follow it so that the data are consistent. To participate in a larger project, such as one of the Cornell citizen science projects, you would have to follow their counting method. The index of abundance counting method works like this:

Each time you see a certain bird species within your count site during a scheduled counting time, you count the number of individuals you see at one time and record that number on your tally sheet. If you see a greater number of individuals of this species together later during your counting time, you revise your tally sheet to reflect the larger number, but you do not add your counts together—this ensures that you will never count an individual bird more than once on the same day. You should count all birds that visit your count site whether they eat or not, but do not count birds that just happen to fly over the count site.

Back in the Classroom

Think about ways that you could display your count data. Make tables and graphs and discuss how they represent the data and what patterns or trends they show.

Prepare a presentation on your project and share it with other classes in your school or in a neighboring school.

Consider taking the next step and participating in a citizen science project so that your bird count data can actually contribute to ongoing scientific research. Information on the Cornell Lab Feederwatch project can be found at http://www.birds.cornell.edu/pfw/.

THINKING LIKE A SCIENTIST—CAUSE AND EFFECT

Bird populations change from year to year. Sometimes there are also longer trends that cause populations of certain species to expand greatly or to decline toward extinction. What might some of the causes be for annual fluctuations in bird populations? What might some of the causes be for longer-term changes in a given bird population?

Imagine that you are a scientist in the Cornell Ornithology Lab and you are getting feeder data from students at schools all around the country. What could you do with these data?

What questions could they help you answer?

What are some of the problems that you might encounter with the students' data?

SAMPLE GRADE-LEVEL MODIFICATION—EARLY ELEMENTARY

Counting objects and creating histograms (picture bar graphs) is a common math activity in the early grades. Teachers survey students about their favorite type of pet or their favorite food or flavor of ice cream and then place pictures on the board to create a histogram. Conducting a bird census and then creating a histogram from the bird count is a similar activity but with an authentic science purpose.

SAMPLE INTERDISCIPLINARY CONNECTION—MATHEMATICS

There is a wide range of math applications that can be studied based on bird census data. At the simplest level, this could be counting birds of different species and creating a histogram (see above). At an intermediate level, means, medians, and modes can be calculated for different species over time. At the middle school level, basic algebra can be used to describe the slopes of graphs of changing bird populations.

SCIENTISTS IN YOUR COMMUNITY

Individuals in your community who might be knowledgeable about birds and bird populations could include amateur bird watchers, professional biologists, zoo employees, and wildlife management workers. Invite one or more of these individuals to your class to ask them questions about local birds and other animal populations and to share what you have learned.

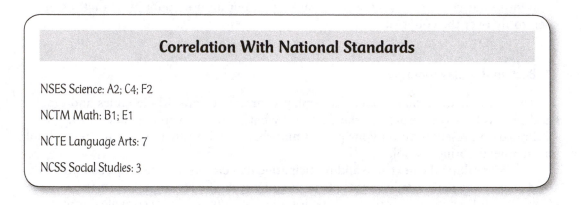

Correlation With National Standards

NSES Science: A2; C4; F2

NCTM Math: B1; E1

NCTE Language Arts: 7

NCSS Social Studies: 3

Activity 21

Adopt a Tree

Students often have very little idea of the plants—particularly trees—that surround their school or where they live. What trees are typical on and around the school grounds (deciduous, evergreen)? What trees provide the best animal and insect habitats? Which trees are preferred in terms of shade and ornamentation? What types of trees bear fruit or nuts? These are just a few of the types of questions students can ask about the trees that live in and surround their school.

Explore with students how trees contribute to the environment where they live. Have students explore how the neighborhood and grounds around their school would be different without trees. What would be missing (shade, animal habitats, etc.)?

Discuss with students the trees that are most common to the region in which they live. Additionally, find out which trees are native to their region and which were brought from somewhere else (Chinese elms, maleluca, etc.).

CULTURAL CONNECTIONS

Trees play an important part in the mythology of many cultures. Have students go online and to learn about the role that trees played in the mythology of Ancient Egypt, Greece, Rome, and India. How were these ancient ideas about trees similar to and different from the way we consider trees in modern times?

ADOPT A TREE

MATERIALS YOU WILL NEED FOR THIS ACTIVITY

- Paper
- Pencil
- A computer with an Internet connection
- Camera (optional)

Tree

WHAT YOU WILL DO

Each student in the class will choose a tree and spend the year studying it.

Before the Trip

Survey with students the grounds of their school to determine what trees are there. Divide the school grounds into quarters or eighths, and have students compile careful lists of the trees in their assigned grids. Have them take photographs of their trees, bring back sample leaves, or do drawings of the plants they have found. Back in class, have groups report the results of their "tree census." Have them compile a master list of the trees that surround the school. If possible, have them map on a black or whiteboard or on a poster board all of the trees that surround the school.

Student Discovery and Research

Have students adopt a specific tree. If you like, they can work with a partner. Have students give their tree a name (Brown Bark, Fred the Fir, Sad Limbs, etc.). Have them write a poem describing their tree. Have them research what species their tree is by looking at the characteristics of its leaves or other identifiers such as fruit or nuts. Have them measure the circumference of their tree at its base. Have them measure its height using a sextant and the Pythagorean theorem. Have them draw and/or photograph their tree, as well as determine if the leaves from their tree are opposite or alternate, simple or compound. Have them record signs of animal life such as insects or birds in their trees.

Back in the Classroom

Students can create a bulletin board with poems, photographs, drawings, and descriptions of their trees. Have them research information online about their trees such as where they are found, how big they can grow, and so forth.

THINKING LIKE A SCIENTIST—CAUSE AND EFFECT

Discuss how trees have adapted to live in different climates. How have different species of trees evolved to live in hot or cold, wet or dry, sunny or shady environments? What are the causes of these differences and what are the effects? For example, why do some trees drop their leaves while others don't? Why are leaves different on different types of trees? What trees do best in what regions of the country? For example, why do palm trees grow in southern climates, while pine trees are found largely in the northern regions? How does this relate to the trees found on your school grounds?

SAMPLE GRADE-LEVEL MODIFICATION—MIDDLE SCHOOL

Dichotomous keys are commonly used by biologists and other scientists to identify species that may look somewhat similar. Have students create their own dichotomous keys to identify the different species of trees on the school grounds. Share these keys with another class of students and see if they can use the keys to correctly identify different trees around the school.

Sample Interdisciplinary Connection—Mathematics

How high is your tree? You probably can't climb your tree to measure how high it is with a ruler or measuring tape. But there are a few different ways that you can use mathematics to help you figure out how tall your tree is. You will need to use some geometry and maybe even some trigonometry to do this. Do some research as a class about ways to use math to calculate the heights of tall objects. Once you learn the strategy, you can measure the height of your tree and other tall objects like your school building, an electrical pole, or a local church steeple.

Scientists in Your Community

Individuals in your community who might be knowledgeable about trees could include local forestry workers, biologists, tree removal service employees, and conservation advocates. Invite one or more of these individuals to your class to ask them questions about trees and to share what you have learned.

Correlation With National Standards

NSES Science: C1; C5

NCTM Math: D2

NCTE Language Arts: 5

Activity 22

One Square Meter of Ground Survey

SCIENCE BACKGROUND

A single square meter of ground, in almost any environment, can yield incredible amounts of information of a scientific nature. On the grounds of a local school in suburban Miami where both of the authors have worked with beginning teachers, one can observe land crabs, iguanas, and even foxes. In the canal adjacent to the school, fish such as barracudas and gar are plentiful, making their way from the ocean in the brackish water. Alligators and even manatees come up the canal. Birds such as great blue herons, ibises, and loons are common sights, as are kingfishers and ospreys. There is an abundant variety of insects, from spiders to beetles and butterflies. Dragonflies zoom across the playground and snakes occasionally slither through the grass. Plants of all varieties and forms can be found growing, and at the microscopic level there are all sorts of plants and animals to observe.

While the animal and plant life in southern Florida is particularly diverse and abundant, you will be amazed at what can be found on a small patch of ground in any environment. Students engaged in place-based science learning should become familiar with their local environment at this microscale level as well as more broadly. In the following activity, students explore a single square meter of land, cataloguing everything on it, large and small, plant and animal, rock, water, and soil.

CULTURAL CONNECTIONS

There is a great deal of art that has been created to illustrate things at the microscopic level. Look online for electron microscope photographs. Have students search for "early microscopic illustrations and/or drawings." Have them look in particular at the work of the English scientist Robert Hooke (1635–1703). Discuss scientific illustration both as scientific data and as pieces of art.

CONDUCTING A MICRO STUDY OF A SQUARE METER OF SCHOOL GROUNDS

MATERIALS YOU WILL NEED FOR THIS ACTIVITY

- Tweezers
- Collecting bottle for specimens
- Bottle or jar for water samples
- Envelops for plant samples
- Notebook for field observations and notes
- Pencil and/or pen
- Tape measure
- Magnifying glass
- Microscope
- Digital camera

WHAT YOU WILL DO

In this activity, you will carefully study the plants, animals, soil, and other materials found in a single square meter of the grounds of your school. You will catalogue the plants and animals, study soil and water samples, and note any human-made materials you find.

Nymphalis polychloros butterfly

Before the Trip

Organize your collecting equipment so that you can work with it easily in the field. Take all of the items listed above with you into the field, except for the microscope.

On the Trip

Find an interesting square meter of the school grounds in which it is safe for you to conduct observations and collect samples. Stay away from busy traffic areas and places that could be dangerous (too near a parking space, etc.). Look for a spot with at least some plant life. The base of a tree can be a good spot, or along the edge of the school building, but any safe spot that attracts your attention will be fine.

Use your tape measure to mark off the boundaries of your square meter of space.

Observe your space carefully. What do you see? Use the magnifying glass to observe more closely. Are there patterns that you can see in terms of how plants are growing or how insects are organized or move around? Are these patterns consistent across the square meter or do the patterns change? Why?

Collect samples of plants, insects, soil, and, if possible, water and carry them back to the classroom.

Visit your plot at different times of the day. Are there patterns that you can observe? Does anything change according to the time of day or because of weather or the changing seasons?

Back in the Classroom

Make a list of the different things you collected or observed. Divide them up according to whether they are animal, plant, or mineral. Use online field guides or books to identify the different things you have found by name. Are there further subdivisions that you can make (grasses versus flowering plants, for example)?

Look at your various samples under the microscope. Can you identify other things that were not visible with the naked eye or the magnifying glass?

Create a report, a bulletin board display, a notebook, or a website that details what you have found in your square meter microsystem.

Thinking Like a Scientist—Hypothesis and Evidence

What types of things are common in almost any microsystem? What things are unique? Come up with a hypothesis about how and why your microsystem would be different from a microsystem in another part of the country or another part of the world. Using your key pal or some other contact with students at a school in a different place, discuss what evidence they could provide so that you can evaluate and refine your hypothesis. What do the similarities and differences between these microsystems imply about the place-based nature of ecosystems?

Sample Grade-level Modification—Early Elementary

This study of a microenvironment can be used as an extension and elaboration upon basic studies of classification. Students can begin by classifying objects in the microsystem as living or nonliving, then elaborate to distinguish between plant, animal, fungus, and so on, and finally come up with their own systems for subdividing their classifications of plants, animals, rocks, and the like.

Sample Interdisciplinary Connection—Social Studies

As students compare what they find in their own microsystems with what their key pals find in their microsystems in another part of the country or world, this provides a context for further exploration of how the natural world influences the social world and vice versa. What about the things found in the microsystem would influence the way people in that area live? What do you find in the microsystem (if anything) that is evidence of human culture or activity?

SCIENTISTS IN YOUR COMMUNITY

Individuals in your community who might be knowledgeable about the things found in a square meter of the school grounds could include local biologists, botanists, anthropologists, plant nursery workers, or other teachers in the school. Invite one or more of these individuals to your class to ask them questions about the types of things you found in your microsystem study.

Correlation With National Standards

NSES Science: A1; C4; C5

NCTM Math: D2; E3

NCTE Language Arts: 4; 5

NCSS Social Studies: 3

Activity 23

Insects All Around You

SCIENCE BACKGROUND

Insects are everywhere. In terms of numbers, they are the most successful animals on the Earth. More than one million different insect species have been identified in the world, representing about half of all the animal species that are known to exist. Some scientists believe that there may actually be ten million different species of insects and perhaps as many as 200 million insects for every human alive on the planet.

Insects come in all shapes and sizes. The acteon beetle (*Megasoma acteon*) from South America is nearly 5 inches in length, while the North American feather-winged beetle (*Nanosella fungi*) is one tenth of an inch. In Africa, swarms of desert locusts (*Schistocerca gregaria*) have been estimated to contain as many as 28,000,000,000 individuals. While each locust only weighs about 2.5 grams, when added together, the weight of the swarm would equal 70,000 tons. One colony of ants in Japan of the species *Formica yessensis* has been reported to have 1,080,000 queens and 306,000,000 workers. It is estimated that 20% of the biomass (the mass of living things, including trees and all other plants) of the world is made up of ants and termites.

While many of the more exotic insect species live in the tropical regions of the planet, no matter where you live, insects are literally all around you. Insects play an important role in local food chains and have other important roles that may often go unnoticed. A study of insects is an important part of any place-based science study.

CULTURAL CONNECTIONS

Have students go online and search for "insects in art." Materials that they find can be used to create a classroom bulletin board display. Have them consider the idea of compiling an exhibit of ant art or bug art. If they are interested, have them create insect art of their own.

INSECTS ALL AROUND YOU

MATERIALS YOU WILL NEED FOR THIS ACTIVITY

- Tape measure
- Pencil
- Paper or notebook

WHAT YOU WILL DO

In this activity, students will estimate the number of insects on the surface of their school grounds. This activity should be done in warm weather and when the ground is reasonably dry, not after a rain.

Before the Trip

Try to obtain the exact measurements for the dimensions of the school grounds. Check with the school office to see if they have the lot survey. If this not available, students will have to measure the grounds themselves. This can be estimated by pacing off the perimeter of the grounds by foot or with a surveyor's wheel and then using the perimeter to calculate an estimate of the area. If the lot is an irregular shape, try dividing the lot into a series of regular shapes.

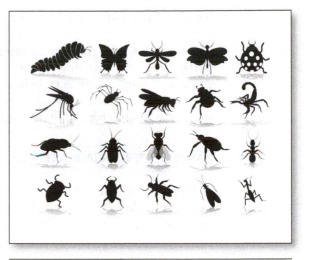

Insects

On the Trip

Have each student mark off a square foot area at least 4 or 5 feet from any other student. Have them count the insects they can find in that area. If insect activity is intense, have them measure a smaller space such as a 6-inch square or a 3-inch square and then multiply accordingly to get a count per square foot.

Back in the Classroom

Have students combine their figures to determine the average number of insects per square foot for the selected observations they have made. The average is determined by the total number of observations made of individual insects in all of the observations made divided by the total number square feet observed.

Take the square foot measure and multiply it times the number of square feet on the grounds of the school. This will provide students with an estimate of the total number of insects *on the surface* of their school grounds.

Have students consider what might lie underneath the ground and how they could go about estimating a cubic measure of insects per cubic foot. Discuss whether more insects are likely to live on the surface or below ground. How could you find out? Might this vary from place to place? Discuss how you could estimate the total biomass of insects on the school grounds based on the estimated number of insects.

THINKING LIKE A SCIENTIST—CONTROL OF VARIABLES

Have students consider what it means to sample something in order to approximate a measure on a much larger scale. What are the most important variables that you need to consider when doing sampling of this kind? How can these variables lead to errors in your results? What are some of the things sampling and estimating are particularly useful for? How much of the work that scientists do involves sampling and making estimates? Is this process scientific? What problems can exist with sampling? How is sampling related to controlling variables?

SAMPLE GRADE-LEVEL MODIFICATION—MIDDLE SCHOOL

To consider the number of insects below the surface as well as those visible on the surface requires thinking about three-dimensional geometry as well as actually doing some sampling for insects below the surface. Decide how to account for the insect populations that are not visible on the surface and then revise your calculations accordingly (see the interdisciplinary connection below).

SAMPLE INTERDISCIPLINARY CONNECTION—MATHEMATICS

How would you revise your insect count to consider the insects below the surface? How far below the surface should you consider? How do the numbers of insects increase or decrease with depth? How could you take this into account in your calculations? A mathematics problem that seems very simple at first can become increasingly complex as you attempt to increase the accuracy of the estimate.

SCIENTISTS IN YOUR COMMUNITY

Individuals in your community who might be knowledgeable about insects could include local biologists, entomologists (either professional or amateur), farmers, gardeners, or other teachers in your school. Invite one or more of these individuals to your class to ask them questions about insects and to share what you have learned.

Correlation With National Standards

NSES Science: C4

NCTM Math: B1; E1; E3

NCSS Social Studies: 3

Acid Rain

Water pollution comes in many forms. Some are obvious and highly visible, like an oil spill or trash floating in a lake. Other forms of water pollution are less obvious and may be more difficult to detect, such as hot water discharge from a factory (thermal pollution) or acid rain. Acid rain is not obviously pollution, but it can cause great damage to water ecosystems by lowering the pH of the water. Acid rain is rain that has been made acidic by certain pollutants in the air. An acid is a substance that has a low pH. The scale for measuring pH runs from zero (the most acidic) to 14 (the most basic or least acidic). A substance that has a pH of 7 is neither basic nor acidic and is called "neutral." Under normal circumstances, water has an approximately neutral pH and is generally in the pH range of 6 to 8. Water with a pH below 6 has been affected by some sort of acid.

Human activities are the main cause of acid rain. Cars, power plants, and factories release many different chemicals into the air that change the mix of gases in the atmosphere. These pollutants cause acid rain.

Acid rain can be extremely harmful to forests and other plant life. Acid rain that seeps into the ground dissolves nutrients and makes it difficult for plant roots to absorb water. A low pH affects different plants in different ways. Young roots and leaf shoots are typically the most sensitive to low pH, but more mature parts of the plant can be harmed as well. Acid rain also affects the composition and makeup of soil water. Soil water is the water trapped in soil, which is a main source of nutrients for plants. Acidic water, when added to soil, can break down soil particles, leading to erosion, and reduce the ability of plants' roots to absorb important trace metals and nutrients. Different plant species will respond differently to low pH and some species are more tolerant to changes in environment than other species. Most plants, however, when exposed to acid rain, will become weaker and more prone to damage from infections, insects, and cold weather.

Acid rain is also very harmful to lakes and streams. Most lakes and streams are usually slightly acidic, with a natural pH level between 6 and 7. Acid rain, however, has caused many lakes and streams to have much lower pH levels. This increase in acidity (a decrease in pH) can be deadly to aquatic wildlife, including fish, insects, frogs, plankton, and aquatic plants. For example, at a pH of 6, trout, which are very susceptible to acidity, may begin to die. At a pH of 5, frog eggs, tadpoles, and crayfish, among other aquatic species, will begin to die. At a pH of 4, nearly all fish and aquatic species will die. There have been numerous recorded cases of acid rain causing the pH in ponds, lakes, and marshes to temporarily fall below 5, causing the loss of some species and a reduction of biodiversity. While acid rain has traditionally been a more severe problem in the northeastern United States and Canada, its effects can be seen in many parts of the world. In the following activity, you will monitor the pH of your local rainwater as well as test the effects of simulated acid rain on growing plants.

CULTURAL BACKGROUND

Have students research how acid rain is a problem, and have them create a 36 × 24-inch poster calling for the reduction of the causes of acid rain. Suggest that they create slogans to go along with their posters ("Acid rain is a bane that's plain."). Create a display of students' acid rain posters.

MEASURING ACID RAIN

MATERIALS YOU WILL NEED FOR THIS ACTIVITY

- Rain gauge
- pH test strips or other pH monitoring test
- Radish seeds
- Small pots
- Potting soil
- Graduated cylinder
- Ruler
- Access to your school garden

Coal power plant

WHAT YOU WILL DO

Before the Trip

Research in your local newspaper or other local sources to see if acid rain has been discussed as a local environmental concern.

Conduct the following lab activity in the classroom on the effects of simulated acid rain on young radish plants:

1. Fill one clean cup with tap water and the other cup with vinegar.

2. Using the pH strips, measure and record the pH of each liquid.

3. Label three small pots A, B, and C.

4. Fill each pot with potting soil and poke several small holes in the bottom for drainage.

5. Make a hole 4 cm deep in the soil in each cup.

6. Place five radish seeds in each hole and cover the seeds with soil.

7. Use the graduated cylinder to water the seeds in pots A and B with 50 ml of water.

8. Water the seeds in pot C with 50 ml of vinegar.

9. Place all three pots in the same growing area.

10. Check the plants each day, using the ruler to measure and record their growth.

11. Every other day, add 20 ml of water to pots A and B and add 20 ml of vinegar to pot C.

12. After 1 week, continue to water pot A with 20 ml of water every other day, but change pot B from 20 ml of water to 20 ml of vinegar. Continue to water pot C with 20 ml of vinegar.

13. Continue measuring and recording plant growth in each pot every day for a 3-week period.

14. Create a bar graph from your data to compare the growth of the plants in the three pots.

On the Trip

During the 3-week period that you are conducting the radish plant experiment in the classroom, place the rain gauge outside to collect any rain that falls.

Using the pH strips or other pH meter, test the pH of any rain that falls.

Continue to collect and test the pH of rain samples until there have been several different rainfalls.

If you have a school garden with radish plants, monitor the health of the plants and collect growth data in the same way that you did for the classroom experiment.

Back in the Classroom

Compare the radish plants from the school garden with the radish plants from your classroom experiment. Compare the pH levels of the rain outside with the pH levels of the artificial rain from the classroom experiment.

Construct tables and graphs to show these comparisons.

THINKING LIKE A SCIENTIST—CONTROL OF VARIABLES

In a controlled experiment such as this one, your results will only be as accurate as your procedures. Understanding your independent variable, dependent variable, and other potential variables that must be controlled or held constant is a crucial part of your experimental design. For the pH experiment, what is your independent variable? How do you know? What is your dependent variable? How do you know? What other variables need to be controlled?

Based on your data, what conclusions can you draw about the relationship between pH and radish plant growth? How might your data for radish plants be similar to or different from data on the effects of pH on trees in a nearby forest?

SAMPLE GRADE-LEVEL MODIFICATION—MIDDLE SCHOOL

Based on the findings from your class experiment, what modifications or extensions could you test to learn more about the effects of acid rain on plant growth? In small groups, propose an extension experiment that takes what you have learned from the initial experiment and builds upon it. Could you try different types of seeds? Seeds versus already sprouted plants? Further variations on pH level? What other variations could you test?

SAMPLE INTERDISCIPLINARY CONNECTION—LANGUAGE ARTS

As individual students or as a class, write a letter to your city council or other government agency that summarizes your findings and assesses the local environmental health in terms of risk of harm from acid rain. Practice your persuasive writing, but also make sure that you use your data to help make your case. Depending on where you live, this could be a critical issue or an issue that is not yet critical but could become so in the future.

SCIENTISTS IN YOUR COMMUNITY

Individuals in your community who might be knowledgeable about acid rain and its effects on the environment could include chemists, environmental scientists, farmers, gardeners, ecologists, or local historians. Invite one or more of these individuals to your class to ask them questions about acid rain in your community and to share what you have learned.

Correlation With National Standards

NSES Science: A1; C4; F5

NCTM Math: D2; E3

NCTE Language Arts: 4; 8

NCSS Social Studies: 3; 8

PART IV

Activities to Promote Place-Based Science Teaching in the Neighborhood

This chapter focuses on science in the neighborhood, when the transportation needed for a traditional field trip is not possible but when students are able to take walking trips in the neighborhood. Students can discover that there is still a lot of exploring to be done on foot in one's neighborhood. While the advantage of more traditional field trips (discussed in Part V) is that it allows students to participate in memorable activities that might otherwise be beyond their experience, the value of studying science in the neighborhood is that it allows for ongoing studies and projects that take place over multiple visits.

A fundamental part of science is the planning for and collecting of data. Good data collection almost always involves multiple trials or measures. If you visit a certain location one time and collect data on some aspect of what you observe, you cannot be sure whether your data were typical or unusual. For example, if you visit a place where you have never been and the temperature is 100 degrees Fahrenheit, what can you conclude? Maybe it is frequently 100 degrees and this is a typical day. On the other hand, it could be the hottest day on record for the given time of year. Repeated visits on different days would allow you to get a more accurate picture of your data and how to interpret them. If you measure the pH of a pond one time and find that it is acidic, what can you conclude? Perhaps the pond is always acidic, but perhaps it just rained for 4 straight days (or, conversely, has not rained in 2 months) and these atypical conditions are affecting the pH of the water in unusual ways. Additionally, there may be regular and typical seasonal variations, such as how the weather changes throughout the year. In either case, repeated measures over time will allow a clearer picture to emerge.

Neighborhood walking field trips can be taken repeatedly throughout the year and allow for observation and data collection over time. A second advantage of neighborhood field trips is that they highlight the notion of place-based teaching and learning on the local scale. Studying science in the students' own neighborhood adds another level of engagement. When the topics being studied are related to social challenges, such as neighborhood health problems or pollution, student motivation for learning can be doubly enhanced. In this chapter, we will consider a series of activities using topics and projects that are conducive to neighborhood study. Additionally, because these topics are contextualized in the students' neighborhoods, they provide the potential for projects with a social action component.

Stream Study, Monitoring, and Restoration

Activity
25

The majority of schools, nationwide, are situated within walking distance of at least one small body of water—a creek, stream, pond, or lake. This small body of water makes a perfect setting for an ongoing study of water quality and a corresponding cleanup and restoration project.

When planning a project for conserving or restoring a small body of water, monitoring is an essential first step. Monitoring can help students to understand how a water system works and can also be used to assess the health of the system. The main idea of monitoring a water system is to document changes over time and to detect stress on the system. Professional and governmental organizations such as the Environmental Protection Agency monitor many of the waterways around the country, but many other waterways, especially smaller streams and ponds, are generally unmonitored unless volunteers do it. This sort of volunteer work can be important for local governments and local law enforcement. Voluntary monitoring projects have been responsible for detecting such problems as sewer leaks, chemical spills, and illegal dumping of waste.

Stream or pond monitoring before a restoration or cleanup project is undertaken can help to focus the project on particular areas of cleanup that are most needed. Ongoing monitoring after a restoration or cleanup project can help to show the benefits of that project and can help in the planning of additional projects. Monitoring of a pond or stream can take several forms and may include measurements of water quality, study of organisms in the water, study of physical characteristics of the area, and study of human impact on the area.

CULTURAL CONNECTIONS

Place name geography is a fascinating topic. The Hudson River is named after the English explorer Henry Hudson (c. 1560/70s—1611?), the name Missouri in the Native American Algonquin language means "river of the big canoes," and the city of Buffalo is a corruption on the French phrase *beau fleuve,* "beautiful river"—a reference to the Niagara River, which much of the downtown city boarders. Have students explore the connection between the names of the rivers in their region and their local history.

STREAM MONITORING

MATERIALS YOU WILL NEED FOR THIS ACTIVITY

- Observation log
- Chemical testing kit
- Scoop net
- Hand lens
- Sample vials
- Microscope (Back in the Classroom)

Autumn river

WHAT YOU WILL DO

Before the Trip

Do some research on the body of water you will be studying. An initial walking tour may be helpful. Looking at a local map can be helpful as well. Consider questions such as the following:

- Where does the water come from that you see in your monitoring site?

- Is there significant seasonal variation in when and how the water comes to the site?

Describe the physical features of the area around your study site such as the shape and slope of the land that drains water into the site (watershed), the kind and amount of plant cover around the site, the kind of soil around the site, and so forth.

Consider whether there are obvious possible sources of pollution such as urban runoff, agricultural runoff (from farms, parks or lawns), or other toxic substances being used close to the site.

Take the following stream survey:

How do you and your family currently dispose of the following:

Soda bottles

Auto fluids

Paint

Pool water

Yard waste

On the Trip

In small groups, fill out a data collection form that includes the following:

- Location, date, and time of observation
- Weather conditions during observation
- Temperature, depth, and flow of the water
- Odor and color of water
- Presence and description of algae
- Sampling and description of bottom surface
- Stream/pond bank composition and erosion
- Water organisms observed and approximate count
- Water chemistry depending on the testing kits you have available (i.e., water temperature, pH, dissolved oxygen, ammonia, chlorine, metals, etc.)
- Description of land use in the area surrounding stream or pond (i.e., housing, forest, urban uses, parking, agriculture, active construction, etc.)
- Other observations and comments

Plan to return for additional data collection on a regular basis (once a month or so) to allow for repeated data measures.

Back in the Classroom

In your groups, conduct research that will help you interpret the data you collected. For example, research what are sensitive, less sensitive, and tolerant organisms when it comes to water quality. Research the normal variation of water chemistry for a healthy pond or stream in your area and compare this with your readings.

THINKING LIKE A SCIENTIST—CAUSE AND EFFECT

Do environments like streams or ponds adapt to changing conditions? Does it matter if those changes happen quickly or slowly? Describe the condition of your pond or stream environment in terms of the forces or changes that might have caused it to have the characteristics it currently does. For example, what does it mean if all the organisms you saw during your water monitoring were considered tolerant to pollution? What would have caused this to be the case?

SAMPLE GRADE-LEVEL MODIFICATION—EARLY ELEMENTARY

There are a number of potential safety concerns involved with stream studies, including walking to and from the site, slipping or falling on wet surfaces, and potential sickness from ingesting water that may be contaminated. Sometimes teachers (or administrators) are hesitant to allow younger grades to go on these sorts of walking trips for these or other safety reasons. With proper supervision and precautions, however, such trips can generally be made safe, and the value to be gained by starting young children out practicing place-based science from the early grades is quite high. Teachers should feel comfortable advocating for such trips with young children.

SAMPLE INTERDISCIPLINARY CONNECTION—SOCIAL STUDIES

The interaction between people and their environments is an important theme in social studies at any grade level. Look at your responses on the stream survey. Are there other disposal methods for some of the items that would reduce the risk of damage to your local watershed? What evidence could you use to convince your family members or neighbors to change their disposal methods? Ask every student to commit to talking with three other people about the effects of pollution on watersheds and some simple actions that can help reduce these risks.

SCIENTISTS IN YOUR COMMUNITY

Individuals in your community who might be knowledgeable about stream studies and monitoring could include local biologists, geographers, geologists, park rangers, and fishermen. Invite one or more of these individuals to your class to ask them questions about stream monitoring and to share what you have learned.

Correlation With National Standards

NSES Science: A1; C4; F2

NCTM Math: E1

NCTE Language Arts: 4

NCSS Social Studies: 3

Pollution in the Neighborhood

One of the values of doing place-based science activities is that they create opportunities for social action in which students learn what it feels like to make a difference. Many of the environmental problems we hear about on the news or in science class seem too large for any one person, class, or school to help improve. We can study about the hole in the ozone layer, but we can't close it. We can learn about how expansion of human settlements is driving more and more endangered species to the brink of extinction, but we cannot prevent that spread from occurring. When it comes to pollution in our neighborhood, however, there are specific problems that we can address that can make a concrete difference.

Pollution is generally classified as being either point-source pollution or non-point-source pollution. The difference is whether there is a single specific location and activity (a point-source) that is responsible for producing pollution or if there are multiple locations and/or activities that are causing the problem. For example, a factory that is releasing dangerous chemicals into a river or into the air is causing point-source pollution. It is possible to trace the pollutant (chemicals in the water or the atmosphere) back to the source (the factory). New laws can be passed or existing laws enforced to force the factory to change how it deals with its waste products.

Non-point-source pollution can be harder to track because it is coming from many different sources. For example, if many homeowners apply fertilizers to their lawns and then a hard rain falls and washes those fertilizers into a local stream, the stream ecosystem can be damaged. The source of the pollution is not one factory or one individual but many sources in small amounts that combine to make a large impact. Common non-point-source pollutants include:

- Oil and other chemicals from cars, roads, and parking lots
- Fertilizers, herbicides, and insecticides from farms, homes, and towns
- Litter and trash that are not properly disposed of
- Animal waste from livestock and pets
- Soil and other sediment that is eroded from farms, construction sites, and stream banks

These non-point-source pollutants then end up in our community's streams, rivers, lakes, and other waters. While large point-source polluters like big factories can create a lot of pollution, non-point-source pollution is actually a greater cause of water quality

135

problems. These pollutants can have harmful effects on our drinking water supplies as well as on water used for recreation, fisheries, and wildlife.

As you can see, many of the common non-point-source pollutants can be easily reduced if everyone pays more attention to what they, their fairly members, and the other people around them are doing. When we become more aware of non-point-source pollution, we can do many things to lessen its harm on the environment. As students engage in the following pollution-in-the-neighborhood activity, they should come to see how we all play a part in contributing to non-point-source pollution, often without realizing it. Students can then commit to concrete actions they will take to reduce water pollution.

CULTURAL CONNECTIONS

Lawns are a common feature in the American landscape. They are not as common in many other countries. Why do Americans love their lawns so much? Are lawns a good thing, or are they wasteful? Are there good alternatives to lawns? Have students discuss these issues as well as explore the history of lawns and their use. How are lawns in your community different than lawns in other communities? How can you account for these differences?

TRACKING NON-POINT-SOURCE POLLUTION

MATERIALS YOU WILL NEED FOR THIS ACTIVITY

- Non-point-source Pollution Checklist
- Notebook
- Camera (optional)

Lawn sign for fertilizer

WHAT YOU WILL DO

Before the Trip

Review the concepts of point-source and non-point-source pollution.

Review the Non-point-source Pollution Checklist and address any student questions.

On the Trip

Students should complete the Non-point-source Pollution Checklist as they tour the neighborhood.

Take notes in the notebook and pictures with the camera to document pollution.

ITEMS FOR THE NON-POINT-SOURCE POLLUTION CHECKLIST

Yards and Landscaping

- Is the soil in the neighborhood sandy or gravelly, allowing water to drain quickly, or clayey, causing water to pool?

- Are there many bare areas of soil that are susceptible to erosion?

- Are there many native plants with low requirements for water, fertilizers, and pesticides or many exotic plants that require a lot of special care?

- Are trees and bushes planted along streams or creeks to help prevent erosion?

- Are lawn clippings and leaves left in the yard so that the nutrients are recycled and less yard waste goes to the landfill?

- Does the neighborhood take action to prevent trash, lawn clippings, leaves, and automobile fluids from entering storm drains?

- Do people in your neighborhood wash their cars in the street or driveway so the soaps and chemicals run into the storm drain?

- Do people in the neighborhood conserve the water they use on their lawns by only watering in the morning and evening to reduce evaporation?

- Do the downspouts from your roof gutters empty onto paved surfaces instead of grass or gravel?

Roads and Streets

- Do people in your neighborhood always pick up after their pets?

- Are storm drains stenciled to alert people that they drain directly to a local body of water?

- Do people in your neighborhood drive their cars only when necessary?

- Do you see evidence of leaking car fluids like oil in driveways, in parking lots, or on the street?

- When it rains, is the water washing down the storm drains muddy (evidence of erosion)?

- Is there new construction in the neighborhood resulting in the clearing of trees, shrubs, and grass? Are any new trees or bushes being planted?

- Are there any golf courses, parks, or farms near the neighborhood that may be adding to local pollution either from chemicals or animal wastes?

Back in the Classroom

Discuss students' responses to the Non-point-source Pollution Checklist and compile a list of possible pollution sources that students discovered in their neighborhood.

List students' concerns and suggestions for how to address the pollution sources they found.

Ask each student to commit to one concrete action to help prevent non-point-source pollutants from entering local waterways in their neighborhood.

THINKING LIKE A SCIENTIST—HYPOTHESIS AND EVIDENCE

Before going on the walking trip, record your hypothesis about what the most common sources of non-point-source pollution will be and why you think those will be the most common. Does the evidence you gather on the trip support or refute your hypothesis? Why do you think that is?

Is it easier for people to take action to reduce point-source or non-point-source pollution? Why?

How might the non-point-sources of pollution be similar and different between a rich neighborhood and a poor neighborhood? Between an urban, suburban, and rural neighborhood?

SAMPLE GRADE-LEVEL MODIFICATION—MIDDLE SCHOOL

Middle school students could go out with partners or in small groups to collect additional data by making additional surveying trips outside of school time. They could survey other nearby neighborhoods to compare the non-point-source pollution they find in those neighborhoods to those found on your class trip.

SAMPLE INTERDISCIPLINARY CONNECTION—LANGUAGE ARTS

How does multimedia help to create more persuasive presentations? In small groups, create posters to convince people that there are simple steps that they can take to reduce non-point-source pollution in their neighborhoods. How can you use multimedia to enhance the power of your poster? Do you think that learning to use multimedia is a language arts skill? Why or why not?

SCIENTISTS IN YOUR COMMUNITY

Individuals in your community who might be knowledgeable about non-point-source pollution could include environmental protection agency workers, local government workers involved in city planning and development, and concerned citizens. Invite one or more of these individuals to your class to ask them questions about non-point-source pollution and to share what you have learned.

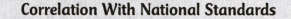

Correlation With National Standards

NSES Science: F1; F3; F4

NCTM Math: E1

NCTE Language Arts: 7; 8

NCSS Social Studies: 3; 8

Traffic Patterns

SCIENCE BACKGROUND

There are traffic patterns in all sorts of places in the local communities where we live. Think for a moment about airports. Traffic is routed into them in very controlled ways. To a lesser extent, the same is true of ports and canals, roadways and streets, and even sidewalks and paths.

Most people take traffic patterns for granted. They give little thought to how they shape our day-to-day lives. Discuss with students how natural patterns shape man-made environments. Highways in mountainous areas, for example, follow geographical contours using valleys and passes to their advantage. Tunnels only are dug through mountains when there is no other convenient way to build around them.

Have students look at a map of the United States. See if they can identify why cities have developed in certain locations based on how local geography has determined traffic patterns. For example, Buffalo, New York, is at the mouth of the Niagara River, at the most eastern end of Lake Erie. It is there because until the Welland Canal was built, it was the farthest point that things could be shipped by boat from the western Great Lakes (Michigan, Superior, and Huron). Buffalo became a major rail-road hub as a result, since for a long time goods could only be shipped by boat to Buffalo and then had to be transferred overland. The opening of the St. Lawrence Seaway in 1957, which connected the Great Lakes to the Atlantic Ocean, eliminated this problem and, in turn, changed commercial shipping patterns from the Great Lakes region.

Students can learn a lot about their community by identifying and studying the local traffic patterns.

CULTURAL CONNECTIONS

Why are roads laid out in different ways in different communities? What happened when superhighways were built through central city locations such as St. Louis or

Chicago? How do roads and their design conform to local geology and geography? Have students discuss and explore these and related issues.

TRAFFIC PATTERNS

MATERIALS YOU WILL NEED FOR THIS ACTIVITY

- Paper and pencil
- Computer
- Digital camera

School zone sign

WHAT YOU WILL DO

Students will record the traffic pattern that occurs in their school drop-off area each morning and afternoon. From a safe location, they will record when cars arrive, who is in the cars, who is dropped off, and so forth. They will count the total number of cars and try to observe any special patterns that exist in the traffic flow.

Before the Trip

Students should discuss and create a data matrix on which to record information. This might consist of things like: (1) Type of car; (2) number of passengers; (3) people dropped off, and so on. Students should discuss types of data that would be useful to observe and record and what types of tools can be used to help them keep a record.

On the Trip

Students should go to positions assigned by their teacher to make their observations. Safety considerations should be paramount. Students may want to conduct a microanalysis using a video camera that records how long it takes to drop students off, what causes delays or difficulties (i.e., people talking on cell phones, conversations with other drivers, etc.), and whether more efficient means could be used to control the flow of traffic. General reference photographs can be used as well. Emphasis should be placed on students doing careful and systematic observations. Once you have done a detailed study of the traffic patterns at the school, plan a similar study of a large street intersection near your school. (Always remember, safety first!)

Back in the Classroom

Students should discuss various ways that the data they have collected can be analyzed. Have them explore whether there are specific patterns in what they have observed that can be teased out of their data (i.e., is there a rush of drop-offs at a certain time?). Have them consider solutions (i.e., staggered arrival times for different student populations).

Compare and contrast the traffic patterns at the school with the patterns at the intersection you observed. Why are they different? Are there ways they are similar?

Thinking Like a Scientist—Cause and Effect

Why do animals (including people) tend to move in certain patterns? What are the causes of these patterned movements? What are some of the effects? Consider why horses run in specific patterns in herds, why birds maintain certain flight patterns in flocks, and why fish maintain certain swimming patterns in schools. Are there connections in these patterns? What were the patterns of human movement before the invention of cars and other vehicles? How have vehicles changed human movement patterns?

Sample Grade-level Modification—Middle School

Middle school students could go in small groups to the neighborhood elementary school (that many of them probably attended) and to the neighborhood high school (that they are likely to attend) to compare the traffic patterns at each of these schools. How are they different? Do more students take the bus? Do more students walk or bike? At the high school, what is the impact on traffic patterns of students being able to drive themselves?

Sample Interdisciplinary Connection—Social Studies

Animals generally have survival reasons for their movement patterns. Human movement patterns may likewise be connected to survival, but there may be social reasons for these movement patterns as well. Discuss possible social reasoning for movement patterns and the social conventions or norms that have developed with those patterns. When it comes to traffic, what are the social norms? What constitutes breaking those norms (cutting in line, running a traffic light, etc.)? What are the consequences for breaking the norms? How are the norms of human movement continuing to evolve?

Scientists in Your Community

Individuals in your community who might be knowledgeable about traffic patterns could include city engineers, city planners, police officers, fire and rescue workers, and frequent commuters. Invite one or more of these individuals to your class to ask them questions about traffic and its evolution in your city or town and to share what you have learned.

Correlation With National Standards

NSES Science: F2; F5

NCTM Math: B1

NCTE Language Arts: 4

NCSS Social Studies: 3; 8

Activity
28

Survey of Local Plants

The plants one finds in a local neighborhood can be either native (original to one's area) or imported (brought from somewhere else). Most students have little idea of what plants are native to their region or imported from elsewhere. Often plants (like animals) that have been brought from other parts of the world can prove to be highly invasive and destructive to native species. For example, in South Florida, melaleuca trees were brought in the 19th century as ornamental plants and used to draw water from wetlands such as the Everglades. The trees have become pests, causing nearly $200 million in environmental losses each year, as they eliminate, on average, approximately 15 acres of local wetlands each day. In places such as North Carolina, Georgia, and South Carolina, kudzu, a type of climbing vine from southern Japan and southeastern China, has become a pest, pushing out native species of plants and coming to be described as "the vine that ate the South."

For any region in the country, you should be able to find a listing of regional native plant species. For example, in South Florida an excellent site, Natives for Your Neighborhood (http://www.regionalconservation.org/beta/nfyn/default.asp), provides lists of both plants and animals native to the South Florida area. A web search for "native plants" along with the name of your region or state is likely to direct you to similar lists.

CULTURAL CONNECTIONS

What is a weed and what is a desirable type of plant? Have students consider this question and how certain plants come to be considered desirable flowers and ground covers. Discuss with them the potential problems with importing plants from outside of native sources. When does a seemingly desirable plant become a weed? (Answer: When it is too successful and pushes out the native species!)

SURVEY OF LOCAL PLANTS

MATERIALS YOU WILL NEED FOR THIS ACTIVITY

- Paper and pencil
- Computer

- Digital camera
- Chart for recording plants observed

Neighborhood garden

WHAT YOU WILL DO

Students will go on a neighborhood walking tour and keep a record of the various plant species that they observe. The class will determine which of the species they observed are native species and which are nonnative species.

Before the Trip

Students should use a regional plant guide, either online or a book, to review what plants they are likely to find locally. If possible, make copies to consult on your trip.

As a class, prepare an observation sheet that you can use to record the different plant types you observe.

On the Trip

Lead the students on a walking tour of the neighborhood around the school.

Based on the plant guides you have plus the knowledge of the group, identify as many plant species as you can. Record them on the observation sheet you have prepared.

Where possible, collect leaves or small clippings from the plants. (Make sure that you do not damage plants, and ask permission where appropriate.)

Photographs can also be taken of plants, and drawings can be made of them as well.

Back in the Classroom

Determine which of the plants you have listed on your observation sheet are local (native) and which have been imported from somewhere else (nonnative). If imported, where did they come from? Remember, all plants are native somewhere. Divide the list into native and nonnative plants, highlighting any that are particularly invasive or destructive.

Using this information, create a neighborhood plant guide that identifies common local plants, their native or nonnative status, other important information, and includes a sample of the plant or a photo or a drawing.

Share your neighborhood plant guide with another class in your school and see if they can use it to identify a sample of the plants that you brought back from your neighborhood walk.

THINKING LIKE A SCIENTIST—CAUSE AND EFFECT

How is it that nonnative plants get introduced into different regions? What are some of the possible causes of this and what are the potential effects? Discuss with students what a weed is and what a desirable plant is. Are weeds native or nonnative? Are they a mix? Could something that is considered a weed in one place be considered a desirable plant somewhere else? Why might this be?

Sample Grade-level Modification—Early Elementary

Early-elementary-grade students can create a simplified local plant guide by taking leaf samples and laminating them (or preserving them in some other way). Each student can then create a page on one local plant with a drawing of the entire plant and the preserved leaf. Label the page and then assemble the class guidebook, including each student's page.

Sample Interdisciplinary Connection—Social Studies

When European explorers, conquerors, and settlers traveled from the Old World to the New World, they brought many plants from Europe to the Americas and took many plants from the Americas back to Europe. This exchange of plants (as well as animals and diseases) is known as the Columbian Exchange. Do some research about the Columbian Exchange and make a poster of New World and Old World plants that can now be found on both sides of the Atlantic Ocean. Are all of these nonnative species a bad thing? Why or why not?

Scientists in Your Community

Individuals in your community who might be knowledgeable about native and nonnative species of plants could include botanists, local historians, gardeners, farmers, and agricultural extension workers. Invite one or more of these individuals to your class to ask them questions about native and nonnative plants in the local community and to share what you have learned about this topic.

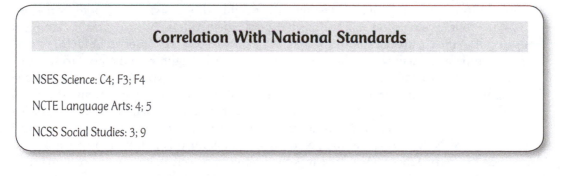

Correlation With National Standards

NSES Science: C4; F3; F4

NCTE Language Arts: 4; 5

NCSS Social Studies: 3; 9

Activity
29

Science in Swimming Pools

SCIENCE BACKGROUND

In the summer when the weather is hot, almost everyone likes to go swimming. For many people, this means a trip to the neighborhood swimming pool. Swimming pools provide an interesting setting to study science, especially chemistry. Without careful monitoring of the chemistry of a swimming pool, the water can quickly become full of bacteria, algae, and other potentially harmful organisms. Swimmers accidently drink enough pool water every time they swim to become sick from these organisms. On the other hand, if too many chemicals are added, the water can burn swimmers' eyes and irritate their skin.

Learning how to monitor pool chemistry is an important part of the job of pool lifeguards and pool managers. Chlorine is the most common chemical that is added to pool water to kill off microorganisms. Other factors, such as the pH and temperature of the water, affect how much chlorine is needed to effectively control the microorganisms. Thus, other chemicals are sometimes added to the pool water to modify, or balance, the pH level. Chlorine is a dangerous chemical and not suitable for use in school science lab activities. However, water quality testing at a neighborhood swimming pool is a safe activity (as long as everyone follows normal pool safety rules). Bringing water samples from a pool to the classroom for testing can also be done; however, important factors such as water temperature will change by the time the water is brought from the pool to school.

Using chlorine to kill microbes has a long history, both in swimming pools and in drinking water (the amount of chlorine added to drinking water is obviously significantly lower than the amount added to swimming pools). It was more than 100 years ago, in 1908, that chorine was first added to a city's drinking water to destroy germs. The city was Jersey City, New Jersey, and the person responsible for this innovation was a scientist named Harriette Chick. Dr. Chick was the first woman scientist to work at England's famous Lister Institute, where research is done on the cause, prevention, and treatment of diseases. Harriette Chick did groundbreaking work on the factors that affect the rates of germ killing by disinfectants such as chlorine. Thus, she was able to determine how much chlorine would be needed to add to water under certain conditions to make it safe to drink (or to swim in). Her work, known as the Law of Disinfection or Chick's Law, is still used today by water treatment plant operators to determine how much disinfectant to add to our drinking water under different conditions. It is also used as the basis for determining how much chlorine needs to be added to swimming pool water.

Many towns, cities, and villages are named after local sources of fresh water (springs). Have students list and map out the major towns and cities in their region with the name *Springs*. Are there patterns in the locations of springs that are revealing when looked at on a state or regional basis? If springs are not common in the region in which students live, have them look at a state or region where they are common such as Massachusetts, New York, or Colorado.

HOW CLEAN IS THE POOL WATER?

MATERIALS YOU WILL NEED FOR THIS ACTIVITY

- Thermometer

- Basic pool water testing kit—at the minimum should include testing materials for pH and chlorine

- (Optional) Advanced test kit—to test for total alkalinity, total dissolved solids, and hardness

WHAT YOU WILL DO

Before the Trip

Discuss the history of using chlorine to disinfect water.

Prepare a data collection table for the various measures you will take of the pool water.

Study the use of the pool water test kit and practice the procedures for each of the tests using water from the tap or the water fountain.

Water testing

On the Trip

Complete the following tests of the pool water:

- Temperature—Stick the thermometer at least 6 to 8 inches deep in the pool to take the water temperature (the first few inches at the surface are artificially warm from the sunlight and are not representative of the average temperature of the pool). Wait at least 30 seconds to get the most accurate reading.

- pH—Fill the sample vial provided for the pH test with water from 8 to 12 inches' depth in the pool. Add the tablet or liquid indicator to the water sample in the specified amount (depending on the kit that is used). Compare the color of the water sample with the color standards that are provided in the test kit and determine the closest match.

- pH too low—Chlorine loses its effectiveness and more must be added. Red and burning eyes can result.

- pH too high—Pool becomes cloudy. Skin and eyes can become dry and itchy.

- Chlorine—There are actually three different aspects of chlorine that can be measured. Some test kits can test for all three, while others test only for free available chlorine, which is the most important to monitor.

- Free available chlorine—This is the amount of chlorine that exists in a state that can disinfect the water.

- Combined chlorine—This is a chlorine compound that forms when there isn't enough free available chlorine. Combined chlorine causes eye and skin irritation.

- Total chlorine—This includes both free available and combined chlorine.

- The recommended level of free available chlorine in a swimming pool is 1.0 to 3.0 parts per million (ppm).

- **Too little chlorine**—Promotes algae and bacteria growth and waterborne illnesses can spread

- **Too much chlorine**—Causes eye, nose, and skin irritations and, in more extreme cases, can cause chemical burns

- If you have a kit that tests for total alkalinity, total dissolved solids, and hardness, follow the testing directions that come with the kit.

- Total alkalinity—This is a measure of the alkaline substances, such as bicarbonates, in the water. Total alkalinity of between 80 and 120 ppm is recommended because at that amount it tends to stabilize the pH of the water.

- Total dissolved solids (TDS)—This is a measure of all the dissolved materials in the water. It includes the chemicals that are intentionally added as well as unintentional solids such as dirt, pollen, and so forth. The maximum acceptable level of TDS for swimming pools is 1,500 ppm.

- Mineral hardness—This is a measure to the total mineral content of the water. The ideal range for mineral hardness in a swimming pool is between 250 and 350 ppm.

Back in the Classroom

Compare the results that the different groups got for each test. Are the test results identical? What could account for some of the differences?

Create a scenario about a public pool where kids have been getting sick. Give some sample water readings and ask students to figure out why the people are getting sick and what needs to be done to the water to prevent further cases of illness.

Thinking Like a Scientist—Cause and effect

Most kids know that chlorine is added to pool water to kill germs and bacteria, but they generally don't know much about the details. What does chlorine actually do and how effective is it? Check out the American Chemical Society's Global Bug Conspiracy:

http://www.americanchemistry.com/bugconspiracy/

What are some of the common microbes that can be killed by chlorine? What common microbes cannot be killed by chlorine?

Public baths and pools have existed in cultures around the world for thousands of years. Do some research to find out what, if anything, was done to control the spread of sickness through microbes in the water in public baths prior to the work of Harriette Chick. How did cause-and-effect reasoning influence Harriette Chick's research?

SAMPLE GRADE-LEVEL MODIFICATION—MIDDLE SCHOOL

Students could check out the pool test kits and take them around to different pools in the community to test the water. Are there differences between indoor and outdoor pools? Between private and public pools? Between large and small pools? Between pools and hot tubs? See how widely students can collect data. What patterns do you see in the data?

SAMPLE INTERDISCIPLINARY CONNECTION—MATHEMATICS

Part of the mathematics necessary to make sense of science is the question of scale and units. What does it mean when we say that the measure of chlorine is 2 ppm or that the measure of alkalinity is 110 ppm or that the TDS is 1,300 ppm? How can we compare this to units of measurement that students are more familiar with? Ask students to come up with a way to model or demonstrate the concept of parts per million. Challenge them to come up with a model or demonstration that is clear enough to explain the concept to students who are younger than they are. Ask them to explain the concept to family members who may be unfamiliar with it.

SCIENTISTS IN YOUR COMMUNITY

Individuals in your community who might be knowledgeable about pool chemistry and water-borne illnesses could include pool maintenance providers, pool and spa store employees, chemists, and microbiologists. Invite one or more of these individuals to your class to ask them questions about pools and water quality and to share what you have learned about this topic.

Correlation With National Standards

NSES Science: A1; B1; F1

NCTM Math: B1; D2

NCTE Language Arts: 7

NCSS Social Studies: 3; 8

Activity
30
Patterns in Nature

SCIENCE BACKGROUND

Patterns are basic to natural forms. We can see patterns in the reflection of an object like a tree on the surface of a lake, in landscapes, in flowers and plants, in rocks, and in animals. The British biologist D'Arcy Thompson argues in his classic 1917 book *On Growth and Form* that "everything is the way it is because it got that way." According to him, "the form of an object is a 'diagram of forces,' in this sense, at least, that from it we can judge or deduce the forces that are acting or have acted upon it." What this means is that a turtle's shell is the shape it is and is divided up into hexagonal plates because it is the most efficient and evolutionally sound shape possible. It is not an accident that cell structures "pack" themselves the same way, that the cells of a honeybee's hive are shaped as hexagons, or that riverbeds or creeks fracture along similar lines.

Patterns are literally everywhere in the natural and human-designed environment. Finding patterns is a way to find meaning and continuity between all natural things and man-made things. The Italian mathematician Leonardo Fibonacci's (1175–1250) book the *Liber Abaci,* which was first published in 1202 and introduced Arabic numbers into Europe, describes a number sequence in which two numbers in the sequence equal the third number in the sequence. For example:

0, 1, 1, 2, 3, 5, 8, 13, 21, 34, 55, 89, 144

This *Fibonacci sequence* appears in many different biological contexts in nature, such as the branching in trees, the arrangement of leaves on a stem, the flowering of an artichoke, and the pattern on a pinecone, to name just few. The pattern of a spiral galaxy is actually a Fibanoccian sequence, as is the shape of a chambered nautilus.

In the following activity, students will explore how patterns occur in many of the day-to-day things that surround them.

CULTURAL CONNECTIONS

Built structures in local communities often have clear parallels to natural forms. Explore with students some of the natural forms that appear in the built environment that surrounds them. Discuss with them which of these parallels are done for artistic reasons and which are done for practical design reasons.

HEXAGONS IN NATURE AND MAN-MADE OBJECTS

Hexagons are found many places, both in nature and in man-made things. Why are hexagons so common? Why do we like to use hexagons when we design things? Have you ever looked at bubbles in a dish of soap and how they form into hexagons? Have you ever looked at a honeycomb from a beehive and how its cells are made up hexagons? Have you ever taken a careful look at chicken wire, a chain-link fence, or the back of a turtle? They are all made up of hexagons.

MATERIALS YOU WILL NEED FOR THIS ACTIVITY

- A computer with an Internet connection
- A computer printer with paper
- A digital camera

WHAT YOU WILL DO

Before the Trip

Search the web and find at least 10 examples of things found in nature that are shaped hexagonally (soap bubbles when they are packed together, a turtle's shell, etc.). Print a small picture (no larger than 3 by 5 inches) of each thing you find.

Brainstorm with students why hexagons are so commonly found in nature and why we use them so often in things we design and build.

Bees working on honeycomb

On the Trip

Take a digital camera and photograph something in your local environment that has a hexagonal pattern. (Stop signs don't count— that's an octagon!) If possible, find something that is man-made and something that is from the natural environment.

Back in the Classroom

Using the images found on the Internet as well as the pictures you took on your walking field trip, create a class hexagon bulletin board or album.

THINKING LIKE A SCIENTIST—HYPOTHESIS AND EVIDENCE

What is your hypothesis about why certain shapes or forms are easier to pack together than others? What evidence could you gather to test your hypothesis? Do the data you collected on your trip of examples of natural and man-made hexagons serve as evidence to support or refute your hypothesis? Why or why not?

Why is it that so many things that surround us in the natural environment have patterns? Why do humans seem to like to adapt these patterns into our construction of our designed world? Are there particular types of patterns that humans seem more or less likely to try to adopt in our designs of buildings and other objects? What hypothesis do you have to explain these behaviors? What additional evidence could you gather to test your hypothesis?

SAMPLE GRADE-LEVEL MODIFICATION—EARLY ELEMENTARY

Before engaging in the study of hexagons in nature and human design, begin with more familiar geometric shapes. Where do we see triangles or pyramids in the world around us? Squares and cubes? Rectangles and rectangular prisms? These are simpler forms, but do they seem to be more common than hexagons in nature? Why or why not?

SAMPLE INTERDISCIPLINARY CONNECTION—LANGUAGE AND VISUAL ARTS

While the connections to mathematics in this activity are obvious (and discussed above) the study of patterns in nature provides rich connections to language and visual art as well. How could you develop poems about geometry in nature using similar patterns in the poem? What would a "hexagon-inspired" poetic form look like? Try to write a hexagonal-form poem about hexagons or triangle-inspired poetic form about triangles in nature and design. Combine visual art as well as poetry to create a geometrically inspired poster.

SCIENTISTS IN YOUR COMMUNITY

Individuals in your community who might be knowledgeable about geometry and patterns in the natural and designed worlds could include artists, architects, engineers, mathematicians, biologists, and construction workers. Invite one or more of these individuals to your class to ask them questions about patterns in design. Share and discuss your hexagon bulletin board with your guests.

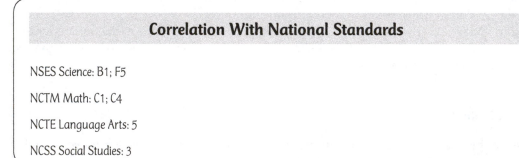

Correlation With National Standards

NSES Science: B1; F5

NCTM Math: C1; C4

NCTE Language Arts: 5

NCSS Social Studies: 3

Wildlife Census in a Neighborhood Park

What animals are the most common in your neighborhood? Which ones do you see most often? Are there other animals that are common but are rarely seen? Every neighborhood, whether rural, suburban, or urban, has wildlife living there. Some wildlife is more obvious and some is less obvious. Some wildlife is present year round and other animals are more seasonal in when they appear.

Conducting a wildlife census is an important part of monitoring the health of an environment. When environments or ecosystems change as a result of human development, climate change, or other factors, this is likely to impact local wildlife, often in negative ways. However, there are a number of challenges in conducting a wildlife census. First, wild animals often must be secretive to survive. They may spend much of their time in thick undergrowth or otherwise use vegetation to hide their movements. Many species will also actively flee from human observers. During some seasons, certain species are more active and more visible than during other seasons. Additionally, the patterns of daily activity for some species may not correspond with ours. They may be nocturnal or most active at dawn and dusk. In fact, there are few species that are most active during the typical hours of the school day when we are best able to do our data collection.

Other typical problems with conducting a local wildlife census are that many species are mobile and do not remain in the same area year round and that their distribution may be uneven—that is, some species stay together in groups, others remain spread out, and others exhibit different grouping behaviors at different times of year. Also, there are seasonal population variations for many species, such as a certain season when young are born or a season when mortality is high. When conducting a wildlife census, all of these challenges and their potential impact on our data need to be considered.

There are several different census methods that are routinely used by wildlife biologists. A direct count census is an attempt to count all the individuals of a species in a given place and at a given time. It may be fairly easy to count all the ducks that live in the pond in a neighborhood park but significantly harder to count all the catfish that live in that same pond. A temporal census is an attempt to count all the members of a species that pass through a given location during a set amount of time. This approach is often used in the study of migratory or wandering species. An auditory census relies on hearing the calls or vocalizations of a particular animal. This technique is used for some bird species that are difficult to observe directly because they tend to stay well hidden. Track counts (footprints) and pellet counts (animal droppings) are two other census approaches that are used to verify the presence of species that may be difficult to observe directly. These approaches do not provide accurate information about the number of animals of a species in a given area but do verify the presence of that species. Other census methods involve the capture, tagging, and release of animals, but these approaches are not recommended for students.

One of the values of neighborhood field trips is that they can be repeated on a semi-regular basis. This allows students to observe variations over time as factors such as season, weather, and habitat change. A critical part of science is the idea of repeated observations. This increases the reliability of the observations, provides consistency, and allows the observer to see changes over time.

In the following activity, you will conduct a neighborhood wildlife census in a local park or other open space that is within walking distance of your school. The area does not have to be large. Some species of wildlife will be found in even the smallest of parks or open spaces.

CULTURAL CONNECTIONS

Have students think about possible interesting population counts in human settings. For example, have them count the people who drop off and pick up children in their cars from schools—count numbers of males and females, estimated age ranges, and any other notable characteristics. What conclusions can you draw? Observe who buys drinks from a vending machine and what they buy. Do you see any patterns? Do you think these are cultural or natural phenomena that you are observing? Explain.

NEIGHBORHOOD WILDLIFE CENSUS

MATERIALS YOU WILL NEED FOR THIS ACTIVITY

- Census sheet
- Binoculars
- Digital camera

Squirrel eating a nut

WHAT YOU WILL DO

Before the Trip

Research and discuss local species that are likely to be living in the park or open space that will be the site of the study.

Discuss the potential challenges to observing and counting each of these species and ideas you have for dealing with these challenges.

Using the descriptions above, discuss and decide upon which type(s) of census you will use during your study and what species of animals you will include in your census (you can do a plant census as well if students are interested). You may choose to let different groups of students conduct different kinds of census and focus on different species.

Design and agree upon a census sheet that will allow you to record the data that you think are important to collect.

Make a schedule for when and how often you will visit the census site to collect data.

On the Trip

Follow the schedule you have created and go to the park or open space for the first time to collect your census data.

The procedure you will use depends on the type of census you are conducting.

If you are doing a direct count census, you will need to decide if you will remain in one place for your count, walk a transit line, or use some other approach.

If you are doing a temporal census, you will need to decide how long a period of time you will observe during each visit.

If you are doing an auditory census, it is normal to walk transit lines back and forth across the area listening for animal calls.

If you are doing a track count or a pellet count, you will need to decide on the area you will examine for tracks or droppings.

Return to your data collection site according to the schedule that your class has set.

Back in the Classroom

Discuss the various ways that your census data can be represented. Begin with a data table and a graph. Consider what type of graph (bar, line, pie, pictogram, etc.) is best for representing your census data. Continue to add data to your table and graph as you follow your data collection schedule.

Think about other complimentary ways that you can add details to the census data. How could photos, video, sketches, and other representations of your observations add to your census data?

Look for trends in the data over time. Which species' populations change significantly over time and which stay more or less constant? What other patterns do you see in the data? What explanations can you offer?

THINKING LIKE A SCIENTIST—CAUSE AND EFFECT

Which population changes seem to be correlated (i.e., when one population goes up, the other goes up as well, or when one population goes up, the other goes down)? What possible explanations are there for these relationships? What are the causes and what are the effects of such population changes?

Create a movie from still shots taken over a course of the school year. What story does your movie tell about the organism(s) you have been studying in your census?

SAMPLE GRADE-LEVEL MODIFICATION—EARLY ELEMENTARY

Think with your students about different ways that they can keep track of the animals they see during their census trips. They could create a chart and make tally marks. They could draw a picture of the animal, make copies, and then glue a copy in their notebook each time they count an animal. They could take a picture using a camera. There are many more possibilities—be creative!

SAMPLE INTERDISCIPLINARY CONNECTION—SOCIAL STUDIES

What is the human effect on animal species due to our ongoing population increase and technological development? Using local archives, look for old city or town maps that include the area where you are collecting your animal census data. What did the area look like 20 years ago? 50 years ago? 100 years ago? How do you think those environmental differences would influence the data for the kind of animal census that you conducted? Look up national data on the population of animals such as the American bison, the bald eagle, and the grey wolf. What does this say about the relationship between humans and other animals?

SCIENTISTS IN YOUR COMMUNITY

Individuals in your community who might be knowledgeable about local animal populations could include local biologists, park rangers, and citizens who spend a lot of time visiting the park where you will conduct your animal census. Invite one or more of these individuals to your class to ask them questions about local animal populations. Share and discuss the data you collected with your guests.

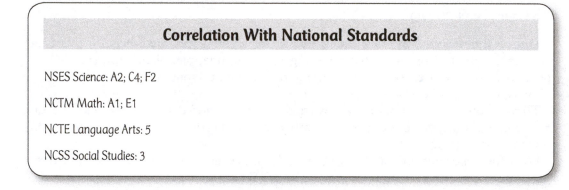

Correlation With National Standards

NSES Science: A2; C4; F2

NCTM Math: A1; E1

NCTE Language Arts: 5

NCSS Social Studies: 3

Who Gets Sick and Why?

Activity 32

A pandemic (from the Greek *pan* "all" + *demos* "people") is an infectious disease that spreads itself by means of human and animal populations across large areas. The flu is a type of pandemic or infectious disease, as is the Black Death (plague), smallpox, cholera, and tuberculosis.

Pandemics have not been well understood until very recently. For example, the infectious disease cholera, an acute diarrheal illness that can lead to severe dehydration and death, was not very well understood until the mid-19th century, when the English physician John Snow (1813–1858) determined that somehow the disease was spread through drinking water. He did this by mapping the home address of all of the people who died of the disease in the city of London during a specified period of time in the 1840s. Snow mapped the home of each person who died from the disease and discovered that they were clustered around certain neighborhoods. Working like a detective, he discovered that the people who died were all using the same water well to get their drinking water. When he prevented people from drawing water from the well, he stopped the spread of the disease.

Snow's actions, which were first reported in an 1849 article, "On the Mode of Communication of Cholera," is considered the beginning of the modern science of epidemiology—the study of infectious diseases. While much has changed since 1849, people are still concerned about the spread of infectious diseases. Recently, worry about the spread of the H1N1 virus, or "swine flu," has been a worldwide concern. Schools have been closed, businesses have been temporarily shut down, and travel between certain countries has been restricted. People have worn protective facial masks out in the streets, the public has been taught to "cough into your elbow," and everyone has been encouraged to wash their hands with soap more frequently. All of these practices, some perhaps more necessary than others, were aimed at controlling the spread of the virus.

It is important for students to be aware of infectious diseases and how they can spread in their local community. Students can also improve their community by helping to educate others. Many people may have incorrect or partially correct ideas about the H1N1 virus, how it spreads, and what the risks are. Students can gather community members' ideas about the spread of the H1N1 virus and then create a poster campaign to separate correct information from misinformation.

CULTURAL CONNECTIONS

Have students explore how major pandemics have affected their community or other communities around the country. For example, what was the impact of the 1918 flu epidemic on their local region, the country, or the world? Have them explore similar topics for diseases such as polio.

WHO GETS SICK AND WHY?

MATERIALS YOU WILL NEED FOR THIS ACTIVITY

- Interview questions
- Poster board
- Markers
- A computer with an Internet connection and a printer

Student with a cold

WHAT YOU WILL DO

Before the Trip

Visit the website for the Centers for Disease Control and Prevention (CDC) (http://www.cdc.gov/). There, you will find the most up-to-date information on the H1N1 flu virus and regular seasonal flu viruses, as well as appropriate steps for controlling their spread. Besides getting the flu vaccine, you can review everyday preventative measures such as covering your nose and mouth with a tissue when you or someone else sneezes and then disposing of the tissue, washing your hands frequently with soap and, especially after you cough or sneeze, avoiding touching your eyes, nose, and mouth with your hands as much as possible, and staying home when you are sick with flu-like symptoms and for at least 24 hours after your fever is gone.

Using the information you find, prepare some questions that you can ask people in your community to get a sense of what they know about the H1N1 flu and how to control it. Some sample questions could include:

- Why is the H1N1 flu sometimes called the swine flu?
- Should you go to work or school if someone else in your family is sick with the flu?
- Why is it important to stay home for 24 hours after your fever has gone?

Come up with additional questions based on your research.

On the Trip

Take a walking trip to a place in your community where people are coming and going and where they might have a couple of spare minutes to answer your questions. A supermarket, the lobby of an office building, and a community center are just a few possibilities.

Ask people you meet if they will take a few minutes to talk with you about the flu and how to prevent it. Don't be pushy—if someone says no, thank him or her anyway. If someone says yes, be sure to thank the person for his or her time. Ask a few of your questions (three is usually a good number) and record or take notes about the responses.

Back in the Classroom

Based on the information gathered from the community interviews, students should plan a community campaign on how to prevent the spread of the flu virus. Groups of students should make posters that will educate people about the flu. The posters could include statements such as:

Some people may think _____ about the swine flu, but you should know this _____.

It's not true that _____. Really, _____.

Be creative and artistic!

A useful resource for designing posters is the Library of Congress's Prints and Photography Division (http://www.loc.gov/rr/print/catalog.html). Ask the students to look at various types of posters used in American history. Topics they should search under, using the site's search engine, include "WPA posters," "World War I posters," and "health posters."

Students can put their posters up around the school, but even better, take some of the posters back to the place or places in the community where you conducted the interviews. Ask if you can put up the posters there for at least a few days. Then they can be returned and posted in the school. When you go to reclaim the posters from the community site, ask someone who works there if they noticed people looking at or talking about the posters.

THINKING LIKE A SCIENTIST—HYPOTHESIS AND EVIDENCE

Everyone has theories about how and why people get sick. Many times, however, they do not have good evidence to support those theories. What were some of the theories you heard about the H1N1 virus when you were conducting your interviews? Did people provide evidence to support their theories? If so, what kind of evidence did they offer? As you design your posters, make sure you provide evidence for the claims that you make.

Have students discuss how maintaining good public health is dependent on good information and people being educated in correct health habits. How do other people's health habits affect your health? How do your health habits affect other people?

SAMPLE GRADE-LEVEL MODIFICATION—UPPER ELEMENTARY

Expand the data set you collected as a class by continuing to interview additional people in your neighborhood, such as family members and neighbors. Look for patterns in the responses. Do kids think about the cause and spread of illness differently than adults? Do senior citizens think about it differently than younger adults? Do people from different cultures or countries of origin think about it differently?

Sample Interdisciplinary Connection—Language Arts

As the class creates its public service announcement posters to educate the community about reducing the spread of the flu, identify and use very different styles of posters. Use examples from the Library of Congress's Prints and Photography Division (mentioned above) to begin thinking about the various styles of persuasive posters that are possible (authoritative, friendly, scary, comical, threatening, etc.). When the posters are designed, take them to another class and let students respond do the different styles. Which ones do they like the best and least? Which ones are most likely to get them to change their behaviors?

Scientists in Your Community

Individuals in your community who might be knowledgeable about the cause and spread of illnesses such as the flu virus could include nurses, doctors, epidemiologists, and other local health care workers. Invite one or more of these individuals to your class to ask them questions about the H1N1 virus and other seasonal illnesses. Share and discuss the results of your survey with your guests.

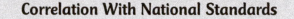

Correlation With National Standards

NSES Science: A1; F1; F5

NCTM Math: E1; E3; E4

NCTE Language Arts: 4; 12

NCSS Social Studies: 3; 8; 9

PART V

Activities to Promote Place-Based Science Teaching in the Broader Community

All of us probably remember field trips we took when we were in school. These were big events that got us out of our daily school routine. These "real" field trips—as opposed to the neighborhood- or schoolyard-based fieldwork that we have been talking about in previous chapters—involved permission slips, usually some financial cost, and a bus trip (or maybe even a plane flight). You may have gone away for several days, such as on a trip to our nation's capital, or just for the day to go see a musical performance or to go to a museum. These experiences stand out in our memories years or even decades later exactly because they were something out of the ordinary. The experience of leaving school to go somewhere "special" provides an opportunity to engage all students in meaningful learning because, as a teacher, you already have student motivation on your side.

There are many things that a teacher can do to help her students get the most out of a field trip experience. Even though the field trip is likely to be a one-time event, there are activities that can (and should) be done both before and after the trip to support and enhance the learning experience. Especially when it comes to place-based teaching and learning, context matters. Before the trip, relevant background should be explored. What is the history behind the museum/water treatment plant/hospital/etc. that is being visited? When was it built? Why, by whom, and with what funding? Who benefits the most from this facility and who is left out? What could be done to make access, use, or the benefits of the facility more equitable? Questions on a variety of topics relevant to the trip location should be considered and should be prepared as interview questions that can be asked during the trip.

During the trip itself, there are many more things that can be done to enhance the learning experience. In addition to the regular tours/presentations that are a standard part of a visit to the site, students should seek information from as many people as they can who are associated with the site. These might be formal interviews based on specific prepared questions or simply informal conversations. In a museum, for example, don't have your students limit themselves to the tour guide. Encourage them to ask the security guard, the exhibit constructor, and so forth about their experiences working at the facility and how they make sense of the science they are surrounded by on a daily basis. Talking with as many people as possible will create a more robust place-based learning experience.

Once the field trip is over, there is still much that can be done back in the classroom to build on the experience. Compare experiences and data, discuss how the experience was unique because of its context, and brainstorm about how it might be similar to and different from a related trip in another context—another city, state, or country. Consider how some aspects of what was experienced on the field trip could be modeled for others in your classroom or school. Could you and your students create an exhibit, a working model, or a multimedia presentation based on what you experienced and then share it with other students or community members who did not go on the trip?

The activity suggestions we present in this chapter require more logistical planning than most of the activity suggestions presented in earlier chapters. However, trips of this kind can make a big difference in motivating students to engage in further place-based learning. Schools traditionally save field trips of this kind for later in the year to serve as a reward. We suggest that you flip that paradigm and use such a trip early in the year to serve both as a motivator and as a shared point of reference for future place-based exploration.

Activity
33

Science in Museums

Most communities have access to some type of science museum. In a large city such as New York, there is a choice of museums to visit ranging from the American Museum of Natural History in Manhattan to the New Hall of Science in the Queens and the Staten Island Institute of Arts and Science. In smaller communities, the possibilities will be much more limited, and may include sites that combine multiple topics, such as local history and science. For example, the Museum of Science and History in Jacksonville has exhibits and activities on Florida history and science, as does the Cape Fear Museum of History and Science in Wilmington, North Carolina.

Whether the museum is large or small, students can almost always go online, either before or after the trip, to find extensive information about the museum's history and exhibits. Many science museums also have virtual tours on their websites that give you a sense of actually walking through a specific exhibit. Websites can also provide students with opportunities to map out what they are going to visit in the museum. This provides an opportunity to create mini-guides before the exhibit or bulletin board displays in the classroom. A fun activity is to have students keep a brief diary on their museum visit, as well as take photographs and even record sounds from their visit. These can be used later on to create websites, podcasts, and audio-visual presentations. Having students engage in this kind of advance planning will greatly enhance their museum visit and give them a sense of ownership during the field trip.

Students visiting a museum should be well versed in proper museum etiquette and behavior. The behavior guidelines presented here apply not only to trips to a museum but to most all of the trips discussed in this book, even if the trip is just a walk around the school grounds.

Most museums have specific rules on what can or cannot be done inside them. Food is not permitted inside most museum exhibit areas, though there is probably a cafeteria. Unless they are interactive in nature, exhibits should not be touched. Yelling and shouting is generally not permitted. Indoor voices should be used. Music should not be played, particularly if it can be heard by others. Essentially, one should not be imposing on others because of one's behavior. Photography is permitted in some museums but not permitted in others, and sometimes pictures are permitted but flashes are not.

If a guide is providing a tour, students should listen carefully, be polite, not talk to others in the group while the guide is presenting, and not listen to devices such as iPods. Pets of any type are usually not allowed (except for guide animals). Animals in living exhibits should not have their windows tapped on or be otherwise provoked in order to gain their attention.

Cell phones should be shut off and only used in an emergency. In this context, it is probably a good idea to let students have a contact number to call a teacher or parent assistant in case they get lost or separated from the group. Horseplay and running around of any type should be forbidden. It is all too easy for someone to slip and fall, not only hurting themselves and others but also potentially damaging an exhibit.

CULTURAL CONNECTIONS

Most communities, even very small ones, have museums. Even when they are not found in an individual community, they will almost certainly be found nearby. Students should understand that museums not only include temporary and permanent exhibits, but that they are often sites for performances and special events, as well as places where research and investigation can be conducted (historical archives, etc.).

VISITING A MUSEUM AND CREATING A REPORT OR DISPLAY BASED ON ONE'S VISIT

MATERIALS YOU WILL NEED FOR THIS ACTIVITY

- A computer with an Internet connection
- Interview or discussion questions to be used during the visit
- Still camera, video camera, and/or voice recorder (optional)

Girl in museum

WHAT YOU WILL DO

Before the Trip

Students should visit the website of the museum they are going to visit as part of a field trip. They should see if a map for the museum and its exhibits is available on the museum's website. Using the website, they should try to find out as much as possible about the exhibits at the museum, particularly the ones they wish to focus on with their field trip. Students can copy images and information into a file they think might help them prepare the creation of a bulletin board, poster board, or Power-Point presentation about their visit to the museum.

On the Trip

If permitted, take photographs and make sound recordings of the things that interest you most and that you think are most important about the exhibit or museum you are visiting. Take careful notes in order to remember important things. Talk to as many people as you can while you are there to learn about the exhibits but also about the history, the mission, and the future plans of the museum.

Back in the Classroom

Have students work by themselves or in groups to develop a creative response to their museum visit. This could be a PowerPoint slide show, a bulletin board or poster board, a letter or other communication back to the museum, a realistic fiction story set in the museum, or any other type of creative project that you can imagine.

Another approach would be to have students create a podcast describing their museum visit. This can be planned out beforehand and can include recorded sounds, interviews with teachers and students who went on the trip, and so forth. Podcasts can be posted to a website or kept on a computer in the classroom to be shared and listened to at convenient times. Reports from field trips can be shared between classes and with students from one year to the next.

THINKING LIKE A SCIENTIST—CAUSE AND EFFECT

Many of the interactive exhibits at a science museum focus on cause-and-effect relationships— you spin in a chair to experience centrifugal force, you stare at a figure for several minutes to experience an optical illusion, or you stand on a series of special scales to see how much you would weigh on other planets, to name just a few. Why do you think that cause-and-effect exhibits are much more popular in science museums than controlling variables or hypothesis and evidence exhibits?

SAMPLE GRADE-LEVEL MODIFICATION—UPPER ELEMENTARY

Have students draw a map or make a 3-D model or diorama of their ideal science museum and its exhibits. Have them explain why they have decided to create the museum and its exhibits the way they did.

SAMPLE INTERDISCIPLINARY CONNECTION—SOCIAL STUDIES

While you are at the museum, observe how other groups or families interact with each other and with the museum exhibits. Think about how learning in a museum setting is different from learning in a school setting. Psychologists who study learning that takes place between parents and children have often found museums to be very good places to study this type of learning. Why do you think that is?

SCIENTISTS IN YOUR COMMUNITY

Individuals in your community who might be knowledgeable about the science that can be learned in museums would include museum guides, museum designers, psychologists who study learning and development, and parents who spend a lot of time in museums with their children. Invite one or more of these individuals to your classroom to interview them about their experiences with learning in museums and to share with them what you have learned doing your project.

Correlation With National Standards

NSES Science: G1; G2; G3

NCTE Language Arts: 1; 6; 8

NCSS Social Studies: 1; 2; 3

Activity

34

Science in Zoos and Aquariums

SCIENCE BACKGROUND

Zoos and aquariums are available in most middle- and large-sized towns and cities. Even many rural areas are within a reasonable traveling distance of a zoo, aquarium, or wildlife sanctuary. Such facilities offer students a way to connect with the natural world and its wildlife, while also gaining a better understanding of why it is important that humans live in balance with nature.

Many zoos include examples of animals from the region's local environment. Create, with your students, a regional zoo list (possibly with student reports of the type described below) that focuses on animals that can be found living within 100 miles of your school. In a place like Miami, this list would include alligators, crocodiles, great blue herons, deer, armadillos, dolphins, and iguanas. In San Francisco, local animals would include bears, wolves, sea lions, coyotes, mountain lions, and otters. Compare the animals found in your part of the country with another region (Northern Maine versus South Florida or Arizona, for example).

Aquariums, although less common than zoos, provide many similar educational opportunities for students. Have students become expert on different types of marine life. Ask them to explore issues of conservation and protection. Talk with them about sports such as fishing and how recreational fishing is different from commercial fishing. Have students discuss issues involving what are fair and humane catches, as well as the need to protect the environments in which aquatic animals live. Students can also learn about aquaculture and the commercial raising of fish and other animals such as clams, oysters, and shrimp.

If possible, have a zookeeper or aquarium educator visit your school. Almost all zoos and aquariums have education outreach staff. If this is not possible, see if you have a parent who works with animals (raising them, protecting them, etc.) who can come talk with your students.

If at all possible, students should go on an actual field trip to their local zoo or aquarium. If this is not possible, then go to your local zoo's website or to a national zoo such as the Smithsonian National Zoological Park (http://nationalzoo.si.edu/Animals/AnimalIndex/) and create an online visit to the zoo for your students. Many such tours can easily be found online if you don't have the time or desire to create a tour yourself. (See, for example, the Smithsonian's tour of animals from around the world, which is available at http://nationalzoo.si.edu/Animals/WorldTour/default.cfm.)

CULTURAL CONNECTIONS

Certain animals are connected with local communities. In Southern Florida, manatees are special to the region. In California, the grizzly bear and the condor are popular animals associated with the region. Have students think about what plants and animals are unique or special in their part of the country and why that may be.

CREATING ANIMAL PROFILES

MATERIALS YOU WILL NEED FOR THIS ACTIVITY

- A computer connected to the Internet

WHAT YOU WILL DO

Before the Trip

Go online and create a list of local animals that are found at your local zoo or aquarium. Many zoos and aquariums will include a list of the animals they have on exhibit. (See, for example, the Animal Index at the Smithsonian National Zoological Park http://nationalzoo.si.edu/Animals/AnimalIndex/ or the Who Zoo at Fort Worth Zoo in Texas http://www.whozoo.org/listodate.htm.) Similar lists can be found using an Internet search for "zoo animal lists" or "zoo index." If possible, try to find an animal list online from your local zoo.

Feeding a giraffe

Create a list of local animals that the children in your class can study and become experts about. Let pairs of students pick an animal to study.

Have each student compile an animal biography, including:

1. The animal's common name

2. Its scientific name

3. Range and habitat

4. Population status (endangered, rare, etc.)

5. Diet

6. Typical behaviors

7. Unique or interesting facts or features

8. Location at your local zoo

Have students add photographs, maps, links to websites, and general information. Presentations can be compiled in a large class notebook, published to an Internet site, or displayed on a bulletin board.

On the Trip

Have students map out where their animals are in their local zoo. Ask them to each introduce their animal to their classmates as they tour the zoo. Students can take turns being tour guides and sharing what they know but also asking questions about the animal's appearance, behavior, and so forth that the class can try to answer together as they observe the animal photograph. Students can take pictures or make drawings of the animals they are expert on while visiting the zoo or aquarium or else designate several zoo photographers to take pictures or video while you are touring.

Back in the Classroom

Photographs and drawings obtained on the zoo or aquarium field trip can be added to students' animal biographies after returning from the class field trip. As a class, create a virtual zoo of local animals with all of the students' animal biographies. Share your virtual zoo with students in other classes in your school.

THINKING LIKE A SCIENTIST—HYPOTHESIS AND EVIDENCE

Discuss with students whether zoos and aquariums are good places for animals to live. What is one hypothesis about why zoos are good places for animals? What evidence, if any, did you see on your trip to the zoo to support this hypothesis? What is one hypothesis about why zoos are not good places for animals to live? What evidence, if any, did you see on your trip to the zoo to support this hypothesis? Have students consider why zoos might be important in terms of preserving rare and endangered animals. Discuss what makes a good zoo where animals can best grow and thrive.

SAMPLE GRADE-LEVEL MODIFICATION—EARLY ELEMENTARY

Ask students to carefully observe any pets they have at home, such as cats or dogs. Have them compare and contrast the behaviors of the domesticated animals at home with the behaviors of the wild animals they saw at the zoo. How are they different and how are they similar? Ask students if they think the behavior of wild animals in the zoo is the same as that of wild animals in the wild. Why?

SAMPLE INTERDISCIPLINARY CONNECTION—SOCIAL STUDIES

If possible, encourage children to make a return visit to the zoo with their families. Have them share what they learned on their school trip and find out what other information about the animals at the zoo that their parents or other older relatives know. Have the children ask their parents or older family members what they remember about zoos from when they were children. How have zoos changed in recent years? What do these changes say about the way that people relate to animals?

SCIENTISTS IN YOUR COMMUNITY

Individuals in your community who might be knowledgeable about the science that can be learned in zoos or aquariums would include zookeepers, wild animal veterinarians, zoo tour guides, and parents who frequently take their children to the zoo. Invite one or more of these individuals to your classroom to interview them about their experiences with zoo animals and to share with them what you have learned from your animal biographies and your virtual zoo.

Correlation With National Standards

NSES Science: C2; C4; C5

NCTM Math: D1

NCTE Language Arts: 1; 4; 11

NCSS Social Studies: 3; 8; 9

Activity
35
Surveying Local Parks

SCIENCE BACKGROUND

Local parks are an outstanding resource for science teachers. They provide a common open space that is readily accessible to students and teachers for various explorations and activities. Almost every community has some kind of park, whether a vest-pocket park in a place like downtown Chicago or a national park in a rural community such as Buena Vista, Virginia, which is adjacent to the George Washington National Forest.

An exciting way to have students become aware of the layout as well as the topological and physical characteristics of a local park is to have them go to Google Maps (http://maps.google.com/maps), where they can actually call up a street map, a satellite map, or a topological map of most towns and cities in the United States. Using Google Maps, students can print out maps of a local park, which they can use any way that they like.

For example, students may want to create a giant wall map of a local park. It can show the terrain of the area, the location of different sites, or both. Wall-size maps or smaller maps can be used to plot out animal populations or to identify places of interest such as monuments, exhibits, and playing fields.

CULTURAL CONNECTIONS

Local history is often associated with parks. In many southern towns, there are two city parks, a relic of past times when the parks were racially segregated. Parks can also be associated with a historical event. For example, Forest Park in St. Louis was built as part of the 1904 World's Fair. Parks are also built to commemorate major events such as wars or independence. Have students explore the cultural and historical connections in the parks in their local community.

SURVEYING LOCAL PARKS

MATERIALS YOU WILL NEED FOR THIS ACTIVITY

- A large piece of paper measuring at least 4 × 4 feet—possibly larger
- Magic markers

- Tape to fix the map to a wall
- A computer with a printer and access to the Internet
- Digital cameras

WHAT YOU WILL DO

Before the Trip

Have students visit Google Maps (http://maps
.google.com/maps) and call up a map of their city and
have them find a park they are interested in studying.
Print out maps in all three available map modes (street
map, satellite map, and terrain map). Students will
carry these maps with them when they visit the park so
that they can record information.

Using these three maps, work together to construct
an accurate, wall-size map of their city park on the
large piece of paper on the classroom wall. Include
details from each of the map modes (i.e. streets, landmarks, buildings, streams or ponds, topography, etc.).

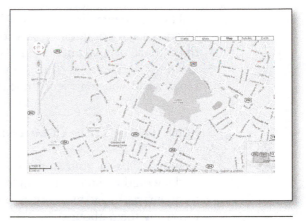

Map of Gypsy Hill Park, Staunton, Virginia

Source: Courtesy of Eric Bryan.

On the Trip

Have students take photographs of major landmarks in the park, both historical and
physical (statues, wildlife areas, ponds, playing fields, etc.). Ask them to record the places
on their maps where they took their photographs. This activity can potentially be combined
with the plant census activity in Part IV (Activity 28) and/or the wildlife census activity also
in Part IV (Activity 31) to further extend and elaborate on the mapping activity. Students can
record where they found different plant and animal species and add photographs to the map.

Back in the Classroom

Students can elaborate on their wall map and create lists of landmarks, plants, and/
or animals they observed and then add these to the maps. Small photographs can also
be added. See how much detail students can add to the map. Try to include things you
observed that would not typically be seen on a map.

THINKING LIKE A SCIENTIST—HYPOTHESIS AND EVIDENCE

How are the sites for city parks chosen? What hypothesis can you come up with to
explain why parks exist where they do? Do these locations have any common features?
Using Google Maps, look at your town or city and any other towns or cities (either near or
far) that you would like to use. What evidence can you gather about where the parks are
located? Does this evidence support or refute your hypothesis about park location? Why?

SAMPLE GRADE-LEVEL MODIFICATION—MIDDLE SCHOOL

Have students use Google Earth and insert images and lists on it electronically and
then save it into a jpg format that can be saved on a school website. A more ambitious

project involves doing the same activity but instead creating an interactive map online, with links to additional information.

Sample Interdisciplinary Connection—Mathematics

Have students discuss why it is important to conduct censuses of plants and animals in one's local community. Ask them to plan a similar census in the area right around their house or apartment. Have students look for patterns as to when animals feed and are most active, as well as how they interact with other animals, as well as humans. How could you represent these patterns graphically or visually?

Scientists in Your Community

Individuals in your community who might be knowledgeable about surveying city parks would include park employees, city employees, local environmental scientists, and frequent park patrons. Invite one or more of these individuals to your classroom to interview them about their experiences with the park and to share with them your class park map and what you learned from creating it.

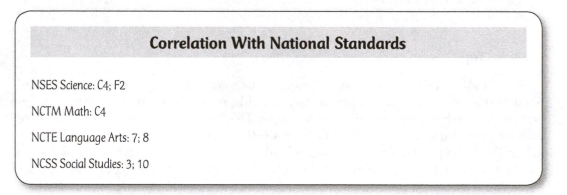

Correlation With National Standards

NSES Science: C4; F2

NCTM Math: C4

NCTE Language Arts: 7; 8

NCSS Social Studies: 3; 10

Geology and Buildings

Activity
36

SCIENCE BACKGROUND

Humans have been using stone for building purposes for thousands of years. All over the world, we continue to use many types of stone for the construction of roads, bridges, buildings, and monuments. In almost any city or town, you can find a wide variety of building stones. Students study and learn to identify different rocks and minerals as part of Earth science in elementary and middle school, but they usually see only small samples and textbook pictures in the classroom. An urban geology field trip can allow students to see and touch much more impressive examples of these rocks and minerals while also having an opportunity to discuss other place-based topics related to construction, city planning, and environmental and eco-justice issues. Additionally, a field trip looking at rocks and minerals in buildings can easily be added as part of another field trip to a particular location in a city or town. An extra stop or two can be made to examine rocks, minerals, and building materials. Downtown areas with large and historic buildings provide the best opportunities for observing a range of rock and mineral types in a compact area. Cemeteries also provide access to a range of rock types as well as a context for local history study.

As with many field trips, it is important to plan your trip in advance. You should visit possible stops and look at the buildings. Look for igneous rocks that have large grain size so that students will be able to observe and distinguish the different mineral components or contrasting grain sizes so that you can discuss the relationship between grain size and cooling rate. Look for metamorphic rocks that show banding and other metamorphic features. Look for sedimentary rocks that show cross-bedding. Limestone, which is commonly used in building, frequently contains a range of marine fossils. Compare stone that has been treated in different ways, such as polished and unpolished, exposed to more weathering and more protected from weathering, and so on. When possible, compare natural samples of the same or similar rock type with the finished rock used in the building. Studying local buildings, statues, gravestones, and the like can also foster connections between geology and architecture and between geology and art.

CULTURAL CONNECTIONS

Buildings and the materials they are constructed of are often connected to the geology of their region. In Denver, Colorado, many buildings are constructed from the red sandstone found in the nearby Rocky Mountains. In places like South Florida, many early homes were made from oolite, a type of sedimentary rock found in the region. Have students explore how local geology has shaped their community and its structures. In addition to buildings, have them consider the types of roads, tunnels, and/or bridges they see in their local area and how these are related to unique local geography and geology.

Geology and Buildings

Materials You Will Need for This Activity

- Sketch pad or lab book
- Colored pencils
- Natural samples of rocks, minerals, and fossils for comparison
- Magnifying glasses or hand lenses
- Rock and mineral identification guide
- Historical drawings or photographs of the area when possible

Smithsonian Institution National Museum of Natural History

What You Will Do

Before the Trip

Introduce and observe samples of the rocks and minerals students are likely to see on the field trip. Introduce topics of rock and mineral classification and weathering. Discuss the history and construction of specific buildings you will visit on the trip. Look at pictures of the buildings online or pictures from past trips and have students make predictions about the rock and mineral types that the buildings might be made of, including explanations for why they made these predictions.

On the Trip

Using a hand lens, students should make careful observations of the stone that is used in the construction of the buildings. Students should also take descriptive notes and make sketches and/or rubbings of the rocks and minerals they observe at each stop. Additionally, they should take close-up digital photos for later use.

Back in the Classroom

Students should compare and contrast their observations, notes, and drawings, revisit their predictions about rock types, look again at classroom samples, look at pictures that were taken on the trip, and draw conclusions about the types of rocks and minerals that were observed at each site.

THINKING LIKE A SCIENTIST—HYPOTHESIS AND EVIDENCE

What hypotheses do you have about why certain types of rocks are commonly used in the construction of large buildings and other types of rocks are not? What are some of the factors that would influence these decisions by architects and builders? What evidence could you gather to test your hypotheses? Where did the rocks used to construct this building come from? How were they transported? By whom? How resistant to wear and erosion are they? How do they look when polished? Do these questions influence building decisions?

SAMPLE GRADE-LEVEL MODIFICATION—MIDDLE SCHOOL

Additional library research can be done to determine the geologic age of the rocks that were used and the geologic names of the rock formations the materials came from. Can you find information about other places where rocks from this same formation were used in the construction of other buildings?

SAMPLE INTERDISCIPLINARY CONNECTION—MATHEMATICS

Using the research done on the age of the rocks used in the construction of the building, compare the age of the rocks with the age of the building itself. Calculate how many times older the rocks are than the building. Create a visual representation to model this ratio.

SCIENTISTS IN YOUR COMMUNITY

Individuals in your community who might be knowledgeable about the local urban geology would include professional and amateur geologists, structural and civil engineers, architects, and local history buffs. Invite one or more of these individuals to your classroom to interview them about their knowledge of the rocks used to build local buildings and to share with them your research, pictures, and findings.

Correlation With National Standards

NSES Science: F1; F5; G5

NCTM Math: E1

NCTE Language Arts: 4; 5

NCSS Social Studies: 8

Activity
37

Science in Hospitals and Health Clinics

SCIENCE BACKGROUND

Living a healthy lifestyle and making healthy choices have not traditionally been major foci of science education. However, a number of growing health crises in this country have been linked to personal lifestyle issues such as diet, exercise, and smoking. This has led to increased calls for a greater emphasis on heath education in schools. In addition to physical education class, science class is the natural place to address these health topics. In addition to overall negative trends in illnesses and diseases such as cancer, asthma, and diabetes that have been linked to poor diet and lack of exercise, there are also significant health disparities and health-care inequalities between ethnic and racial groups and between social classes.

Research has shown that personal, socioeconomic, and environmental differences across ethnic and racial groups can be linked to health disparities and health-care inequalities. For example, African Americans and Hispanic Americans are more likely, on average, to live in poorer neighborhoods with more environmental health risks, less access to healthy food choices, less access to safe places to exercise, and less access to nonemergency health care when compared to their White peers. Thus, people living in poverty and people of color face greater heath risks with fewer health-care options to combat those risks. Not surprisingly, very different health outcomes result from these differences in risk and access to quality medical care across demographic groups.

For example, studies have found that:

- Within each racial/ethnic group, the amount of exercise and other leisure-time activity people engage in is related to income—people with lower incomes get less exercise and engage in less leisure-time activity.

- The risk of allergic diseases, such as asthma, is related to social class. People living in poverty have higher exposure to allergens and higher rates of asthma and other allergic diseases.

- People living in poverty have a greater chance of dying prematurely from stroke or heart attack. This difference is related to differences both in diet and in access to preventive heath care.

- The higher rates of diabetes among African Americans when compared to Whites have been shown to have less to do with genetic differences (as was previously thought) and more to do with differences in living conditions. A recent study at Johns Hopkins School of Public Health found that when African Americans and Whites live in similar environments and have similar incomes, their diabetes rates are similar.

The research makes it clear that public health issues are place-based issues and are also issues of eco-justice. While these issues can be studied and discussed in the classroom setting, a field trip through different neighborhoods and to a hospital or public health clinic can make these discrepancies more real for students. Discussion and interviews with health-care providers and community members can provide information in ways that are more meaningful than reading about these topics in a book.

Most hospitals are used to giving group tours, but other smaller heath clinics may not be. Additionally, the individuals who facilitate these tours are unlikely to be prepared to answer the sorts of questions about health disparities, health-care inequalities, and eco-justice that are likely to be the focus of your discussions. Thus, you should discuss these topics with a representative of the hospital or health clinic in advance so that they can make someone available to engage your class in this discussion.

CULTURAL CONNECTIONS

Names found on buildings are often associated with famous people in science. In many parts of the country, there are schools named after the African American scientist George Washington Carver (1864–1943). Hospital and medical complexes are often named after famous doctors. Learn about and help students become aware of who local institutions are named after and what role these individuals may have played in the local community or even in the history of the nation.

AN OUNCE OF PREVENTION IS WORTH A POUND OF CURE

MATERIALS YOU WILL NEED FOR THIS ACTIVITY

- Survey questions

- A notebook or journal

WHAT YOU WILL DO

Before the Trip

Create a KWL chart (what you *know*, what you *want* to know, and what you *learned*) or other graphic organizer to assess prior knowledge and interest around the topic of health concerns, including health disparities and health-care inequalities between ethnic and racial groups and between social classes. Copy down questions from the KWL chart to take with you on the trip.

Discuss students' experiences in hospitals and health clinics and predict what will be seen on the field trip.

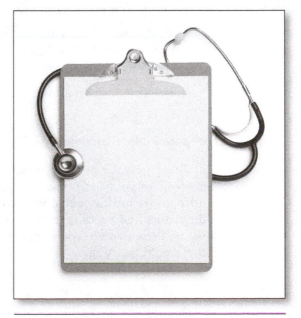

Doctor's stethoscope and chart

Develop a list of interview questions for health-care providers based on the student interests that have been expressed. Students should feel free to create their own questions, but the following list can help get them started. These questions are based on the health data given above:

- How are exercise and other leisure-time activities related to physical and emotional health and well-being? What evidence do you see of this relationship in your practice?

- Do you see evidence in your practice that exercise and other leisure-time activity are related to income? Please describe this evidence.

- What factors do you see in your practice that increase the risk of allergic diseases, such as asthma?

- Do you see evidence in your practice that the risk of allergic diseases, such as asthma, is related to social class? Please describe this evidence.

- What factors do you see in your practice that increase the risk of patients dying prematurely from stroke or heart attack?

- Do you see evidence in your practice that people living in poverty have increased risk of dying prematurely from stroke or heart attack? Please describe this evidence.

- What factors do you see in your practice that increase the risk of patients developing diabetes?

- Do you see evidence in your practice of higher rates of diabetes among African Americans when compared to Whites? If so, do you see evidence that these differences are due partially to differences in living conditions? Please describe this evidence.

On the Trip

- Take notes and pictures (when you are given permission) to document your visit in detail.

- During the tour, ask questions related to the topics that your class put on the KWL chart. You should have these questions in your notebook.

- Find time to interview one or more health-care workers using the interview questions that you developed in the classroom. Either take careful notes during the interview or make an audio or video recording.

- See as many things and ask as many questions as you can on the trip.

Back in the Classroom

Compare your observations, your notes, the answers to the KWL questions, and the answers to your interview questions. What patterns do you see? Discuss how well the hospital or health center was prepared for dealing with the growing issues of health disparities and health-care inequalities. In what ways were they being proactive in working on these issues through preventive measures? Discuss suggestions for other strategies they could be using.

THINKING LIKE A SCIENTIST—HYPOTHESIS AND EVIDENCE

What hypotheses did your class have about community health issues at the start of this activity (as described on the KWL chart)? What evidence did your class collect during the course of the activity to support or challenge those theories?

How did your class discussions about public health issues differ before and after your trip to the hospital or health clinic?

What choices are available to people in your community in terms of where to have their health-care needs addressed?

The federal government has tried for many years to create a comprehensive health-care reform. What are some of the reasons why this reform has been so difficult to enact?

SAMPLE GRADE-LEVEL MODIFICATION—UPPER ELEMENTARY

Plan a family health night for parents and other community members. Make posters and other displays with information on community heath issues. Set up stations to take basic health measures such as blood pressure and heart rate. Invite family members and use the evening as an opportunity to educate them about the issues you have been studying and to celebrate the benefits of living a healthier lifestyle.

SAMPLE INTERDISCIPLINARY CONNECTION—MATHEMATICS

Collect data on the change in life expectancy in your state over the past several decades. See if you can find this data broken down by demographic categories such as family income, gender, and racial/ethnic group. Describe the patterns you see in the data and relate these patterns to the health and wellness factors that you have been studying during this activity.

SCIENTISTS IN YOUR COMMUNITY

Individuals in your community who might be knowledgeable about the local community health issues would include doctors, nurses, community health workers, and patients with some of the illnesses that have been discussed in this activity. Invite one or more of these individuals to your community health night along with family members and ask them to share their experiences with health issues in the community.

Correlation With National Standards

NSES Science: F1; F5; G5

NCTM Math: E1

NCTE Language Arts: 4; 5

NCSS Social Studies: 8

Activity 38

Where Does Your Food Come From?

SCIENCE BACKGROUND

In the last activity, we alluded to people's food choices and the negative health impacts of an unhealthy diet. We considered how people living in poverty have fewer healthy food choices due to issues such as cost, availability, and time. Still, everyone has some choice about the food they eat, and as children grow older, they have more opportunities to make choices. The eating habits we form when we are young, however, influence the choices we make later. As we have seen, those choices can then affect our health and well-being.

The current generation of schoolchildren has grown up eating more fast food and "convenience meals" than any prior generation. These foods contain more sugars and more fats and are more highly processed than typical home-cooked meals. Typical breakfast foods like cold cereals are very high in sugar and the typical lunch foods served in school cafeterias often contain high-fat and high-sugar items like chips and "juice" drinks that are mostly sugar water. These unhealthy meals are usually supplemented with candy and other unhealthy snacks several times a day.

While it is true that people's purchasing choices are a major cause of these unhealthy food options being so widely available, there are other factors that drive questions of food availability. There are issues of cost, convenience, habit, advertising, and taste on the part of consumers. There is also the driving issue of profit margin on the part of producers. The huge increase in recent years in the use of corn syrup as a sweetener in many of our foods is a result of companies realizing how much money they can save through this process. Companies claim that they just produce what people want to buy, but they fail to mention some of the cost-saving decisions that are made about ingredients that generally happen without the knowledge of consumers.

Given our dietary habits, it should not be surprising that many students have very little idea about what they are actually eating and where their food comes from. Food production and distribution is now a worldwide enterprise. The banana you ate with your breakfast cereal most likely came from Central America, your coffee or tea from Brazil or Asia. The hamburger you had for lunch was likely to contain a combination of beef from North American and South American cattle, and the vegetables you had with your dinner probably came from Mexico or California. These are just a few examples. If you are a typical American, it is highly unlikely that a single food item that you ate today came from a plant or animal that was raised within 20 miles of where you live. This was not the case just a few generations ago. Transportation has become a much larger part of the food industry.

There are three basic parts of our modern food system that get food to you: production, processing, and transportation. Production involves the initial raising of the food product such as the growing of a fruit in an orchard or the raising of beef cattle on a feedlot. Processing involves picking, slaughtering, grading, packaging, and other such processes that get the food ready for sale. Transportation involves getting the food from where it is produced to where it is processed and then from where it is processed to where it is sold.

A trip to a farmer's market in your local area is an ideal way to explore local food options in relation to the international corporate food system.

CULTURAL CONNECTIONS

Food, like geology, architecture, and other topics we have discussed, typically has distinct regional connections. Peaches are associated with Georgia, oranges with Florida, maple syrup with Vermont, and corn with Nebraska, to give just a few examples. Have students explore regional cultural associations and connections with foods. Consider other associations with farm-grown or hunted products such as Virginia and ham or Alaska and salmon.

WHAT GROWS IN YOUR STATE?

MATERIALS YOU WILL NEED FOR THIS ACTIVITY

- Map of your state
- Reference books
- Colored pencils

WHAT YOU WILL DO

Before the Trip

Students should begin by researching the major agricultural products grown in their state. Check out the United States Department of Agriculture's Census of Agriculture website at http://www.agcensus.usda.gov/ as one source of information and maps about agricultural production. There are many other sources of information you can find online.

Next, get a printout of a blank map of your state and create a state agricultural map by adding pictures of locally grown food items to the parts of your state where each item is most common.

Based on your agriculture map, predict and make a list of the food items you are likely to see at your local farmer's market. Do you think you would see different items at a farmer's market in a different part of the state? Explain.

Prepare interview questions to ask farmers and other vendors at the farmer's market—questions should focus on issues of production, processing, and transportation of their crops and products. Remember that production involves the initial raising of the food, processing involves

Shopping for vegetables

picking, packaging, and getting the food ready for sale, and transportation involves getting the food from where it is produced and processed to where it is sold. As a class, come up with several questions based on each of these three parts of the modern food system.

On the Trip

Walk around and observe the farmer's market. How is it similar to and different from the supermarket? Take pictures of what you see.

Look at your list of products that you expected to see based on your research in the classroom. Which of those items are actually for sale? What other items are for sale that are not on your list?

There will probably be free samples of things to try. Describe and record how they taste.

Ask questions of the farmers and vendors at the market—use your interview questions as a guide, but feel free to ask other questions based on what you see around you.

Back in the Classroom

Make a graphic organizer that compares and contrasts issues of production, processing, and transportation for food you saw at the farmer's market and the same or similar food items found at the supermarket.

Using the state agricultural map that you made before the trip, add the products that you saw at the farmer's market that you had not included at first and where they come from—how does this alter your map?

Display your maps and pictures in the hallway or some other location where other classes can see them. Add some signs in large text that make some point about local agriculture and local farmer's markets, such as "Support local agriculture—shop at the farmer's market!"

THINKING LIKE A SCIENTIST—CAUSE AND EFFECT

Since each region of the country is suited for specific agricultural products, how will this influence what you see for sale at farmer's markets in different parts of the country? During different times of year? What, specifically, causes these differences? What has the effect been of globalizing the production and distribution of agricultural products? Use the Internet to research farmer's markets in different parts of the country. How are they similar to and different from your farmer's market?

What are the pros and cons of "eating locally"? What are the pros and cons of "eating with the seasons"?

SAMPLE GRADE-LEVEL MODIFICATION—EARLY ELEMENTARY

Use the trip to the farmer's market as an opportunity to learn more about the senses. Have students describe everything they see, hear, smell, taste, and touch in as much detail as they can. Work on using the most descriptive language and adjectives that they can.

Sample Interdisciplinary Connection—Social Studies

Do you think your great-grandparents ate locally? Do you think they ate with the seasons? Why or why not? If you have some elderly relatives who you can interview, either in person or by phone, ask them to share with you what they remember about the fresh foods that were available when they were children. How were they different from what's currently available? Share what you find out with your class. Especially, try as a class to identify relatives who grew up in other countries and compare their experiences with relatives who grew up in the United States.

Scientists in Your Community

Individuals in your community who might be knowledgeable about local agriculture and local farmer's markets could include local farmers, local trucking companies, farmer's market organizers, food store purchasing agents, and local historians. Invite one or more of these individuals to your classroom and ask them to share their experiences with local agriculture and farmer's markets and share with them what you have learned.

Correlation With National Standards

NSES Science: F2; G1

NCTM Math: C4

NCTE Language Arts: 1; 4

NCSS Social Studies: 1; 2; 3; 8

Activity 39

Where Does Your Water Come From?

SCIENCE BACKGROUND

In this country, we think of water as being plentiful and cheap. This is not true in many other parts of the world. Some people predict that in the next century, wars will be fought over the rights to water that countries need for agriculture and hydroelectric power. We may be able to avoid this prediction if people work together to use water more efficiently. Think about your own water use on an average day. What are some of the ways that you use water? For example, drinking, washing, flushing, cooking, recreation, irrigation, fighting fires, cooling engines, and so on.

The typical person in the United States uses about 125 gallons of water every day. That does not count the water that is used to produce the things you eat and use through farming and manufacturing. This can be more than 1,000 gallons of additional water per person every day! For more on these direct and indirect uses of water, see the activity on water usage (Activity 4). Where does your local water come from? It may be from a lake, an aquifer, a river, a reservoir, or some other source. Do some research to find out.

Now think about where water goes once you use it. Water that goes down your sink or toilet most likely goes to a water treatment plant and then into a river or ocean. It may be cleaned at the plant and then used again in a factory or maybe even returned to the public water supply. Visiting a water treatment plant can help you get the answers to some of these questions and also give you a better sense of all the work that goes into having clean water come out when you turn on your sink.

CULTURAL CONNECTIONS

Water treatment plants and water towers are often icons in local communities. Generally they occupy or become the highest point in the town. Why do you think this is? Have students imagine how their town would be different if they did not have a centralized water system. Where would their water come from? How would activities and the layout of the local community change? Could water towers be made to look more interesting or more artistic? (Most water towers simply have the name of their town painted on the side.) Have students draw pictures of more creatively designed water towers.

TRIP TO A WATER TREATMENT PLANT

MATERIALS YOU WILL NEED FOR THIS ACTIVITY

- Community map
- Treatment plant schematic diagram
- Interview questions

WHAT YOU WILL DO

Before the Trip

Hand out a community map that shows the major community features (roads, airport, rivers, lakes, major buildings, etc.).

Have the students attempt to locate the water source for the community, the water treatment facility, water storage tanks, and any other physical features that are related to the water treatment operations in the community.

If possible, have someone from the water treatment plant or another knowledgeable community official come to class to talk about the operation of the water treatment plant.

Develop a list of questions that you can ask while you are visiting the plant. Use the sample questions below as a guide.

Water purification plant

On the Trip

Look at a schematic diagram of the plant and talk about the process of water treatment.

Take a tour of the plant and compare what you are actually seeing to the schematic of the plant.

Using your question sheet, ask the guide or other people you meet on the tour questions about the functioning of the plant.

SAMPLE QUESTIONS FOR TRIP TO WATER TREATMENT PLANT

- What is the source of the raw water that is used?
- What is the basic type of treatment used?
- How many homes are served by the distribution system?
- How many people (population) are served by the distribution system?
- How much water (in gallons per day) is produced by the plant?
- What method of disinfection is used?
- How many people are required to operate the system?

- How many person-hours/week are required to operate the system?

- How much energy (kilowatts of electrical power) is used per month?

- What chemicals are used in the treatment process?

- What special treatment processes are used?

- Are bacteriological samples tested for coliforms? How often?

- What is the pH of the raw water? Of the treated water?

- What is the hardness of the raw water? Of the treated water?

- What is the alkalinity of the raw water? Of the treated water?

- What training or certification is required of the operators?

Back in the Classroom

As a class, build a 3-D model of the water treatment system you saw. Break into small groups and assign each group one component of the system. Each group should remember to talk to other groups to be sure that the size and scale of what they are doing is compatible. When the model is built, have another class come and see it and give them a virtual version of the tour that you took at the plant, explaining the system to them and answering their questions.

THINKING LIKE A SCIENTIST: CONTROL OF VARIABLES

Water purification is high-stakes science—if the process is not done correctly, many people can get sick or even die. What are some of the variables that water treatment plant scientists and engineers need to be aware of when treating the water? What do they do to try to control those possible variables? What safety features are in place in the plant in case there is a problem controlling one or more of the variables?

SAMPLE GRADE-LEVEL MODIFICATION—MIDDLE SCHOOL

There is a lot of chemistry involved in the water treatment process. Based on what you learned at the water treatment plant, what are some of the areas of chemistry that someone needs to know to understand what happens in the plant? What chemical elements are involved in the treatment process? What sorts of chemical processes take place?

SAMPLE INTERDISCIPLINARY CONNECTION—SOCIAL STUDIES

Do some research on the history of water treatment in your city, town, or community. What was done to purify water in your local area before the technology that you saw at the water treatment plant was available? See if you can find out. How effective was it? What is currently done in developing countries to purify drinking water? Does this vary depending on where in the country one lives? Why?

SCIENTISTS IN YOUR COMMUNITY

Individuals in your community who might be knowledgeable about local water treatment efforts could include engineers and other workers at the water treatment plant, city workers at the sewage and water board, local civil engineers, and city planners. Invite one or more of these individuals to your classroom and ask them to share their experiences working with water treatment and share with them your model of the water treatment plant and what you learned on the field trip.

Correlation With National Standards

NSES Science: E1; E2; F1

NCTM Math: A3; E1

NCTE Language Arts: 4; 8

NCSS Social Studies: 2; 3; 8

Activity

40

Where Does Your Garbage Go?

SCIENCE BACKGROUND

The term *sanitary landfill* was first used in the 1930s to refer to the compacting of solid waste materials. This system was initially adopted by New York City and Fresno, California, where heavy earth-moving equipment was used to compress waste materials and then cover them with soil. The practice of covering solid waste with soil is actually much older and was evident in Greek civilization more than 2,000 years ago. However, the Greeks did not compact the waste, perhaps because they lacked the technology needed to have considered this part of the process.

Today, sanitary landfills are the major method of disposing of solid waste materials in North America and other developed countries, even while considerable efforts are being made to find alternative methods of waste disposal, such as recycling, incineration, and composting. Landfills are likely to remain a popular choice for the foreseeable future because of their simplicity and versatility. Landfills are not sensitive to the shape, size, or weight of a particular waste material—most anything can be put in. Additionally, because landfills are constructed of soil, they are usually unaffected by the chemical composition of waste that is added. Other waste disposal options, such as composting and incineration, require that the waste be more uniform in its composition and cannot be used if potentially toxic chemicals are present in the waste.

About 67% of the solid waste generated in the United States is still dumped in landfills. This corresponds to several tons of waste per landfill daily, based on an average of 4.5 pounds of solid waste per person per day in this country. This year, Americans will create approximately 250 million tons of solid waste, and two thirds of this waste that is dumped in a landfill will not decompose for about 30 years. It is possible to create more environmentally sustainable landfills. For example, newer landfills are being engineered to recover the methane gas that is generated during decomposition of waste, while some older landfills are being mined for useful products. Efforts to restrict what goes into landfills have increased in recent years. This is because landfills that have been filled and closed have gone on to be used in creative ways, including industrial parks, airport runways, recreational parks, ski slopes, ball fields, golf courses, and playgrounds.

About 70% of the solid waste that is typically disposed of in landfills could be recycled instead. More than 30% of bulk municipal garbage collection consists of paper products that could be remanufactured, while other materials such as plastic, metal, and glass are also readily reused in manufacturing. These changes could greatly reduce the amount of waste materials disposed of in landfills, as well as preserving sources of non-renewable raw materials.

CULTURAL CONNECTIONS

Have students explore how some landfills, after they were filled, have been used creatively as the sites for parks and recreation centers. What are the potential benefits of doing this? What are the potential risks? Have students consider other creative ways to use the principles of recycling to improve their local community.

VISITING A RECYCLING CENTER

MATERIALS YOU WILL NEED FOR THIS ACTIVITY

- Local telephone directory
- Recycling interview questions
- Books and other resources for studying recycling

WHAT YOU WILL DO

Before the Trip

Have students define the word *cycle*.

Create a class KWL chart on what they know about recycling. Then ask the following or similar questions:

- Why is recycling important?
- How does recycling affect our daily lives?
- What products do we find in stores that use the word *recycled*?
- What part can you play to support recycling?

Recycling plant

Give each group of students a telephone directory and ask them to find any evidence of community, county, or state groups involved in recycling efforts.

Have students create a list of questions that they would use to interview neighbors, parents, and relatives about their feelings on recycling.

Divide the class into groups to research the recycling processes used for one of the different materials that can be recycled: newspapers, glass, plastic, aluminum cans, and steel cans. The small groups can then report back to the rest of the class with their findings. Each group should also make a list of questions for things they don't understand about their process.

If students' families or the school already have a recycling project, the class could observe and record the amount and type of recycled items that are collected for 1 week (perhaps the week prior to the field trip). Students could graph the different items on a class chart. This will provide some idea of the vast amount of recyclables that are collected for their whole town or city over the course of a week.

Look up and discuss "Mt. Trashmore" in Virginia Beach, Virginia. This is a beautiful park that was created from wastes and trash and then covered by dirt, grass, and so forth.

On the Trip

Observe an assembly line for separating and sorting items. Have students discuss how an assembly line helps the recycling process in the center and whether such a system would be useful in a classroom or school-wide recycling program.

Ask students to use their senses to describe the site. Were the odor, sounds, and visual appearance of the recycling center what they expected? What sorts of protective gear do the employees wear to protect them from any of the processes or effects of recycling?

Have students tally the number of employees involved in the recycling process and ask about the amount of material that is recycled. Calculate how much material each employee is responsible for recycling each day.

Take note of the huge pile of items waiting to be recycled and ask about the period of time it took to collect it and how long it will take to recycle it. Estimate the weight of the material in the pile.

Each group of students should ask questions about the process of recycling for the specific type of recyclable items that they researched in class before the trip.

Back in the Classroom

Have students pick one or more of the these extension projects as a follow-up to the trip to the recycling center:

- Find products at home or at school that are made primarily from recycled materials, and have them write letters to the companies praising them for their efforts.

- Find products that are overpackaged at home and at school, and have students write letters to the companies asking them to be aware of resources and try to be more frugal and limit the amount of unnecessary packaging.

- Reuse something for the same or for a different purpose. Is this better than recycling? Why or why not? Write about it.

- Set up a mock recycling business. Decide upon the product, cost, number of employees, location, and so on.

- Write a letter to a family member, friend, or another schoolmate persuading them to recycle, informing them about the importance of recycling and how it can save our environment.

Thinking Like a Scientist—Cause and Effect

Reusing is a much older idea than recycling. Research ways that people have been reusing items throughout history. What do you think caused the shift in people's practices leading to less reusing now than in the past? What have been the effects of those changes? Think about things that are produced locally in your state or community and then think about alternative uses for those products that would allow them to be reused.

SAMPLE GRADE-LEVEL MODIFICATION—UPPER ELEMENTARY

What would someone from a historical time period who is used to reusing think about our current recycling practices? Create a skit in which this person travels forward in time to the present day and tries to convince people of the value of reusing materials when possible. Go perform this skit in classes of younger students in your school and then have a discussion with those students about the benefits of reusing materials.

SAMPLE INTERDISCIPLINARY CONNECTION—MATHEMATICS

Recycling took some time to catch on in many parts of the country because it was not profitable for recycling companies to make money collecting and recycling household goods. Based on data you collect on your trip to the recycling plant and other research you conduct back in the classroom, try to determine the costs and the profits of starting a recycling business. To make a living at it, try to estimate how much material you would have to recycle in a year. Does this help to explain why there are still only a limited number of for-profit recycling businesses?

SCIENTISTS IN YOUR COMMUNITY

Individuals in your community who might be knowledgeable about local recycling efforts could include engineers and other workers at the recycling plant, city workers who collect the recycling, city planners, local environmental activists, and local historians. Invite one or more of these individuals to your classroom and ask them to share their experiences with local recycling efforts and share with them your recycling projects and what you learned on the field trip to the recycling center.

Correlation With National Standards

NSES Science: E2; F2; F5

NCTM Math: A3; D2; E1

NCTE Language Arts: 4; 5; 12

NCSS Social Studies: 1; 3; 8; 10

Conclusion

Throughout this book, we have considered how science teaching and learning can foster a sense of place for students—how exploring science can be connected to exploring the world around us. We have proposed a model of place-based teaching and provided numerous examples of what this model could look like in practice. We have also provided models to assess what it is that students have learned.

Underlying our approach is our strongly held belief that science at the elementary and middle school levels is best learned by engaging students in hands-on experiences drawn from the real world that surrounds them. In an age when education is driven by standards documents and the accountability mandates of No Child Left Behind, it is critical for us to remember why it is that we are teaching children: to prepare them for meaningful lives, not just to perform well on tests.

Today's students will be forced to deal with significant global economic and ecological challenges that our generation has found ways to postpone addressing. For example, we have continued to use federal deficit spending to postpone looming economic crises such as with Social Security and Medicare, and we have resisted making hard choices and significant lifestyle changes to proactively curb greenhouse gas emissions, hoping that some technological fix will be discovered that allows us to continue to live as inefficiently as we have grown used to. Place-Based teaching and learning can challenge us to think about these choices and how they play out in our local communities.

In this context, we find ourselves going back not only to John Dewey's ideas about making science meaningful to the lived experience of the child but also to the constructivist hands-on models promoted by figures such as the Swiss educator Jean Piaget (1896–1980), the Russian psychologist Lev Vygotsky (1896–1934), and more contemporary figures such as the American psychologist Jerome Bruner (1915–). In the case of Bruner, his involvement with science reform in the post-Sputnik era (after 1956) emphasized constructivist models in which children learned science by a process of personal self-discovery and literally, as Piaget suggested, understanding through inventing (Bruner, 1962; Piaget, 1971).

In summary, the essence of place-based education (i.e., learning connected to the local community and the lived experiences children) is rarely, if ever, enacted in the typical science classroom today. Place-Based education is not just an interesting alternative but a powerful means of improving science instruction. The model of place-based education we propose in this book can simultaneously enhance students' conceptual understanding and their engagement in science. These outcomes cannot help but increase students' test performance as a byproduct of these efforts.

In this context, we believe that the object of all education is to make students more knowledgeable and aware of the world around them, that it should provide students with real skills that will help them as adults, and that it should be both exciting and intellectually engaging. We do not believe in teaching to tests but instead in using tests and standards to make sure that we are achieving the goal of educating the whole child. In this context, we feel that Place-Based science education can and should play an important role in the reform of our schools, their curricula, and the education and well-being of our children.

Appendix

*Resources for Place-Based Science
Teaching and Learning*

Every community, whether rural or urban, has extensive resources for place-based education. In the following appendix, we provide a suggested set of resources for pursuing place-based science education. Most of these resources are available for free or at very little cost and many are available online. Clearly, each community is unique, so finding out what is available in your own community and local setting will require that you to do a bit of exploring. Yet having said this, many types of resources that are found in one community will be available in other locations as well. Additionally, comparing your local resources to the resources in other communities in your state, in the nation, or in other countries can provide students with fruitful topics of discussion. Consider this appendix to be a starting point for your own explorations of museums, parks, and web-based resources that will assist you in developing place-based science activities for your classroom.

SCIENCE MUSEUMS

Some of the best general resources for place-based science are science museums. Most major urban centers have at least one science museum. Besides providing general background on science concepts, these museums often focus on regional issues. In the case of Miami, for example, the Miami Museum of Science (http://www.miamisci.org/) has extensive exhibits dealing with sharks, reptiles, and the Everglades. If you happen to be geographically close to Washington, D.C., you can take advantage of the Smithsonian museum system, including sites such as the Smithsonian Museum of Natural History. Exhibits at national museums such as the Smithsonian or other large museums like the Museum of Natural History in New York City or the Field Museum in Chicago will tend to be more national or global in emphasis, but smaller museums are more likely to highlight local issues. If you are not physically close to any natural history museum, all of the museums listed here have interactive and engaging websites that can provide ideas for making local connections. Consider using ideas from big museums to make your own classroom into a

Chicago Science Museum

local natural history museum or interactive science museum. Then have a gala museum party for families and other community members.

Smithsonian National Museum of Natural History
http://www.mnh.si.edu/onehundred years/brief_history.htm

American Museum of Natural History
http://www.amnh.org/

Field Museum of Natural History
www.fieldmuseum.org

Examples of more regional natural history museums that might be of potential interest for use in place-based education include:

Denver Museum of Nature and Science
www.dmns.org

Fairbanks Museum and Planetarium
www.fairbanksmuseum.org

Houston Museum of Natural Science
www.hmns.org

Museum of Science, Boston
www.mos.org

New Mexico Museum of Natural History and Science
www.nmnaturalhistory.org

North Carolina Museum of Natural Sciences
www.naturalsciences.org

Peabody Museum of Natural History
www.peabody.yale.edu

San Diego Natural History Museum
www.sdnhm.org

LINKS TO NATURAL HISTORY MUSEUMS AND COLLECTIONS CAN BE FOUND AT:

Natural History Museums and Collections
www.lib.washington.edu/sla/natmus.html

At more specialized museums such as the Museum of Health and Medical Science in Houston, visitors can explore a giant body from the inside, as well as learn how the body works and ways to live a healthier life.

Museum of Health and Medical Science
www.mhms.org

Links to more than 400 science and technology museums worldwide can be found at the Association of Science-Technology Centers.

Association of Science-Technology Centers
http://www.astc.org/

MuseumsUSA provides a database searchable by museum type, state, ZIP code, or city. Find the museums in your area that may be relevant to place-based science education.

MuseumsUSA
www.museumsusa.org

Many museums in the United States emphasize hands-on exploration and learning. For science education, there is probably no better example of this type of museum than San Francisco's Exploratorium.

Exploratorium
www.exploratorium.edu

LIVING HISTORY MUSEUMS

Living history museums are outstanding resources for teachers interested in place-based education. Many of their exhibits and activities relate to place-based science education as it is connected to local and regional history. In Staunton, Virginia, for example, the Frontier Culture Museum has a series of working farms including a German American farm from the 1820s, an Irish American farm from the late 18th century, and a frontier settlement farm from the 1750s. Visits to a living history museum of this type can provide students with an understanding of the basics of agricultural science, cloth production (flax and wool), and regional food ways and customs, as well as a basic understanding of mechanics involving simple machines and water power.

There are a total of approximately 550 living history museums in the United States. Some of the most interesting are included below:

Frontier Culture Museum, Staunton, Virginia

http://www.frontiermuseum.org/

Colonial Williamsburg
www.history.org

Old Sturbridge Village
www.osv.org

Independence Mine State Historical Park
http://www.travelalaska.com/Regions/
ParksDetail.aspx?ParkID=18

Jamestown Settlement & Yorktown Victory Center
www.historyisfun.org

Jarrell Plantation State Historic Site
http://www.georgiaparks.org/info/jarrell/

New Mexico Farm & Ranch Heritage Museum
http://www.nmfarmandranchmuseum
.org/

Old City Park: The Historical Village of Dallas
www.oldcitypark.org

Ozark Folk Center
www.ozarkfolkcenter.com

Historic Cold Spring Village
www.hcsv.org

Rough and Tumble Engineers Historical Association
www.roughandtumble.org

Shaker Village at Sabbathday Lake
http://www.shaker.lib.me.us/

Stuhr Museum of the Prairie Pioneer
www.stuhrmuseum.org

Examples of other living history museums can be found at the *Step Into History* web portal, which includes links to nearly all of the major living history museums in the United States. Check here to discover the living history museums that are in your community or nearby to you.

Step Into History
http://www.stepintohistory.com/index.htm

For links to living history museums from around the world, visit:

Midwest Open Air Museums Coordinating Council
www.momcc.org

CAVES AND CAVERNS

Caves and caverns exist in many parts of the country. Humans have been exploring caves both out of necessity, for shelter and protection, and out of curiosity for tens of thousands of years. In the last century, caving, or spelunking, has developed into both a tourist attraction and an athletic pastime. While most cave systems are undeveloped and require elaborate preparation and safety equipment to explore (hardhats, protective overalls, head lamps, ropes, poles, etc.), a number of cave systems have been developed as tourist destinations, or "show caves," that can be entered safely and without the need for protective gear by people of all ages and abilities.

Natural entrance of Carlsbad Cavern

Caves and cavern systems contain an amazing variety of geological features and are also home to interesting and unusual animals and plants. In addition to bats (often in incredible numbers), cave-dwelling life forms include cave shrimp, salamanders, snails, and crayfish. Because the light quickly disappears when entering a cave, plant life is generally found only near the entrance of caves. Cave organisms are specially adapted to low-light environments and are typically pink in color with large eyes. It is the geological features, however, that attract most people to caves. Perhaps most distinctive are stalactites—icicle-shaped deposits hanging from the roof of caves that form when calcium carbonate is deposited by mineralized water solutions. Stalagmites are cone-shaped deposits of calcite that are formed on the cave floor by the dripping of mineral-rich water solutions. Over time, stalactites and stalagmites can grow large enough so that they meet to form columns.

To find more information about caves and cave exploring, and to find a list of caves near you, check out the website of the National Caves Association.

National Caves Association
http://cavern.com/

Some of the more well-known caves in the United States are the following:

Mammoth Cave National Park
http://www.nps.gov/maca

Carlsbad Caverns National Park
http://www.nps.gov/cave/index.htm

Ape Cave at the Mount Saint Helens National Volcanic Monument
http://www.fs.fed.us/gpnf/mshnvm/

Luray Caverns
http://www.luraycaverns.com/

WEATHER AND CLIMATE RESOURCES

Understanding, tracking, and predicting the weather and climate can provide many opportunities for creating science-related place-based teaching. Additionally, understanding climate change may be one of the most important science-related topics for the foreseeable future. It is important for students to gain an understanding of weather and climate because of the profound effects they can have on our everyday lives. There are many aspects of weather and climate that can be investigated. What do the different clouds mean? How do I know what kind of clothes to wear for different types of weather? How much has it rained this year and how does this compare with other years? How likely is it for a hurricane or tornado to strike my community and what preparations should we take?

Below we list some of the main Internet resources that can help you to design and carry out local weather and climate studies.

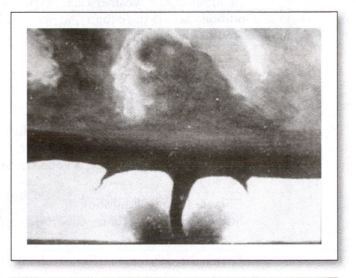

Tornado

National Oceanic and Atmospheric Administration
http://www.education.noaa.gov/

The National Oceanic and Atmospheric Administration provides a wide range of materials for teachers and students to support learning about our oceans, atmosphere, weather and climate. Most of the activities are written in a generic way but can easily be tailored to the specifics of your local context.

American Meteorological Society
http://www.ametsoc.org/amsedu/

The American Meteorological Society sponsors a number of education programs to promote the value of learning about atmospheric, oceanographic, and hydrologic sciences. These include Project ATMOSPHERE and Project DataStream Atmosphere. The society also provides a range of summer teacher workshops and makes available for sale carefully selected, classroom-tested material.

Weatherscope Project
http://www.ciese.org/curriculum/weatherproj2/en/

The Weatherscope project, sponsored by the Center for Innovation in Engineering and Science Education, guides students in an investigation of both local and world weather and climate. Students create their own weather instruments and then locate and gather real-time weather information both locally and from around the world. Participants develop an understanding of how weather can be described in measurable quantities such as temperature, wind, and precipitation.

Nearly every local television station has significant resources for weather prediction and most stations are very welcoming of student groups. Contact your local station to see about arranging a tour. In addition, you can get regular updates on local weather at most newspaper websites.

In addition, the Weather Channel provides extensive information on current weather conditions across the country, as well as documentary information on different topics related to weather history and science.

The Weather Channel
http://www.weather.com/

Climate change is an issue that affects us all and is of particular interest to students. It is a topic that is likely to gain increasing prominence in the coming years. For resources on climate change, a good starting point is:

Climate Change Education
http://www.climatechangeeducation.org/k-12/index.html

Focus the Nation, a climate change awareness and action group (http://www.focusthenation.org/), provides a wide range of lesson ideas for teaching about global climate change for all ages of students and related to each of the major science disciplines.

ZOOS

Nearly every major urban area in the United States has a zoo or animal park, and many smaller cities do as well. In addition to the exotic animals, such as lions or giraffes, that first come to mind when most people think of zoos, many zoos also include collections of local or regional animals. Of course, many species of local animals can also be observed in their natural habitats.

Many of the major U.S. zoos and animal refuge parks also have engaging interactive websites:

Smithsonian National Zoological Park
http://nationalzoo.si.edu/default.cfm

Bronx Zoo
http://www.bronxzoo.com/

Buffalo Zoo
www.buffalozoo.org

Cincinnati Zoo and Botanical Garden
www.cincyzoo.org

Cleveland Metroparks Zoo
www.clemetzoo.com

Detroit Zoological Institute
www.detroitzoo.org

Honolulu Zoo
www.honoluluzoo.org

Houston Zoo
www.houstonzoo.org

Lincoln Park Zoo—Chicago
www.lpzoo.com

Oakland Zoo
www.oaklandzoo.org

Oregon Zoo
www.oregonzoo.org

Feeding a giraffe

Phoenix Zoo
www.phoenixzoo.org

Riverbanks Zoo & Garden
www.riverbanks.org

Saint Louis Zoo
www.stlzoo.org

San Diego Zoo
http://www.sandiegozoo.org/

San Francisco Zoo
www.sfzoo.org

Santa Barbara Zoological Gardens
www.santabarbarazoo.org

For a general directory to zoo sites in the United States, visit:

Zoos in the USA
http://www.officialusa.com/stateguides/zoos/

AQUARIUMS

Similar to zoos, aquariums provide an excellent source of ideas and information for regional science studies. Most aquariums include exhibits from both freshwater and saltwater environments. A selection of major national and regional aquarium websites is below:

Alaska SeaLife Center
www.alaskasealife.org

Audubon Aquarium
http://www.auduboninstitute.org/

At the aquarium

Georgia Aquarium
www.georgiaaquarium.org

Great Lakes Aquarium
www.glaquarium.org

John G. Shedd Aquarium
www.sheddaquarium.org

Long Beach Aquarium of the Pacific
www.aquariumofpacific.org

Monterey Bay Aquarium
http://www.montereybayaquarium.org/

National Aquarium in Baltimore
www.aqua.org

National Aquarium in Washington, D.C.
www.nationalaquarium.com

New England Aquarium
www.neaq.org

North Carolina Aquariums
www.ncaquariums.com

Tennessee Aquarium
www.tennis.org

BIRD WATCHING AND AVIARIES

Flamingos

Bird watching can be done almost anywhere, but aviaries can bring together an incredible range of bird species in one location. Major bird watching centers and aviaries include:

Parrot Jungle and Gardens
www.parrotjungle.com

National Aviary
www.aviary.org

Tracy Aviary
www.tracyaviary.org

Clear Springs Aviaries and Gardens
www.angelfire.com/tx5/clearspgs

Theodore Roosevelt Sanctuary
http://ny.audubon.org/CentersEdu_TRoosevelt.html

INSECTS

Insectariums can be found throughout the country. Among the most popular are Butterfly Pavilions. A few representative websites include:

Butterfly Pavilion and Insect Center
http://www.butterflies.org/

Seattle Bug Safari
http://www.seattlebugsafari.com/

A list of butterfly gardens in the United States and around the world can be found at:

Butterfly Gardens around the World
http://butterflywebsite.com/gardens/index
.cfm

Emerging monarch

PLANETARIUMS AND ASTRONOMY

There are numerous planetariums and observatories around the country. Most are associated with science museums or universities. Some of the more well known are:

Adler Planetarium and Astronomy Museum
www.adlerplanetarium.org

American Museum of Natural History—Frederick Phineas and Sandra Priest Rose Center for Earth and Space
www.amnh.org/rose

Armagh Planetarium
www.armagh-planetarium.co.uk

Planetarium

Clark Planetarium
http://www.clarkplanetarium.org/

Pacific Science Center—Willard Smith Planetarium
www.pacsci.org/planetarium

West Virginia University—Tomchin Planetarium and Observatory
www.as.wvu.edu/~planet

For lists of additional planetariums visit the following site:

Planetarium Web Sites
http://www.lochnessproductions.com/pltweb/pltweb.html

DAMS, POWER PLANTS, AND WATER TREATMENT PLANTS

Most communities have a power plant of some kind nearby, yet most students do not know where their electricity comes from. Power plants are a great resource for

Reservoir dam

place-based science, as are water treatment plants, recycling centers, and hydroelectric dams. Links to some useful websites on these topics include:

Boulder City/Hoover Dam Museum
http://www.bcmha.org/

A local history museum that also chronicles the construction of the Hoover Dam.

Niagara Power Project Power Vista
http://www.nypa.gov/vc/niagara.htm

An extensive educational museum and display highlighting the Niagara Power Project.

A Visit to a Wastewater-Treatment Plant
http://ga.water.usgs.gov/edu/wwvisit.html

This website provides the visitor with a step-by-step guide to what happens during the treatment process in a wastewater-treatment plant and how pollutants are removed to create clean recycled water.

The Recycling Center
http://www.therecyclingcenter.info/

A web portal for finding recycling centers in your community.

Remember that the resources presented in this appendix are meant to provide a starting point for your own investigations into local resources to support place-based teaching and learning. Don't feel limited to this list—head out into your local community and see what other resources for supporting place-based teaching and learning you can find!

Index

About the Authors

Cory A. Buxton is Associate Professor of Education at the University of Georgia. His research uses anthropological and sociolinguistic lenses to explore the interactions of culture and language in science classrooms. He also studies the ways in which students, teachers, and schools both conform to and resist the current political pressures of high-stakes assessment and how such assessments differentially influence "at-risk" and "high-performing" schools. Buxton began his career as a geologist and became interested in teaching science while serving as a U.S. Peace Corps volunteer in Guatemala. He then taught in urban New Orleans and rural Colorado before receiving his PhD from the University of Colorado at Boulder. Buxton currently directs a National Science Foundation-funded project working with middle school teachers to develop strategies for better supporting the academic success of English Language learners. The current collaboration with Provenzo has resulted in the creation of a text that draws upon many of these diverse interests.

Eugene F. Provenzo, Jr., is Professor of Education at the University of Miami. The author of a wide range of books on education and culture, he has a particular interest in technology and the history of science, as well as constructivist models of learning. His book *Video Kids: Making Sense of Nintendo* (1991) was the first scholarly book to look in detail at issues of race, gender, and violence in video games. A national media figure, he has appeared on *Good Morning America,* the *Today Show, ABC World News Tonight,* the *CBS Evening News,* and has been profiled in *People* magazine. He recently edited a three-volume encyclopedia on the social and cultural foundations of education for SAGE Publications and is also the editor for SAGE of *Critical Issues in Education: An Anthology of Readings* (2006). He is an avid sculptor and collage artist, a toy designer and inventor, and divides his time between teaching and researching in Miami and restoring a circa-1850 house in Staunton, Virginia, with his wife Asterie Baker Provenzo and his red tabby Maine Coon cat Fred.

SAGE Research Methods Online

The essential tool for researchers

**Sign up now at
www.sagepub.com/srmo
for more information.**

An expert research tool

- An **expertly designed taxonomy** with more than 1,400 unique terms for social and behavioral science research methods

- **Visual and hierarchical search tools** to help you discover material and link to related methods

- Easy-to-use navigation tools

- Content organized by complexity

- Tools for citing, printing, and downloading content with ease

- Regularly updated content and features

A wealth of essential content

- The most comprehensive picture of quantitative, qualitative, and mixed methods available today

- More than **100,000 pages of SAGE book and reference material** on research methods as well as editorially selected material from SAGE journals

- More than **600 books** available in their entirety online

Launching 2011!

$SAGE research methods online

CPSIA information can be obtained
at www.ICGtesting.com
Printed in the USA
JSHW061706250722
28458JS00003B/24

9 781412 975254